The Theory of Moral Sentiments; or, An Essay Towards an Analysis of the Principles by Which Men Naturally Judge Concerning the Conduct and Character, First of Their Neighbours, and Afterwards of Themselves

THE

THEORY

OF

MORAL SENTIMENTS.

VOL. II

THE

THEORY

OF

MORAL SENTIMENTS;

OR,

An Essay towards an Analysis of the Principles by which Men naturally judge concerning the Conduct and Character, first of their Neighbours, and afterwards of themselves.

TO WHICH IS ADDED,

A Dissertation on the Origin of Languages.

By ADAM SMITH, LL.D.
Fellow of the Royal Societies of London and Edinburgh,
One of the Commissioners of His Majesty's Customs in Scotland,
and formerly Professor of Moral Philosophy in the
University of Glasgow.

THE NINTH EDITION.

IN TWO VOLUMES.

VOL. II.

LONDON:
Printed for A. Strahan; and T. Cadell jun. and W. Davies,
(Successors to Mr. Cadell) in the Strand; and
W. Creech, and J. Bell & Co. at Edinburgh.
1801.

CONTENTS

OF

THE SECOND VOLUME.

PART V.

OF the INFLUENCE of CUSTOM and FASHION upon the Sentiments of Moral Approbation and Disapprobation.

PART

PART VI.

Of the CHARACTER of VIRTUE.

SECTION I.

SECTION II.

SECTION III.

PART VII.

Of Systems of Moral Philosophy.

SECTION I.

SECTION II.

SECTION III.

Of the different Systems which have been formed concerning the Principle of Approbation.

SECTION IV.

THE THEORY OF MORAL SENTIMENTS.

PART V.

Of the INFLUENCE of CUSTOM and FASHION upon the Sentiments of Moral Approbation and Disapprobation.

Consisting of One Section.

CHAP. I.

Of the Influence of Custom and Fashion upon our notions of Beauty and Deformity.

THERE are other principles besides those already enumerated, which have a considerable influence upon the moral sentiments of mankind, and are the chief causes of the many irregular and discordant opinions which prevail in different ages and nations

[illegible] and [illegible] domi- [illegible] our judgments concerning beauty of every kind.

When two objects have frequently been seen together, the imagination acquires a habit of passing easily from the one to the other. If the first appear, we lay our account that the second is to follow. Of their own accord they put us in mind of one another, and the attention glides easily along them. Though, independent of custom, there should be no real beauty in their union, yet when custom has thus connected them [illegible] an impropriety in their [illegible] think is awkward [illegible] usual companion. [illegible] expected to [illegible] of our [illegible] disappointment. A [illegible] seems to want [illegible] accompa- [illegible] or awk- [illegible] of a branch [illegible] property [illegible] of [illegible] appear [illegible]

still more disagreeable than it would otherwise seem to be. Those who have been accustomed to see things in a good taste are more disgusted by whatever is clumsy or awkward. Where the conjunction is improper, custom either diminishes, or takes away altogether, our sense of the impropriety. Those who have been accustomed to slovenly disorder lose all sense of neatness or elegance. The modes of furniture or dress which seem ridiculous to strangers, give no offence to the people who are used to them.

Fashion is different from custom, or rather is a particular species of it. That is not the fashion which every body wears, but which those wear who are of a high rank, or character. The graceful, the easy, and commanding manners of the great, joined to the usual richness and magnificence of their dress, give a grace to the very form which they happen to bestow upon it. As long as they continue to use this form, it is connected in our imaginations with the idea of something that is genteel and magnificent, and though in itself it should be indifferent, it seems, on account of this relation, to have something about it that is genteel and magnificent too. As soon as they drop it, it loses

all

the grace, which it had appeared to possess before, and being now used only by the inferior ranks of people, seems to have something of their meanness and awkwardness.

Dress and furniture are allowed by all the world to be entirely under the dominion of custom and fashion. The influence of those principles, however, is by no means confined to so narrow a sphere, but extends itself to whatever is in any respect the object of taste, to music, to poetry, to architecture. The modes of dress and furniture are continually changing, and that fashion appearing ridiculous to-day which was admired five years ago, we are experimentally convinced that it owed its vogue chiefly or entirely to custom and fashion. Clothes and furniture are not made of very durable materials. A well-fancied coat is done in a twelve-month, and cannot continue longer to propagate, as the fashion, that form according to which it was made. The modes of furniture change less rapidly than those of dress; because furniture is commonly more durable. In five or six years, however, it generally undergoes an entire revolution, and every man in his own time sees the fashion in this respect change many different ways. The productions of the other arts are much more lasting, and,

what

which, happily imagined, may continue to propagate the fashion of their make for a much longer time. A well-contrived building may endure many centuries: a beautiful air may be delivered down by a sort of tradition through many successive generations: a well-written poem may last as long as the world; and all of them continue for ages together, to give the vogue to that particular style, to that particular taste or manner, according to which each of them was composed. Few men have an opportunity of seeing in their own times the fashion in any of these arts change very considerably. Few men have so much experience and acquaintance with the different modes which have obtained in remote ages and nations, as to be thoroughly reconciled to them, or to judge with impartiality between them, and what takes place in their own age and country. Few men therefore are willing to allow, that custom or fashion have much influence upon their judgments concerning what is beautiful, or otherwise, in the productions of any of those arts; but imagine, that all the rules, which they think ought to be observed in each of them, are founded upon reason and nature, not upon habit or prejudice. A very little attention, however, may convince

them in the contrary, and to satisfy them, that the influence of custom and fashion over dress and furniture, is not more absolute than over architecture, poetry, and music.

Can any reason, for example, be assigned why the Doric capital should be appropriated to a pillar, whose height is equal to eight diameters; the Ionic volute to one of nine; and the Corinthian foliage to one of ten? The propriety of each of those appropriations can be founded upon nothing but habit and custom. The eye having been used to see a particular proportion connected with a particular ornament, would be offended if they were not joined together. Each of the five orders has its peculiar ornaments, which cannot be changed for any other, without giving offence to all those who know any thing of the rules of architecture. According to some architects, indeed, such is the exquisite judgment with which the ancients have assigned to each order its proper ornaments, that no others can be found which are equally suitable. It seems, however, a little difficult to be conceived that these forms, though, no doubt, extremely agreeable, should be the only forms which can suit those proportions, or that there should not be five hundred others which, antecedent

ce[illegible]nt to e[illegible]ed [illegible]tom, would [illegible] fitted them e[illegible]ly well. When custom, however, [illegible]ed particular rules of building, [illegible] they are not absolutely unreasonable, [illegible] to think of [illegible] the [illegible] good, or even [illegible] in point of ele[illegible] [illegible] [illegible] [illegible] [illegible] [illegible] [illegible] [illegible] [illegible] [illegible] [illegible] [illegible] [illegible] [illegible] [illegible] [illegible] [illegible] [illegible] [illegible] [illegible].

[illegible], a [illegible] [illegible] [illegible] [illegible], it, [illegible] to [illegible]. [illegible], was [illegible] great, and [illegible] works, [illegible] could [illegible], [illegible], be [illegible] [illegible]ged without the greatest impropriety.

The experience of modern times, however, seems to contradict this principle, though in itself it would appear to be extremely probable. What is the burlesque verse in English, is the heroic verse in French. The tragedies of Racine and the Henriad of Voltaire, are nearly in the same verse with,

Let me have your advice in a weighty affair.

The burlesque verse in French, on the contrary, is pretty much the same with the heroic verse of ten syllables in English. Custom has made the one nation associate the ideas of gravity, sublimity, and seriousness, to that measure which the other has connected with whatever is gay, flippant, and ludicrous. Nothing would appear more absurd in English, than a tragedy written in the Alexandrine verses of the French; or in French, than a work of the same kind in verses of ten syllables.

An eminent artist will bring about a considerable change in the established modes of each of those arts, and introduce a new fashion of writing, music, or architecture. As the dress of an agreeable man of high rank recommends itself, and how peculiar and fantastical soever, comes soon to be ad-

mired

[illegible] and indeed, in the [illegible] of [illegible] [illegible] [illegible] [illegible] [illegible] within th[illegible] [illegible]

practised [illegible], [illegible] works that are written in [illegible], the one in long verses, the other in [illegible] the imitations of Butler [illegible] the plainness of Swift. The [illegible] Dryden, and the correct [illegible] prosaic languor of Addison, are no longer the objects of imitation, but all long verses are now written after the manner of the nervous precision of Mr. Pope.

Neither is it only over the productions of the arts, that custom and fashion exert their dominion. They influence our judgments, in the same manner, with regard to the beauty of natural objects. What various and opposite forms are deemed beautiful in different species of things? The proportions which are admired in one animal, are altogether different from those which are esteemed in another. Every class of things has its [illegible] conformation, which is approved [illegible] has [illegible]

[illegible]

each feature lies in a certain middle, equally removed from a variety of other forms that are ugly. A beautiful nose, for example, is one that is neither very long, nor very short, neither very straight, nor very crooked, but a sort of middle between all these extremes, and less different from any one of them than all of them are from one another. It is the form which Nature seems to have aimed at in them all, which, however, she deviates from in a great variety of ways, and very seldom hits exactly; but to which all those deviations still bear a very strong resemblance. When a number of drawings are made after one pattern, though they may all miss it in some respects, yet they will all resemble it more than they resemble one another; the general character of the pattern will run through them all; the most singular and odd will be those which are most wide of it; and though very few will copy it exactly, yet the most accurate delineations will bear a greater resemblance to the most careless, than the careless ones will bear to one another. In the same manner, in each species of creatures, what is most beautiful bears the strongest characters of the general fabric of the species, and has the most strong resemblance to the greater part of the individuals with which it

it

it is [illegible], on the contrary, or what is [illegible] formed, are [illegible] most singular and odd, and have the least resemblance to the [illegible] of that species to which they [illegible]. [illegible] the beauty of each species, [illegible] the rarest of all things, [illegible] the [illegible] the deviations from it [illegible] than their refemble [illegible]. The [illegible] every form, therefore, [illegible] of things, according to [illegible]. And hence [illegible] [illegible] or [illegible] which [illegible] the [illegible] [illegible]. The [illegible] [illegible] It is [illegible] of [illegible] [illegible] found in [illegible]

different nations concerning the beauty of the human shape and countenance? A fair complexion is a shocking deformity upon the coast of Guinea. Thick lips and a flat nose are a beauty. In some nations long ears that hang down upon the shoulders are the objects of universal admiration. In China if a lady's foot is so large as to be fit to walk upon, she is regarded as a monster of ugliness. Some of the savage nations in North-America tie four boards round the heads of their children, and thus squeeze them, while the bones are tender and gristly, into a form that is almost perfectly square. Europeans are astonished at the absurd barbarity of this practice, to which some missionaries have imputed the singular stupidity of those nations among whom it prevails. But when they condemn those savages, they do not reflect that the ladies in Europe had, till within these very few years, been endeavouring, for near a century past, to squeeze the beautiful roundness of their natural form into a square form of the same kind. And that, notwithstanding the many distortions and diseases which this practice was known to occasion, custom had rendered it agreeable among some of the most civilized nations which, perhaps, the world ever beheld.

Such is the system of this learned and ingenious Father, concerning the nature of beauty; of which the whole charm, according to him, would thus seem to arise from its falling in with the habits which custom had impressed upon the imagination, with regard to things of each particular kind. I cannot, however, be induced to believe that our sense even of external beauty is founded altogether on custom. The utility of any form, its fitness for the useful purposes for which it was intended, evidently recommends it, and renders it agreeable to us, independent of custom. Certain colours are more agreeable than others, and give more delight to the eye the first time it ever beholds them. A smooth surface is more agreeable than a rough one. Variety is more pleasing than a tedious undiversified uniformity. Connected variety, in which each new appearance seems to be introduced by what went before it, and in which all the adjoining parts seem to have some natural relation to one another, is more agreeable than a disjointed and disorderly [illegible] But [illegible]

form fo beautiful as to pleafe, if quite contrary to cuftom, and unlike whatever we have been ufed to in that particular fpecies of things: or fo deformed as not to be agreeable, if cuftom uniformly fupports it, and habituates us to fee it in every fingle individual of the kind.

CHAP. II.

Of the Influence of Cuftom and Fafhion upon Moral Sentiments.

SINCE our fentiments concerning beauty of every kind are fo much influenced by cuftom and fafhion, it cannot be expected that thofe, concerning the beauty of conduct, fhould be entirely exempted from the dominion of thofe principles. Their influence here, however, feems to be much lefs than it is every where elfe. There is, perhaps, no form of external objects, how abfurd and fantaftical foever, to which cuftom will not reconcile us, or which fafhion will not render even agreeable. But the characters and conduct of a Nero, or a Claudius, are what no cuftom will ever reconcile us to, what no

fashion will ever render agreeable; but the one will always be the object of dread and hatred; the other of scorn and derision. The principles of the imagination, upon which our sense of beauty depends, are of a very nice and delicate nature, and may easily be altered by habit and education: but the sentiments of moral approbation and disapprobation, are founded on the strongest and most vigorous passions of human nature; and though they may be somewhat warpt, cannot be entirely perverted.

But though the influence of custom and fashion upon moral sentiments is not altogether so great, it is however perfectly similar to what it is every where else. When custom and fashion coincide with the natural principles of right and wrong, they heighten the delicacy of our sentiments, and increase our abhorrence for every thing which approaches to evil. Those who have been educated in what is really good company, not in what is commonly called such, who have been accustomed to see nothing in the persons whom they esteemed and lived with, but justice, modesty, humanity, and good order; are more shocked with whatever seems to be inconsistent with the rules which those virtues prescribe. Those, on

the

the contrary, who have had the misfortune to be brought up amidst violence, licentiousness, falsehood, and injustice; lose, though not all sense of the impropriety of such conduct, yet all sense of its dreadful enormity, or of the vengeance and punishment due to it. They have been familiarized with it from their infancy, custom has rendered it habitual to them, and they are very apt to regard it as, what is called, the way of the world, something which either may, or must be practised, to hinder us from being the dupes of our own integrity.

Fashion too will sometimes give reputation to a certain degree of disorder, and, on the contrary, discountenance qualities which deserve esteem. In the reign of Charles II. a degree of licentiousness was deemed the characteristic of a liberal education. It was connected, according to the notions of those times, with generosity, sincerity, magnanimity, loyalty, and proved that the person who acted in this manner was a gentleman, and not a puritan. Severity of manners, and regularity of conduct, on the other hand, were altogether unfashionable, and were connected, in the imaginations of the age, with cant, cunning, hypocrisy, and low manners. To superficial minds, the vices of

the great seem at all times agreeable. They connect them, not only with the splendour of fortune, but with many superior virtues, which they ascribe to their superiors; with the spirit of freedom and independency, with frankness, generosity, humanity, and politeness. The virtues of the inferior ranks of people, on the contrary, their parsimonious frugality, their painful industry, and rigid adherence to rules, seem to them mean and disagreeable. They connect them, both with the meanness of the station to which those qualities commonly belong, and with many great vices, which, they suppose, usually accompany them; such as an abject, cowardly, ill-natured, lying, pilfering disposition.

The objects with which men in the different professions and states of life are conversant, being very different, and habituating them to very different passions, naturally form in them very different characters and manners. We expect in each rank and profession, a degree of those manners, which, experience has taught us, belong to it. But as in each species of things, we are particularly pleased with the middle conformation, which, in every part and feature, agrees most exactly with the general standard which nature seems to have established for things of

that kind; so in each rank, or, if I may say so, in each species of men, we are particularly pleased, if they have neither too much, nor too little of the character which usually accompanies their particular condition and situation. A man, we say, should look like his trade and profession; yet the pedantry of every profession is disagreeable. The different periods of life have, for the same reason, different manners assigned to them. We expect in old age, that gravity and sedateness which its infirmities, its long experience, and its worn-out sensibility, seem to render both natural and respectable; and we lay our account to find in youth that sensibility, that gaiety and sprightly vivacity which experience teaches us to expect from the lively impressions that all interesting objects are apt to make upon the tender and unpractised senses of that early period of life. Each of those two ages, however, may easily have too much of these peculiarities which belong to it. The flirting levity of youth, and the immoveable insensibility of old age, are equally disagreeable. The young, according to the common saying, are most agreeable when in their behaviour there is something of the manners of the old, and the old, when they retain something of the gaiety of the

the young. Either of them, however, may easily have too much of the manners of the other. The extreme coldness, and dull formality, which are pardoned in old age, make youth ridiculous. The levity, the carelessness, and the vanity, which are indulged in youth, render old age contemptible.

The peculiar character and manners which we are led by custom to appropriate to each rank and profession, have sometimes perhaps a propriety independent of custom; and are what we should approve of for their own sakes, if we took into consideration all the different circumstances which naturally affect those in each different state of life. The propriety of a person's behaviour, depends not upon its suitableness to any one circumstance of his situation, but to all the circumstances, which, when we bring his case home to ourselves, we feel, should naturally call upon his attention. If he appears to be so much occupied by any one of them, as entirely to neglect the rest, we disapprove of his conduct, as something which we cannot entirely go along with, because not properly adjusted to all the circumstances of his situation. Yet, perhaps, the emotion he expresses for the object which principally inter-

ects him, does not exceed what we ſhould entirely ſympathize with, and approve of, in one whoſe attention was not required by any other thing. A perſon in private life might, upon the loſs of an only ſon, expreſs without blame a degree of grief and tenderneſs, which would be unpardonable in a general at the head of an army, when glory and the public ſafety demanded ſo great a part of his attention. As different objects ought, upon common occaſions, to occupy the attention of men of different profeſſions, ſo different paſſions ought naturally to become habitual to them; and when we bring home to ourſelves their ſituation in this particular reſpect, we muſt be ſenſible, that every occurrence ſhould naturally affect them more or leſs, according as the emotion which it excites, coincides or diſagrees with the fixt habit and temper of their minds. We cannot expect the ſame ſenſibility to the gay pleaſures and amuſements of life in a clergyman, which we lay our account with in an officer. The man whoſe peculiar occupation it is to keep the world in mind of that awful futurity which awaits them, who is to announce what may be the fatal conſequences of every deviation from the rules of duty, and who is

himself to set the example of the most exact conformity, seems to be the messenger of tidings, which cannot, in propriety, be delivered either with levity or indifference. His mind is supposed to be continually occupied with what is too grand and solemn to leave any room for the impressions of those frivolous objects which fill up the attention of the dissipated and the gay. We readily feel therefore, that, independent of custom, there is a propriety in the manners which custom has allotted to this profession; and that nothing can be more suitable to the character of a clergyman, than that grave, that austere and abstracted severity, which we are habituated to expect in his behaviour. These reflections are so very obvious, that there is scarce any man so inconsiderate, as not, at some time, to have made them, and to have accounted to himself in this manner for his approbation of the usual character of this order.

The foundation of the customary character of some other professions is not so obvious, and our approbation of it is founded entirely in habit, without being either confirmed, or enlivened by any reflections of this kind. We are led by custom, for example, to an

nex the character of gaiety, levity, and sprightly freedom, as well as of some degree of dissipation, to the military profession. Yet, if we were to consider what mood or tone of temper would be most suitable to this situation, we should be apt to determine, perhaps, that the most serious and thoughtful turn of mind would best become those whose lives are continually exposed to uncommon danger, and who should therefore be more constantly occupied with the thoughts of death and its consequences than other men. It is this very circumstance, however, which is not improbably the occasion why the contrary turn of mind prevails so much among men of this profession. It requires so great an effort to conquer the fear of death, when we survey it with steadiness and attention, that those who are constantly exposed to it, find it easier to turn away their thoughts from it altogether, to wrap themselves up in careless security and indifference, and to plunge themselves, for this purpose, into every sort of amusement and dissipation. A camp is not the element of a thoughtful or a melancholy man: persons of that cast, indeed, are often abundantly determined, and are capable, by a great effort, of going on [illegible] resolution to the most un-

avoidable death. But to be expoſed to continual, though leſs imminent danger, to be obliged to exert, for a long time, a degree of this effort, exhauſts and depreſſes the mind, and renders it incapable of all happineſs and enjoyment. The gay and careleſs, who have occaſion to make no effort at all, who fairly reſolve never to look before them, but to loſe in continual pleaſures and amuſements all anxiety about their ſituation, more eaſily ſupport ſuch circumſtances. Whenever, by any peculiar circumſtances, an officer has no reaſon to lay his account with being expoſed to any uncommon danger, he is very apt to loſe the gaiety and diſſipated thoughtleſſneſs of his character. The captain of a city guard is commonly as ſober, careful, and penurious an animal as the reſt of his fellow-citizens. A long peace is, for the ſame reaſon, very apt to diminiſh the difference between the civil and the military character. The ordinary ſituation, however, of men of this profeſſion, renders gaiety, and a degree of diſſipation, ſo much their uſual character; and cuſtom has, in our imagination, ſo ſtrongly connected this character with this ſtation of life, that we are very apt to deſpiſe any man, whoſe peculiar humour or ſituation renders him incapable of acquiring it. We

laugh

laugh at the grave and careful faces of a city guard, which ſo little reſemble thoſe of their profeſſion. They themſelves ſeem often to be aſhamed of the regularity of their own manners, and, not to be out of the faſhion of their trade, are fond of affecting that levity, which is by no means natural to them. Whatever is the deportment which we have been accuſtomed to ſee in a reſpectable order of men, it comes to be ſo aſſociated in our imagination with that order, that whenever we ſee the one, we lay our account that we are to meet with the other, and when diſappointed, miſs ſomething which we expected to find. We are embarraſſed, and put to a ſtand, and know not how to addreſs ourſelves to a character, which plainly affects to be of a different ſpecies from thoſe with which we ſhould have been diſpoſed to claſs it.

The different ſituations of different ages and countries are apt, in the ſame manner, to give different characters to the generality of thoſe who live in them, and their ſentiments concerning the particular degree of each quality, that is either blameable or praiſe-worthy, vary, according to that degree which is uſual in their own country, and in their own times. That degree of politeneſs, which

which would be highly efteemed, perhaps, would be thought effeminate adulation, in Ruffia, would be regarded as rudenefs and barbarifm at the court of France. That degree of order and frugality, which, in a Polifh nobleman, would be confidered as exceffive parfimony, would be regarded as extravagance in a citizen of Amfterdam. Every age and country look upon that degree of each quality, which is commonly to be met with in thofe who are efteemed among themfelves, as the golden mean of that particular talent or virtue. And as this varies, according as their different circumftances render different qualities more or lefs habitual to them, their fentiments concerning the exact propriety of character and behaviour vary accordingly.

Among civilized nations, the virtues which are founded upon humanity, are more cultivated than thofe which are founded upon felf-denial and the command of the paffions. Among rude and barbarous nations, it is quite otherwife, the virtues of felf-denial are more cultivated than thofe of humanity. The general fecurity and happinefs which prevail in ages of civility and politenefs, afford little exercife to the contempt of danger, to patience in enduring labour, hunger,

and pain. Poverty may easily be avoided, and the contempt of it therefore almost ceases to be a virtue. The abstinence from pleasure becomes less necessary, and the mind is more at liberty to unbend itself, and to indulge its natural inclinations in all these particular respects.

Among savages and barbarians it is quite otherwise. Every savage undergoes a sort of Spartan discipline, and by the necessity of his situation is inured to every sort of hardship. He is in continual danger: he is often exposed to the greatest extremities of hunger, and frequently dies of pure want. His circumstances not only habituate him to every sort of distress, but teach him to give way to none of the passions which that distress is apt to excite. He can expect from his countrymen no sympathy or indulgence for such weakness. Before we can feel much for others, we must in some measure be at ease ourselves. If our own misery pinches us very severely, we have no leisure to attend to that of our neighbour: and all savages are too much occupied with their own wants and necessities, to give much attention to those of another person. A savage, therefore, whatever be the nature of his distress, expects no sympathy from those about him,

and disdains, upon that account, to expose himself, by allowing the least weakness to escape him. His passions, how furious and violent soever, are never permitted to disturb the serenity of his countenance or the composure of his conduct and behaviour. The savages in North America, we are told, assume upon all occasions the greatest indifference, and would think themselves degraded if they should ever appear in any respect to be overcome, either by love, or grief, or resentment. Their magnanimity and self-command, in this respect, are almost beyond the conception of Europeans. In a country in which all men are upon a level, with regard to rank and fortune, it might be expected that the mutual inclinations of the two parties should be the only thing considered in marriages, and should be indulged without any sort of control. This, however, is the country in which all marriages, without exception, are made up by the parents, and in which a young man would think himself disgraced for ever, if he shewed the least preference of one woman above another, or did not express the most complete indifference, both about the time when, and the person to whom, he was to be married. The weakness of love, which is so much indulged in ages

of humanity and politeneſs, is regarded among ſavages as the moſt unpardonable effeminacy. Even after the marriage, the two parties ſeem to be aſhamed of a connexion which is founded upon ſo ſordid a neceſſity. They do not live together. They ſee one another by ſtealth only. They both continue to dwell in the houſes of their reſpective fathers, and the open cohabitation of the two ſexes, which is permitted without blame in all other countries, is here conſidered as the moſt indecent and unmanly ſenſuality. Nor is it only over this agreeable paſſion that they exert this abſolute ſelf-command. They often bear, in the ſight of all their countrymen, with injuries, reproach, and the groſſeſt inſults, with the appearance of the greateſt inſenſibility, and without expreſſing the ſmalleſt reſentment. When a ſavage is made priſoner of war, and receives, as is uſual, the ſentence of death from his conquerors, he hears it without expreſſing any emotion, and afterwards ſubmits to the moſt dreadful torments, without ever bemoaning himſelf, or diſcovering any other paſſion but contempt of his enemies. While he is hung by the ſhoulders over a ſlow fire, he derides his tormentors, and tells them with how much more ingenuity he himſelf

had tormented such of their countrymen as had fallen into his hands. After he has been scorched and burnt, and lacerated in all the most tender and sensible parts of his body for several hours together, he is often allowed, in order to prolong his misery, a short respite, and is taken down from the stake: he employs this interval in talking upon all indifferent subjects, inquires after the news of the country, and seems indifferent about nothing but his own situation. The spectators express the same insensibility; the sight of so horrible an object seems to make no impression upon them; they scarce look at the prisoner, except when they lend a hand to torment him. At other times they smoke tobacco, and amuse themselves with any common object, as if no such matter was going on. Every savage is said to prepare himself from his earliest youth for this dreadful end. He composes, for this purpose, what they call the song of death, a song which he is to sing when he has fallen into the hands of his enemies, and is expiring under the tortures which they inflict upon him. It consists of insults upon his tormentors, and expresses the highest contempt of death and pain. He sings this song upon all extraordinary occasions, when he goes out

to

to war, when he meets his enemies in the field, or whenever he has a mind to show that he has familiarised his imagination to the most dreadful misfortunes, and that no human event can daunt his resolution, or alter his purpose. The same contempt of death and torture prevails among all other savage nations. There is not a negro from the coast of Africa who does not, in this respect, possess a degree of magnanimity which the soul of his sordid master is too often scarce capable of conceiving. Fortune never exerted more cruelly her empire over mankind, than when she subjected those nations of heroes to the refuse of the jails of Europe, to wretches who possess the virtues neither of the countries which they come from, nor of those which they go to, and whose levity, brutality, and baseness, so justly expose them to the contempt of the vanquished.

This heroic and unconquerable firmness, which the custom and education of his country demand of every savage, is not required of those who are brought up to live in civilized societies. If these last complain when they are in pain, if they grieve when they are in distress, if they allow themselves either to be overcome by love, or to be discomposed by anger, they are easily pardoned. Such weak-

weakneſſes are not apprehended to affect the eſſential parts of their character. As long as they do not allow themſelves to be tranſported to do any thing contrary to juſtice or humanity, they loſe but little reputation, though the ſerenity of their countenance, or the compoſure of their diſcourſe and behaviour, ſhould be ſomewhat ruffled and diſturbed. A humane and poliſhed people, who have more ſenſibility to the paſſions of others, can more readily enter into an animated and paſſionate behaviour, and can more eaſily pardon ſome little exceſs. The perſon principally concerned is ſenſible of this; and being aſſured of the equity of his judges, indulges himſelf in ſtronger expreſſions of paſſion, and is leſs afraid of expoſing himſelf to their contempt by the violence of his emotions. We can venture to expreſs more emotion in the preſence of a friend than in that of a ſtranger, becauſe we expect more indulgence from the one than from the other. And in the ſame manner the rules of decorum among civilized nations, admit of a more animated behaviour, than is approved of among barbarians. The firſt converſe together with the openneſs of friends; the ſecond with the reſerve of ſtrangers. The emotion and vivacity with which the French

French and the Italians, the two moſt poliſhed nations upon the continent, expreſs themſelves on occaſions that are at all intereſting, ſurpriſe at firſt thoſe ſtrangers who happen to be travelling among them, and who, having been educated among a people of duller ſenſibility, cannot enter into this paſſionate behaviour, of which they have never ſeen any example in their own country. A young French nobleman will weep in the preſence of the whole court upon being refuſed a regiment. An Italian, ſays the abbot Du Bos, expreſſes more emotion on being condemned in a fine of twenty ſhillings, than an Engliſhman on receiving the ſentence of death. Cicero, in the times of the higheſt Roman politeneſs, could, without degrading himſelf, weep with all the bitterneſs of ſorrow in the ſight of the whole ſenate and the whole people; as it is evident he muſt have done in the end of almoſt every oration. The orators of the earlier and ruder ages of Rome could not probably, conſiſtent with the manners of the times, have expreſſed themſelves with ſo much emotion. It would have been regarded, I ſuppoſe, as a violation of nature and propriety in the Scipios, in the Leliuſes, and in the elder Cato, to have expoſed ſo much ten-

[illegible] Thefe
[illegible] felves
[illegible] ment;
[illegible] that
[illegible] which was
[illegible] many years
[illegible] the two Grac-
[illegible] This ani-
[illegible] long prac-
[illegible] both in France
[illegible] to be intro-
[illegible] the differ-
[illegible] of felf-command
[illegible] in civilized and in barba-
[illegible] different ftandards
[illegible] of behaviour.
[illegible] to many
[illegible] A polifhed
[illegible] way, in
[illegible] of nature,
[illegible] Barba-
[illegible]
[illegible]
[illegible]
[illegible] by
[illegible] with
[illegible] or
[illegible]
[illegible] to
[illegible]

conceal the truth, no examination is capable of drawing it from them. They cannot be trepanned by the most artful questions. The torture itself is incapable of making them confess any thing which they have no mind to tell. The passions of a Chinese [illegible] they never express them[illegible] [illegible] emotion, but are concealed [illegible] of the [illegible], are, notwithstanding [illegible] mounted to the high[illegible] [illegible]. [illegible]

[illegible]

from them only to aim at no other fatisfaction, but that of convincing the fpectator, that they are in the right to be fo much moved, and of procuring his fympathy and approbation.

All thefe effects of cuftom and fafhion, however, upon the moral fentiments of mankind, are inconfiderable, in comparifon of thofe which they give occafion to in fome other cafes; and it is not concerning the general ftyle of character and behaviour, that thofe principles produce the greateft perverfion of judgment, but concerning the propriety or impropriety of particular ufages.

The different manners which cuftom teaches us to approve of in the different profeffions and ftates of life, do not concern things of the greateft importance. We expect truth and juftice from an old man as well as from a young, from a clergyman as well as from an officer; and it is in matters of fmall moment only, that we look for the diftinguifhing marks of their refpective characters. With regard to thefe too, there is often fome unobferved circumftance which, if it was attended to, would fhow us, that, independent of cuftom, there was a propriety in the character which cuftom had taught us to allot to each profeffion. We cannot com-

plain, therefore, in this case, that the perversion of natural sentiments is very great. Though the manners of different nations require different degrees of the same quality, in the character which they think worthy of esteem, yet the worst that can be said to happen even here, is, that the duties of one virtue are sometimes extended so as to encroach a little upon the precincts of some other. The rustic hospitality that is in fashion among the Poles encroaches, perhaps, a little upon œconomy and good order; and the frugality that is esteemed in Holland, upon generosity and good fellowship. The hardiness demanded of savages diminishes their humanity; and, perhaps, the delicate sensibility required in civilized nations sometimes destroys the masculine firmness of the character. In general, the style of manners which takes place in any nation, may commonly upon the whole be said to be that which is most suitable to its situation. Hardiness is the character most suitable to the circumstances of a savage; sensibility to those of one who lives in a very civilized society. Even here, therefore, we cannot complain that the moral sentiments of men are very grossly perverted.

[illegible] fish [illegible] [illegible] natural [illegible] to parti- [illegible] more [illegible] capable [illegible] par- [illegible] prin- ciples [illegible] and [illegible]

[illegible] be [illegible] ex- amples [illegible] ment [illegible] the [illegible] not [illegible] the [illegible] and cruel [illegible] imagine [illegible] could in- [illegible] a furious [illegible] the exposi- [illegible] born infants, [illegible] almost all the [illegible] the polite and [illegible] whenever the cir- cumstances [illegible] parent rendered it incon- [illegible] to bring up the child, to abandon it [illegible], or to wild beasts, was regarded [illegible] blame or censure. This practice [illegible] begun in times of the most sa- vage

[illegible] barbarians. [illegible] had been [illegible] earliest [illegible] continued [illegible] them [illegible] mity. We [illegible] ties prevail [illegible] in that [illegible] other. The [illegible] is often [illegible] exposed to [illegible] he [illegible] quently [illegible] himself and [illegible] therefore, [illegible] it. One who, [illegible] throw [illegible] his [illegible] would [illegible] In this state of [illegible] so great [illegible] however, [illegible] of [illegible] which could [illegible]

terrupted cuſtom had by this time ſo thoroughly authoriſed the practice, that not only the looſe maxims of the world tolerated this barbarous prerogative, but even the doctrine of philoſophers, which ought to have been more juſt and accurate, was led away by the eſtabliſhed cuſtom, and upon this, as upon many other occaſions, inſtead of cenſuring, ſupported the horrible abuſe, by far-fetched conſiderations of public utility. Ariſtotle talks of it as of what the magiſtrate ought upon many occaſions to encourage. The humane Plato is of the ſame opinion, and, with all that love of mankind which ſeems to animate all his writings, no where marks this practice with diſapprobation. When cuſtom can give ſanction to ſo dreadful a violation of humanity, we may well imagine that there is ſcarce any particular practice ſo groſs which it cannot authoriſe. Such a thing, we hear men every day ſaying, is commonly done, and they ſeem to think this a ſufficient apology for what, in itſelf, is the moſt unjuſt and unreaſonable conduct.

There is an obvious reaſon why cuſtom ſhould never pervert our ſentiments with regard to the general ſtyle and character of conduct and behaviour, in the ſame degree

as with regard to the propriety or unlawfulneſs of particular uſages. There never can be any ſuch cuſtom. No ſociety could ſubſiſt a moment, in which the uſual ſtrain of men's conduct and behaviour was of a piece with the horrible practice I have juſt now mentioned.

THE THEORY OF MORAL SENTIMENTS.

PART VI.

Of the CHARACTER of VIRTUE.

Consisting of three Sections.

INTRODUCTION.

W[illegible] we consider the character of any [illegible]

SECTION I.

Of the Character of the Individual, so far as it affects his own Happiness; or of Prudence.

THE preservation and healthful state of the body seem to be the objects which Nature first recommends to the care of every individual. The appetites of hunger and thirst, the agreeable or disagreeable sensations of pleasure and pain, of heat and cold, &c. may be considered as lessons delivered by the voice of Nature herself, directing him what he ought to chuse, and what he ought to avoid, for this purpose. The first lessons which he is taught by those to whom his childhood is entrusted, tend, the greater part of them, to the same purpose. Their principal object is to teach him how to keep out of harm's way.

As he grows up, he soon learns that some care and foresight are necessary for providing the means of gratifying those natural appetites, of procuring pleasure and avoiding pain, of procuring the agreeable and avoiding the disagreeable temperature of heat and cold.

cold. In the proper direction of this care and foresight consists the art of preserving and increasing what is called his external fortune.

Though it is in order to supply the necessities and conveniencies of the body, that the advantages of external fortune are originally recommended to us, yet we cannot live long in the world without perceiving that the respect of our equals, our credit and rank in the society we live in, depend very much upon the degree in which we possess, or are supposed to possess, those advantages. The desire of becoming the proper objects of this respect, of deserving and obtaining this credit and rank among our equals, is, perhaps, the strongest of all our desires, and our anxiety to obtain the advantages of fortune is accordingly much more excited and irritated by this desire, than by that of supplying all the necessities and conveniencies of the body, which are always very easily supplied.

Our rank and credit among our equals, too, depend very much upon, what, perhaps, a virtuous man would wish them to depend entirely, our character and conduct, or upon the confidence, esteem, and good-will, which these naturally excite in the people we live with.

The care of the health, of the fortune, of the rank and reputation of the individual, the objects upon which his comfort and happiness in this life are supposed principally to depend, is considered as the proper business of that virtue which is commonly called Prudence.

We suffer more, it has already been observed, when we fall from a better to a worse situation, than we ever enjoy when we rise from a worse to a better. Security, therefore, is the first and the principal object of prudence. It is averse to expose our health, our fortune, our rank, or reputation, to any sort of hazard. It is rather cautious than enterprising, and more anxious to preserve the advantages which we already possess, [illegible]

[illegible]

suade other people that he understands it; and though his talents may not always be very brilliant, they are always perfectly genuine. He neither endeavours to impose upon you by the cunning devices of an artful impostor, nor by the arrogant airs of an assuming pedant, nor by the confident assertions of a superficial and impudent pretender. He is not ostentatious, even of the abilities which he really possesses. His conversation is simple and modest, and he is averse to all the quackish arts by which other people so frequently thrust themselves into public notice and reputation. For reputation in his profession he is naturally disposed to rely a good deal upon the solidity of his knowledge and abilities; and he does not always think of cultivating the favour of those little clubs and cabals, who, in the superior arts and sciences, so often erect themselves into the supreme judges of merit; and who make it their business to celebrate the talents and virtues of one another, and to decry whatever can come into competition with them. If he ever connects himself with any society of this kind, it is merely in self-defence, not with a view to impose upon the public, but to hinder the public from being imposed upon, to his disadvantage, by the clamours,

the whispers, or the intrigues, either of that particular society, or of some other of the same kind.

The prudent man is always sincere, and feels horror at the very thought of exposing himself to the disgrace which attends upon the detection of falsehood. But though always sincere, he is not always frank and open; and though he never tells any thing but the truth, he does not always think himself bound, when not properly called upon, to tell the whole truth. As he is cautious in his actions, so he is reserved in his speech; and never rashly or unnecessarily obtrudes his opinion concerning either things or persons.

The prudent man, though not always distinguished by the most exquisite sensibility, is always very capable of friendship. But his friendship is not that ardent and passionate, but too often transitory affection, which appears so delicious to the generosity of youth and inexperience. It is a sedate, but steady and faithful attachment to a few well-tried and well-chosen companions; in the choice of whom he is not guided by the giddy admiration of shining accomplishments, but by the sober esteem of modesty, discretion, and good conduct. But though capable of

friendſhip, he is not always much diſpoſed to general ſociality. He rarely frequents, and more rarely figures in thoſe convivial ſocieties which are diſtinguiſhed for the jollity and gaiety of their converſation. Their way of life might too often interfere with the regularity of his temperance, might interrupt the ſteadineſs of his induſtry, or break in upon the ſtrictneſs of his frugality.

But though his converſation may not always be very ſprightly or diverting, it is always perfectly inoffenſive. He hates the thought of being guilty of any petulence or rudeneſs. He never aſſumes impertinently over any body, and, upon all common occaſions, is willing to place himſelf rather below than above his equals. Both in his conduct and converſation, he is an exact obſerver of decency, and reſpects with an almoſt religious ſcrupuloſity, all the eſtabliſhed decorums and ceremonials of ſociety. And, in this reſpect, he ſets a much better example than has frequently been done by men of much more ſplendid talents and virtues; who, in all ages, from that of Socrates and Ariſtippus, down to that of Dr. Swift and Voltaire, and from that of Philip and Alexander the Great, down to that of the great Czar Peter of Muſcovy, have too often diſtinguiſhed them-

ſelves by the moſt improper and even inſolent contempt of all the ordinary decorums of life and converſation, and who have thereby ſet the moſt pernicious example to thoſe who wiſh to reſemble them, and who too often content themſelves with imitating their follies, without even attempting to attain their perfections.

In the ſteadineſs of his induſtry and frugality, in his ſteadily ſacrificing the eaſe and enjoyment of the preſent moment for the probable expectation of the ſtill greater eaſe and enjoyment of a more diſtant but more laſting period of time, the prudent man is always both ſupported and rewarded by the entire approbation of the impartial ſpectator, and of the repreſentative of the impartial ſpectator, the man within the breaſt. The impartial ſpectator does not feel himſelf worn out by the preſent labour of thoſe whoſe conduct he ſurveys; nor does he feel himſelf ſolicited by the importunate calls of their preſent appetites. To him their preſent, and what is likely to be their future ſituation, are very nearly the ſame: he ſees them nearly at the ſame diſtance, and is affected by them very nearly in the ſame manner. He knows, however, that to the perſons principally concerned, they are very far from being the ſame,

fame, and that they naturally affect *them* in a very different manner. He cannot therefore but approve, and even applaud, that proper exertion of self-command, which enables them to act as if their present and their future situation affected them nearly in the same manner in which they affect him.

The man who lives within his income, is naturally contented with his situation, which by continual, though small accumulations, is growing better and better every day. He is enabled gradually to relax, both in the rigour of his parsimony and in the severity of his application; and he feels with double satisfaction this gradual increase of ease and enjoyment, from having felt before the hardship which attended the want of them. He has no anxiety to change so comfortable a situation, and does not go in quest of new enterprises and adventures, which might endanger, but could not well increase, the secure tranquillity which he actually enjoys. If he enters into any new projects or enterprises, they are likely to be well concerted and well prepared. He can never be hurried or drove into them by any necessity, but has always time and leisure to deliberate soberly and coolly concerning what are likely to be their consequences.

The prudent man is not willing to ſubject himſelf to any reſponſibility which his duty does not impoſe upon him. He is not a buſtler in buſineſs where he has no concern; is not a meddler in other people's affairs; is not a profeſſed counſellor or adviſer, who obtrudes his advice where nobody is aſking it. He confines himſelf, as much as his duty will permit, to his own affairs, and has no taſte for that fooliſh importance which many people wiſh to derive from appearing to have ſome influence in the management of thoſe of other people. He is averſe to enter into any party diſputes, hates faction, and is not always very forward to liſten to the voice even of noble and great ambition. When diſtinctly called upon, he will not decline the ſervice of his country, but he will not cabal in order to force himſelf into it, and would be much better pleaſed that the public buſineſs were well managed by ſome other perſon, than that he himſelf ſhould have the trouble, and incur the reſponſibility, of managing it. In the bottom of his heart he would prefer the undiſturbed enjoyment of ſecure tranquillity, not only to all the vain ſplendour of ſucceſsful ambition, but to the real and ſolid glory of performing the greateſt and moſt magnanimous actions.

Prudence,

Prudence, in ſhort, when directed merely to the care of the health, of the fortune, and of the rank and reputation of the individual, though it is regarded as a moſt reſpectable, and even in ſome degree, as an amiable and agreeable quality, yet it never is conſidered as one, either of the moſt endearing, or of the moſt ennobling of the virtues. It commands a certain cold eſteem, but ſeems not entitled to any very ardent love or admiration.

Wiſe and judicious conduct, when directed to greater and nobler purpoſes than the care of the health, the fortune, the rank and reputation of the individual, is frequently and very properly called prudence. We talk of the prudence of the great general, of the great ſtateſman, of the great legiſlator. Prudence is, in all theſe caſes, combined with many greater and more ſplendid virtues, with valour, with extenſive and ſtrong benevolence, with a ſacred regard to the rules of juſtice, and all theſe ſupported by a proper degree of ſelf-command. This ſuperior prudence, when carried to the higheſt degree of perfection, neceſſarily ſuppoſes the art, the talent, and the habit or diſpoſition of acting with the moſt perfect propriety in every poſſible circumſtance and ſituation. It neceſſa-

nily supposes the utmost perfection of all the intellectual and of all the moral virtues. It is the best head joined to the best heart. It is the most perfect wisdom combined with the most perfect virtue. It constitutes very nearly the character of the Academical or Peripatetic sage, as the inferior prudence does that of the Epicurean.

Mere imprudence, or the mere want of the capacity to take care of one's self, is, with the generous and humane, the object of compassion; with those of less delicate sentiments, of neglect, or, at worst, of contempt, but never of hatred or indignation. When combined with other vices, however, it aggravates in the highest degree the infamy and disgrace which would otherwise attend them. The artful knave, whose dexterity and address exempt him, though not from strong suspicions, yet from punishment or distinct detection, is too often received in the world with an indulgence which he by no means deserves. The awkward and foolish one, who, for want of this dexterity and address, is convicted and brought to punishment, is the object of universal hatred, contempt, and derision. In countries where great crimes frequently pass unpunished, the most atrocious

cious actions become almoſt familiar, and ceaſe to impreſs the people with that horror which is univerſally felt in countries where an exact adminiſtration of juſtice takes place. The injuſtice is the ſame in both countries; but the imprudence is often very different. In the latter, great crimes are evidently great follies. In the former, they are not always conſidered as ſuch. In Italy, during the greater part of the ſixteenth century, aſſaſſinations, murders, and even murders under truſt, ſeem to have been almoſt familiar among the ſuperior ranks of people. Cæſar Borgia invited four of the little princes in his neighbourhood, who all poſſeſſed little ſovereignties, and commanded little armies of their own, to a friendly conference at Senigaglia, where, as ſoon as they arrived, he put them all to death. This infamous action, though certainly not approved of even in that age of crimes, ſeems to have contributed very little to the diſcredit, and not in the leaſt to the ruin of the perpetrator. That ruin happened a few years after from cauſes altogether diſconnected with this crime. Machiavel, not indeed a man of the niceſt morality even for his own times, was reſident, as miniſter from the republic of Florence, at the court of Cæſar Borgia when this crime was

committed. He gives a very particular account of it, and in that pure, elegant, and ſimple language which diſtinguiſhes all his writings. He talks of it very coolly; is pleaſed with the addreſs with which Cæſar Borgia conducted it; has much contempt for the dupery and weakneſs of the ſufferers; but no compaſſion for their miſerable and untimely death, and no ſort of indignation at the cruelty and falſehood of their murderer. The violence and injuſtice of great conquerors are often regarded with fooliſh wonder and admiration; thoſe of petty thieves, robbers, and murderers, with contempt, hatred, and even horror upon all occaſions. The former, though they are a hundred times more miſchievous and deſtructive, yet when ſucceſsful, they often paſs for deeds of the moſt heroic magnanimity. The latter are always viewed with hatred and averſion, as the follies, as well as the crimes, of the loweſt and moſt worthleſs of mankind. The injuſtice of the former is certainly, at leaſt, as great as that of the latter; but the folly and imprudence are not near ſo great. A wicked and worthleſs man of parts often goes through the world with much more credit than he deſerves. A wicked and worthleſs fool appears always, of all mortals, the moſt hateful,

ful, as well as the most contemptible. As prudence, combined with other virtues, constitutes the noblest; so imprudence, combined with other vices, constitutes the vilest of all characters.

SECTION II.

Of the Character of the Individual, ſo far as it can affect the Happineſs of other People.

INTRODUCTION.

THE character of every individual, ſo far as it can affect the happineſs of other people, muſt do ſo by its diſpoſition either to hurt or to benefit them.

Proper reſentment for injuſtice attempted, or actually committed, is the only motive which, in the eyes of the impartial ſpectator, can juſtify our hurting or diſturbing in any reſpect the happineſs of our neighbour. To do ſo from any other motive, is itſelf a violation of the laws of juſtice, which force ought to be employed either to reſtrain or to puniſh. The wiſdom of every ſtate or commonwealth endeavours, as well as it can, to employ the force of the ſociety to reſtrain thoſe who are ſubject to its authority, from hurting or diſturbing the happineſs of one another. The rules which it eſtabliſhes for this

this purpose, constitute the civil and criminal law of each particular state or country. The principles upon which those rules either are, or ought to be founded, are the subject of a particular science, of all sciences by far the most important, but hitherto, perhaps, the least cultivated, that of natural jurisprudence; concerning which it belongs not to our present subject to enter into any detail. A sacred and religious regard not to hurt or disturb in any respect the happiness of our neighbour, even in those cases where no law can properly protect him, constitutes the character of the perfectly innocent and just man; a character which, when carried to a certain delicacy of attention is always highly respectable and even venerable for its own sake, and can scarce ever fail to be accompanied with many other virtues, with great feeling for other people, with great humanity and great benevolence. It is a character sufficiently understood, and requires no further explanation. In the present section I shall only endeavour to explain the foundation of that order which nature seems to have traced out for the distribution of our good offices, or for the direction and employment of our very limited powers of beneficence: first,

towards

towards individuals; and fecondly, towards focieties.

The fame unerring wifdom, it will be found, which regulates every other part of her conduct, directs, in this refpect too, the order of her recommendations; which are always ftronger or weaker in proportion as our beneficence is more or lefs neceffary, or can be more or lefs ufeful.

CHAP. I.

Of the Order in which Individuals are recommended by Nature to our care and attention.

EVERY man, as the Stoics ufed to fay, is firft and principally recommended to his own care; and every man is certainly, in every refpect, fitter and abler to take care of himfelf than of any other perfon. Every man feels his own pleafures and his own pains more fenfibly than thofe of other people. The former are the original fenfations; the latter the reflected or fympathetic images of

of thoſe ſenſations. The former may be ſaid to be the ſubſtance; the latter the ſhadow.

After himſelf, the members of his own family, thoſe who uſually live in the ſame houſe with him, his parents, his children, his brothers and ſiſters, are naturally the objects of his warmeſt affections. They are naturally and uſually the perſons upon whoſe happineſs or miſery his conduct muſt have the greateſt influence. He is more habituated to ſympathize with them. He knows better how every thing is likely to affect them, and his ſympathy with them is more preciſe and determinate, than it can be with the greater part of other people. It approaches nearer, in ſhort, to what he feels for himſelf.

This ſympathy too, and the affections which are founded on it, are by nature more ſtrongly directed towards his children than towards his parents, and his tenderneſs for the former ſeems generally a more active principle, than his reverence and gratitude towards the latter. In the natural ſtate of things, it has already been obſerved, the exiſtence of the child, for ſome time after it comes into the world, depends altogether upon the care of the parent; that of the parent does not naturally depend upon the

care of the child. In the eye of nature, it would ſeem, a child is a more important object than an old man; and excites a much more lively, as well as a much more univerſal ſympathy. It ought to do ſo. Every thing may be expected, or at leaſt hoped, from the child. In ordinary caſes, very little can be either expected or hoped from the old man. The weakneſs of childhood intereſts the affections of the moſt brutal and hard-hearted. It is only to the virtuous and humane, that the infirmities of old age are not the objects of contempt and averſion. In ordinary caſes, an old man dies without being much regretted by any body. Scarce a child can die without rending aſunder the heart of ſomebody.

The earlieſt friendſhips, the friendſhips which are naturally contracted when the heart is moſt ſuſceptible of that feeling, are thoſe among brothers and ſiſters. Their good agreement, while they remain in the ſame family, is neceſſary for its tranquillity and happineſs. They are capable of giving more pleaſure or pain to one another than to the greater part of other people. Their ſituation renders their mutual ſympathy of the utmoſt importance to their common happineſs; and, by the wiſdom of nature, the ſame ſitua-

tion, by obliging them to accommodate to one another, renders that sympathy more habitual, and thereby more lively, more distinct, and more determinate.

The children of brothers and sisters are naturally connected by the friendship which, after separating into different families, continues to take place between their parents. Their good agreement improves the enjoyment of that friendship; their discord would disturb it. As they seldom live in the same family, however, though of more importance to one another, than to the greater part of other people, they are of much less than brothers and sisters. As their mutual sympathy is less necessary, so it is less habitual, and therefore proportionably weaker.

The children of cousins, being still less connected, are of still less importance to one another; and the affection gradually diminishes as the relation grows more and more remote.

What is called affection, is in reality, nothing but habitual sympathy. Our concern in the happiness or misery of those who are the objects of what we call our affections; our desire to promote the one, and to prevent the other; are either the actual feeling of that habitual sympathy, or the necessary con-

consequences of that feeling. Relations being usually placed in situations which naturally create this habitual sympathy, it is expected that a suitable degree of affection should take place among them. We generally find that it actually does take place; we therefore naturally expect that it should; and we are, upon that account, more shocked when, upon any occasion, we find that it does not. The general rule is established, that persons related to one another in a certain degree, ought always to be affected towards one another in a certain manner, and that there is always the highest impropriety, and sometimes even a sort of impiety, in their being affected in a different manner. A parent without parental tenderness, a child devoid of all filial reverence, appear monsters, the objects, not of hatred only, but of horror.

Though in a particular instance, the circumstances which usually produce those natural affections, as they are called, may, by some accident, not have taken place, yet respect for the general rule will frequently, in some measure, supply their place, and produce something which, though not altogether the same, may bear, however, a very considerable resemblance to those affections.

A father

A father is apt to be less attached to a child, who, by some accident, has been separated from him in its infancy, and who does not return to him till it is grown up to manhood. The father is apt to feel less paternal tenderness for the child; the child, less filial reverence for the father. Brothers and sisters, when they have been educated in distant countries, are apt to feel a similar diminution of affection. With the dutiful and the virtuous, however, respect for the general rule will frequently produce something which, though by no means the same, yet may very much resemble those natural affections. Even during the separation, the father and the child, the brothers or the sisters, are by no means indifferent to one another. They all consider one another as persons to and from whom certain affections are due, and they live in the hopes of being some time or another in a situation to enjoy that friendship which ought naturally to have taken place among persons so nearly connected. Till they meet, the absent son, the absent brother, are frequently the favourite son, the favourite brother. They have never offended, or, if they have, it is so long ago, that the offence is forgotten, as some childish trick not worth the remembering. Every account

they have heard of one another, if conveyed by people of any tolerable good nature, has been, in the higheſt degree, flattering and favourable. The abſent ſon, the abſent brother, is not like other ordinary ſons and brothers; but an all-perfect ſon, an all-perfect brother; and the moſt romantic hopes are entertained of the happineſs to be enjoyed in the friendſhip and converſation of ſuch perſons. When they meet, it is often with ſo ſtrong a diſpoſition to conceive that habitual ſympathy which conſtitutes the family affection, that they are very apt to fancy they have actually conceived it, and to behave to one another as if they had. Time and experience, however, I am afraid, too frequently undeceive them. Upon a more familiar acquaintance, they frequently diſcover in one another habits, humours, and inclinations, different from what they expected, to which, from want of habitual ſympathy, from want of the real principle and foundation of what is properly called family-affection, they cannot now eaſily accommodate themſelves. They have never lived in the ſituation which almoſt neceſſarily forces that eaſy accommodation, and though they may now be ſincerely deſirous to aſſume it, they have really become incapable of doing

doing ſo. Their familiar converſation and intercourſe ſoon become leſs pleaſing to them, and, upon that account, leſs frequent. They may continue to live with one another in the mutual exchange of all eſſential good offices, and with every other external appearance of decent regard. But that cordial ſatisfaction, that delicious ſympathy, that confidential openneſs and eaſe, which naturally take place in the converſation of thoſe who have lived long and familiarly with one another, it ſeldom happens that they can completely enjoy.

It is only, however, with the dutiful and the virtuous, that the general rule has even this ſlender authority. With the diſſipated, the profligate, and the vain, it is entirely diſregarded. They are ſo far from reſpecting it, that they ſeldom talk of it but with the moſt indecent deriſion; and an early and long ſeparation of this kind never fails to eſtrange them moſt completely from one another. With ſuch perſons, reſpect for the general rule can at beſt produce only a cold and affected civility (a very ſlender ſemblance of real regard); and even this, the ſlighteſt offence, the ſmalleſt oppoſition of intereſt, commonly puts an end to altogether.

The education of boys at diſtant great ſchools, of young men at diſtant colleges, of young ladies in diſtant nunneries and boarding-ſchools, ſeems, in the higher ranks of life, to have hurt moſt eſſentially the domeſtic morals, and conſequently the domeſtic happineſs, both of France and England. Do you wiſh to educate your children to be dutiful to their parents, to be kind and affectionate to their brothers and ſiſters? put them under the neceſſity of being dutiful children, of being kind and affectionate brothers and ſiſters: educate them in your own houſe. From their parent's houſe they may, with propriety and advantage, go out every day to attend public ſchools: but let their dwelling be always at home. Reſpect for you muſt always impoſe a very uſeful reſtraint upon their conduct; and reſpect for them may frequently impoſe no uſeleſs reſtraint upon your own. Surely no acquirement, which can poſſibly be derived from what is called a public education, can make any ſort of compenſation for what is almoſt certainly and neceſſarily loſt by it. Domeſtic education is the inſtitution of nature; public education the contrivance of man. It is ſurely unneceſſary to ſay, which is likely to be the wiſeſt.

In ſome tragedies and romances, we meet with many beautiful and intereſting ſcenes, founded upon, what is called, the force of blood, or upon the wonderful affection which near relations are ſuppoſed to conceive for one another, even before they know that they have any ſuch connexion. This force of blood, however, I am afraid, exiſts no-where but in tragedies and romances. Even in tragedies and romances, it is never ſuppoſed to take place between any relations, but thoſe who are naturally bred up in the ſame houſe; between parents and children, between brothers and ſiſters. To imagine any ſuch myſterious affection between couſins, or even between aunts or uncles, and nephews or nieces, would be too ridiculous.

In paſtoral countries, and in all countries where the authority of law is not alone ſufficient to give perfect ſecurity to every member of the ſtate, all the different branches of the ſame family commonly chuſe to live in the neighbourhood of one another. Their aſſociation is frequently neceſſary for their common defence. They are all, from the higheſt to the loweſt, of more or leſs importance to one another. Their concord ſtrengthens their neceſſary aſſociation; their

difcord always weakens, and might deftroy it. They have more intercourfe with one another, than with the members of any other tribe. The remoteft members of the fame tribe claim fome connection with one another; and, where all other circumftances are equal, expect to be treated with more diftinguifhed attention than is due to thofe who have no fuch pretenfions. It is not many years ago that, in the Highlands of Scotland, the Chieftain ufed to confider the pooreft man of his clan, as his coufin and relation. The fame extenfive regard to kindred is faid to take place among the Tartars, the Arabs, the Turkomans, and, I believe, among all other nations who are nearly in the fame ftate of fociety in which the Scots Highlanders were about the beginning of the prefent century.

In commercial countries, where the authority of law is always perfectly fufficient to protect the meaneft man in the ftate, the defcendants of the fame family, having no fuch motive for keeping together, naturally feparate and difperfe, as intereft or inclination may direct. They foon ceafe to be of importance to one another; and, in a few generations, not only lofe all care about one another, but all remembrance of their common

mon origin, and of the connection which took place among their anceſtors. Regard for remote relations becomes, in every country, leſs and leſs, according as this ſtate of civilization has been longer and more completely eſtabliſhed. It has been longer and more completely eſtabliſhed in England than in Scotland; and remote relations are, accordingly, more conſidered in the latter country than in the former, though, in this reſpect, the difference between the two countries is growing leſs and leſs every day. Great lords, indeed, are, in every country, proud of remembering and acknowledging their connection with one another, however remote. The remembrance of ſuch illuſtrious relations flatters not a little the family pride of them all; and it is neither from affection, nor from any thing which reſembles affection, but from the moſt frivolous and childiſh of all vanities, that this remembrance is ſo carefully kept up. Should ſome more humble, though, perhaps, much nearer kinſman, preſume to put ſuch great men in mind of his relation to their family, they ſeldom fail to tell him that they are bad genealogiſts, and miſerably ill-informed concerning their own family hiſtory. It is not in that order, I am afraid, that we are to ex-

pect any extraordinary extenſion of, what is called, natural affection.

I conſider what is called natural affection as more the effect of the moral than of the ſuppoſed phyſical connection between the parent and the child. A jealous huſband, indeed, notwithſtanding the moral connection, notwithſtanding the child's having been educated in his own houſe, often regards, with hatred and averſion, that unhappy child which he ſuppoſes to be the offſpring of his wife's infidelity. It is the laſting monument of a moſt diſagreeable adventure; of his own diſhonour, and of the diſgrace of his family.

Among well-diſpoſed people, the neceſſity or conveniency of mutual accommodation, very frequently produces a friendſhip not unlike that which takes place among thoſe who are born to live in the ſame family. Colleagues in office, partners in trade, call one another brothers; and frequently feel towards one another as if they really were ſo. Their good agreement is an advantage to all; and, if they are tolerably reaſonable people, they are naturally diſpoſed to agree. We expect that they ſhould do ſo; and their diſagreement is a ſort of a ſmall ſcandal. The Romans expreſſed this ſort of attach-

ment by the word *necessitudo*, which, from the etymology, seems to denote that it was imposed by the necessity of the situation.

Even the trifling circumstance of living in the same neighbourhood, has some effect of the same kind. We respect the face of a man whom we see every day, provided he has never offended us. Neighbours can be very convenient, and they can be very troublesome, to one another. If they are good sort of people, they are naturally disposed to agree. We expect their good agreement; and to be a bad neighbour is a very bad character. There are certain small good offices, accordingly, which are universally allowed to be due to a neighbour in preference to any other person who has no such connection.

This natural disposition to accommodate and to assimilate, as much as we can, our own sentiments, principles, and feelings, to those which we see fixed and rooted in the persons whom we are obliged to live and converse a great deal with, is the cause of the contagious effects of both good and bad company. The man who associates chiefly with the wise and the virtuous, though he may not himself become either wise or virtuous, cannot help conceiving a certain re-

spect

ſpect at leaſt for wiſdom and virtue; and the man who aſſociates chiefly with the profligate and the diſſolute, though he may not himſelf become profligate and diſſolute, muſt ſoon loſe, at leaſt, all his original abhorrence of profligacy and diſſolution of manners. The ſimilarity of family characters, which we ſo frequently ſee tranſmitted through ſeveral ſucceſſive generations, may, perhaps, be partly owing to this diſpoſition, to aſſimilate ourſelves to thoſe whom we are obliged to live and converſe a great deal with. The family character, however, like the family countenance, ſeems to be owing, not altogether to the moral, but partly to the phyſical connection. The family countenance is certainly altogether owing to the latter.

But of all attachments to an individual, that which is founded altogether upon eſteem and approbation of his good conduct and behaviour, confirmed by much experience and long acquaintance, is, by far, the moſt reſpectable. Such friendſhips, ariſing not from a conſtrained ſympathy, not from a ſympathy which has been aſſumed and rendered habitual for the ſake of convenience and accommodation; but from a natural ſympathy, from an involuntary feeling that the perſons to whom we attach ourſelves are the natural and proper objects

objects of esteem and approbation; can exist only among men of virtue. Men of virtue only can feel that entire confidence in the conduct and behaviour of one another, which can, at all times, assure them that they can never either offend or be offended by one another. Vice is always capricious; virtue only is regular and orderly. The attachment which is founded upon the love of virtue, as it is certainly, of all attachments, the most virtuous; so it is likewise the happiest, as well as the most permanent and secure. Such friendships need not be confined to a single person, but may safely embrace all the wise and virtuous, with whom we have been long and intimately acquainted, and upon whose wisdom and virtue we can, upon that account, entirely depend. They who would confine friendship to two persons, seem to confound the wise security of friendship with the jealousy and folly of love. The hasty, fond, and foolish intimacies of young people, founded, commonly, upon some slight similarity of character, altogether unconnected with good conduct, upon a taste, perhaps, for the same studies, the same amusements, the same diversions, or upon their agreement in some singular principle or opinion, not commonly adopted; those intimacies which a freak be-

gins,

gins, and which a freak puts an end to, how agreeable ſoever they may appear while they laſt, can by no means deſerve the ſacred and venerable name of friendſhip.

Of all the perſons, however, whom nature points out for our peculiar beneficence, there are none to whom it ſeems more properly directed than to thoſe whoſe beneficence we have ourſelves already experienced. Nature, which formed men for that mutual kindneſs, ſo neceſſary for their happineſs, renders every man the peculiar object of kindneſs, to the perſons to whom he himſelf has been kind. Though their gratitude ſhould not always correſpond to his beneficence, yet the ſenſe of his merit, the ſympathetic gratitude of the impartial ſpectator, will always correſpond to it. The general indignation of other people, againſt the baſeneſs of their ingratitude, will even, ſometimes, increaſe the general ſenſe of his merit. No benevolent man ever loſt altogether the fruits of his benevolence. If he does not always gather them from the perſons from whom he ought to have gathered them, he ſeldom fails to gather them, and with a tenfold increaſe, from other people. Kindneſs is the parent of kindneſs; and if to be beloved by our brethren be the great object of our ambition, the

the ſureſt way of obtaining it is, by our conduct to ſhew that we really love them.

After the perſons who are recommended to our beneficence, either by their connection with ourſelves, by their perſonal qualities, or by their paſt ſervices, come thoſe who are pointed out, not indeed to, what is called, our friendſhip, but to our benevolent attention and good offices; thoſe who are diſtinguiſhed by their extraordinary ſituation; the greatly fortunate and the greatly unfortunate, the rich and the powerful, the poor and the wretched. The diſtinction of ranks, the peace and order of ſociety, are, in a great meaſure, founded upon the reſpect which we naturally conceive for the former. The relief and conſolation of human miſery depend altogether upon our compaſſion for the latter. The peace and order of ſociety, is of more importance than even the relief of the miſerable. Our reſpect for the great, accordingly, is moſt apt to offend by its exceſs; our fellow-feeling for the miſerable, by its defect. Moraliſts exhort us to charity and compaſſion. They warn us againſt the faſcination of greatneſs. This faſcination, indeed, is ſo powerful, that the rich and the great are too often preferred to the wiſe and the virtuous. Nature has wiſely judged that the diſtinction

of

of rank, the peace and order of ſociety, would reſt more ſecurely upon the plain and palpable difference of birth and fortune, than upon the inviſible and often uncertain difference of wiſdom and virtue. The undiſtinguiſhing eyes of the great mob of mankind can well enough perceive the former: it is with difficulty that the nice diſcernment of the wiſe and the virtuous can ſometimes diſtinguiſh the latter. In the order of all thoſe recommendations, the benevolent wiſdom of nature is equally evident.

It may, perhaps, be unneceſſary to obſerve, that the combination of two, or more, of thoſe exciting cauſes of kindneſs, increaſes the kindneſs. The favour and partiality which, when there is no envy in the caſe, we naturally bear to greatneſs, are much increaſed when it is joined with wiſdom and virtue. If, notwithſtanding that wiſdom and virtue, the great man ſhould fall into thoſe misfortunes, thoſe dangers and diſtreſſes, to which the moſt exalted ſtations are often the moſt expoſed, we are much more deeply intereſted in his fortune than we ſhould be in that of a perſon equally virtuous, but in a more humble ſituation. The moſt intereſting ſubjects of tragedies and romances are the misfortunes of virtuous and magnanimous

nimous kings and princes. If, by the wisdom and manhood of their exertions, they should extricate themselves from those misfortunes, and recover completely their former superiority and security, we cannot help viewing them with the most enthusiastic and even extravagant admiration. The grief which we felt for their distress, the joy which we feel for their prosperity, seem to combine together in enhancing that partial admiration which we naturally conceive both for the station and the character.

When those different beneficent affections happen to draw different ways, to determine by any precise rules in what cases we ought to comply with the one, and in what with the other, is, perhaps, altogether impossible. In what cases friendship ought to yield to gratitude, or gratitude to friendship; in what cases the strongest of all natural affections ought to yield to a regard for the safety of those superiors upon whose safety often depends that of the whole society; and in what cases natural affection may, without impropriety, prevail over that regard; must be left altogether to the decision of the man within the breast, the supposed impartial spectator, the great judge and arbiter of our conduct. If we place ourselves completely in his situation,

tion, if we really view ourſelves with his eyes, and as he views us, and liſten with diligent and reverential attention to what he ſuggeſts to us, his voice will never deceive us. We ſhall ſtand in need of no caſuiſtic rules to direct our conduct. Theſe it is often impoſſible to accommodate to all the different ſhades and gradations of circumſtance, character, and ſituation, to differences and diſtinctions which, though not imperceptible, are, by their nicety and delicacy, often altogether undefinable. In that beautiful tragedy of Voltaire, the Orphan of China, while we admire the magnanimity of Zanti, who is willing to ſacrifice the life of his own child, in order to preſerve that of the only feeble remnant of his ancient ſovereigns and maſters; we not only pardon, but love the maternal tenderneſs of Idame, who, at the riſque of diſcovering the important ſecret of her huſband, reclaims her infant from the cruel hands of the Tartars, into which it had been delivered.

CHAP. II.

Of the order in which Societies are by nature recommended to our Beneficence.

THE ſame principles that direct the order in which individuals are recommended to our beneficence, direct that likewiſe in which ſocieties are recommended to it. Thoſe to which it is, or may be of moſt importance, are firſt and principally recommended to it.

The ſtate or ſovereignty in which we have been born and educated, and under the protection of which we continue to live, is, in ordinary caſes, the greateſt ſociety upon whoſe happineſs or miſery, our good or bad conduct can have much influence. It is accordingly, by nature, moſt ſtrongly recommended to us. Not only we ourſelves, but all the objects of our kindeſt affections, our children, our parents, our relations, our friends, our benefactors, all thoſe whom we naturally love and revere the moſt, are commonly comprehended within it; and their proſperity and ſafety depend in ſome mea-

ſure upon its proſperity and ſafety. It is by nature, therefore, endeared to us, not only by all our ſelfiſh, but by all our private benevolent affections. Upon account of our own connection with it, its proſperity and glory ſeem to reflect ſome ſort of honour upon ourſelves. When we compare it with other ſocieties of the ſame kind, we are proud of its ſuperiority, and mortified in ſome degree, if it appears in any reſpect below them. All the illuſtrious characters which it has produced in former times (for againſt thoſe of our own times envy may ſometimes prejudice us a little), its warriors, its ſtateſmen, its poets, its philoſophers, and men of letters of all kinds; we are diſpoſed to view with the moſt partial admiration, and to rank them (ſometimes moſt unjuſtly) above thoſe of all other nations. The patriot who lays down his life for the ſafety, or even for the vain-glory of this ſociety, appears to act with the moſt exact propriety. He appears to view himſelf in the light in which the impartial ſpectator naturally and neceſſarily views him, as but one of the multitude, in the eye of that equitable judge, of no more conſequence than any other in it, but bound at all times to ſacrifice and devote himſelf to the ſafety, to the ſervice, and even to the glory

glory of the greater number. But though this facrifice appears to be perfectly juft and proper, we know how difficult it is to make it, and how few people are capable of making it. His conduct, therefore, excites not only our entire approbation, but our higheft wonder and admiration, and feems to merit all the applaufe which can be due to the moft heroic virtue. The traitor, on the contrary, who, in fome peculiar fituation, fancies he can promote his own little intereft by betraying to the public enemy that of his native country; who, regardlefs of the judgment of the man within the breaft, prefers himfelf, in this refpect fo fhamefully and fo bafely, to all thofe with whom he has any connection; appears to be of all villains the moft deteftable.

The love of our own nation often difpofes us to view, with the moft malignant jealoufy and envy, the profperity and aggrandifement of any other neighbouring nation. Independent and neighbouring nations, having no common fuperior to decide their difputes, all live in continual dread and fufpicion of one another. Each fovereign, expecting little juftice from his neighbours, is difpofed to treat them with as little as he expects from them. The regard for the laws of nations,

or for thoſe rules which independent ſtates profeſs or pretend to think themſelves bound to obſerve in their dealings with one another, is often very little more than mere pretence and profeſſion. From the ſmalleſt intereſt, upon the ſlighteſt provocation, we ſee thoſe rules every day, either evaded or directly violated without ſhame or remorſe. Each nation foreſees, or imagines it foreſees, its own ſubjugation in the increaſing power and aggrandiſement of any of its neighbours; and the mean principle of national prejudice is often founded upon the noble one of the love of our own country. The ſentence with which the elder Cato is ſaid to have concluded every ſpeech which he made in the ſenate, whatever might be the ſubject, "*It is my opinion likewiſe that Carthage ought* "*to be deſtroyed*," was the natural expreſſion of the ſavage patriotiſm of a ſtrong but coarſe mind, enraged almoſt to madneſs againſt a foreign nation from which his own had ſuffered ſo much. The more humane ſentence with which Scipio Naſica is ſaid to have concluded all his ſpeeches, "*It is my* "*opinion likewiſe that Carthage ought not to* "*be deſtroyed*," was the liberal expreſſion of a more enlarged and enlightened mind, who felt no averſion to the proſperity even of an

old enemy, when reduced to a ſtate which could no longer be formidable to Rome. France and England may each of them have ſome reaſon to dread the increaſe of the naval and military power of the other; but for either of them to envy the internal happineſs and proſperity of the other, the cultivation of its lands, the advancement of its manufactures, the increaſe of its commerce, the ſecurity and number of its ports and harbours, its proficiency in all the liberal arts and ſciences, is ſurely beneath the dignity of two ſuch great nations. Theſe are the real improvements of the world we live in. Mankind are benefited, human nature is ennobled by them. In ſuch improvements each nation ought, not only to endeavour itſelf to excel, but from the love of mankind, to promote, inſtead of obſtructing the excellence of its neighbours. Theſe are all proper objects of national emulation, not of national prejudice or envy.

The love of our own country ſeems not to be derived from the love of mankind. The former ſentiment is altogether independent of the latter, and ſeems ſometimes even to diſpoſe us to act inconſiſtently with it. France may contain, perhaps, near three times the number of inhabitants which Great Britain

contains. In the great ſociety of mankind, therefore, the proſperity of France ſhould appear to be an object of much greater importance than that to Great Britain. The British ſubject, however, who, upon that account, ſhould prefer upon all occaſions the proſperity of the former to that of the latter country, would not be thought a good citizen of Great Britain. We do not love our country merely as a part of the great ſociety of mankind: we love it for its own ſake, and independently of any ſuch conſideration. That wiſdom which contrived the ſyſtem of human affections, as well as that of every other part of nature, ſeems to have judged that the intereſt of the great ſociety of mankind would be beſt promoted by directing the principal attention of each individual to that particular portion of it, which was moſt within the ſphere both of his abilities and of his underſtanding.

National prejudices and hatreds ſeldom extend beyond neighbouring nations. We very weakly and fooliſhly, perhaps, call the French our natural enemies; and they perhaps, as weakly and fooliſhly, conſider us in the ſame manner. Neither they nor we bear any ſort of envy to the proſperity of China or Japan. It very rarely happens, however, that

that our good-will towards ſuch diſtant countries can be exerted with much effect.

The moſt extenſive public benevolence which can commonly be exerted with any conſiderable effect, is that of the ſtateſmen, who project and form alliances among neighbouring or not very diſtant nations, for the preſervation either of, what is called, the balance of power, or of the general peace and tranquillity of the ſtates within the circle of their negociations. The ſtateſmen, however, who plan and execute ſuch treaties have ſeldom any thing in view, but the intereſt of their reſpective countries. Sometimes, indeed, their views are more extenſive. The Count d'Avaux, the plenipotentiary of France, at the treaty of Munſter, would have been willing to ſacrifice his life (according to the Cardinal de Retz, a man not over-credulous in the virtue of other people), in order to have reſtored, by that treaty, the general tranquillity of Europe. King William ſeems to have had a real zeal for the liberty and independency of the greater part of the ſovereign ſtates of Europe; which, perhaps, might be a good deal ſtimulated by his particular averſion to France, the ſtate from which, during his time, that liberty and independency were principally in danger.

Some ſhare of the ſame ſpirit ſeems to have deſcended to the firſt miniſtry of Queen Anne.

Every independent ſtate is divided into many different orders and ſocieties, each of which has its own particular powers, privileges, and immunities. Every individual is naturally more attached to his own particular order or ſociety, than to any other. His own intereſt, his own vanity, the intereſt and vanity of many of his friends and companions, are commonly a good deal connected with it. He is ambitious to extend its privileges and immunities. He is zealous to defend them againſt the encroachments of every other order or ſociety.

Upon the manner in which any ſtate is divided into the different orders and ſocieties which compoſe it, and upon the particular diſtribution which has been made of their reſpective powers, privileges, and immunities, depends, what is called, the conſtitution of that particular ſtate.

Upon the ability of each particular order or ſociety to maintain its own powers, privileges, and immunities, againſt the encroachments of every other, depends the ſtability of that particular conſtitution. That particular conſtitution is neceſſarily more or leſs altered,

altered, whenever any of its ſubordinate parts is either raiſed above or depreſſed below whatever had been its former rank and condition.

All thoſe different orders and ſocieties are dependent upon the ſtate to which they owe their ſecurity and protection. That they are all ſubordinate to that ſtate, and eſtabliſhed only in ſubſerviency to its proſperity and preſervation, is a truth acknowledged by the moſt partial member of every one of them. It may often, however, be hard to convince him that the proſperity and preſervation of the ſtate require any diminution of the powers, privileges, and immunities of his own particular order or ſociety. This partiality, though it may ſometimes be unjuſt, may not, upon that account, be uſeleſs. It checks the ſpirit of innovation. It tends to preſerve whatever is the eſtabliſhed balance among the different orders and ſocieties into which the ſtate is divided; and while it ſometimes appears to obſtruct ſome alterations of government which may be faſhionable and popular at the time, it contributes in reality to the ſtability and permanency of the whole ſyſtem.

The love of our country ſeems, in ordinary caſes, to involve in it two different principles;

ples; first, a certain respect and reverence for that constitution or form of government which is actually established; and secondly, an earnest desire to render the condition of our fellow-citizens as safe, respectable, and happy as we can. He is not a citizen who is not disposed to respect the laws and to obey the civil magistrate; and he is certainly not a good citizen who does not wish to promote, by every means in his power, the welfare of the whole society of his fellow-citizens.

In peaceable and quiet times, those two principles generally coincide and lead to the same conduct. The support of the established government seems evidently the best expedient for maintaining the safe, respectable, and happy situation of our fellow-citizens; when we see that this government actually maintains them in that situation. But in times of public discontent, faction, and disorder, those two different principles may draw different ways, and even a wise man may be disposed to think some alteration necessary in that constitution or form of government, which, in its actual condition, appears plainly unable to maintain the public tranquillity. In such cases, however, it often requires, perhaps, the highest effort of political

political wisdom to determine when a real patriot ought to support and endeavour to re-establish the authority of the old system, and when he ought to give way to the more daring, but often dangerous spirit of innovation.

Foreign war and civil faction are the two situations which afford the most splendid opportunities for the display of public spirit. The hero who serves his country successfully in foreign war gratifies the wishes of the whole nation, and is, upon that account, the object of universal gratitude and admiration. In times of civil discord, the leaders of the contending parties, though they may be admired by one half of their fellow-citizens, are commonly execrated by the other. Their characters and the merit of their respective services appear commonly more doubtful. The glory which is acquired by foreign war is, upon this account, almost always more pure and more splendid than that which can be acquired in civil faction.

The leader of the successful party, however, if he has authority enough to prevail upon his own friends to act with proper temper and moderation (which he frequently has not), may sometimes render to his country a service much more essential and important

potent than the greateſt victories and the moſt extenſive conqueſts. He may re-eſtabliſh and improve the conſtitution, and from the very doubtful and ambiguous character of the leader of a party, he may aſſume the greateſt and nobleſt of all characters, that of the reformer and legiſlator of a great ſtate; and, by the wiſdom of his inſtitutions, ſecure the internal tranquillity and happineſs of his fellow-citizens for many ſucceeding generations.

Amidſt the turbulence and diſorder of faction, a certain ſpirit of ſyſtem is apt to mix itſelf with that public ſpirit which is founded upon the love of humanity, upon a real fellow-feeling with the inconveniences and diſtreſſes to which ſome of our fellow-citizens may be expoſed. This ſpirit of ſyſtem commonly takes the direction of that more gentle public ſpirit; always animates it, and often inflames it even to the madneſs of fanaticiſm. The leaders of the diſcontented party ſeldom fail to hold out ſome plauſible plan of reformation which, they pretend, will not only remove the inconveniences and relieve the diſtreſſes immediately complained of, but will prevent, in all time coming, any return of the like inconveniences and diſtreſſes. They often propoſe, upon this account, to

new-

new-model the conſtitution, and to alter, in ſome of its moſt eſſential parts, that ſyſtem of government under which the ſubjects of a great empire have enjoyed, perhaps, peace, ſecurity, and even glory, during the courſe of ſeveral centuries together. The great body of the party are commonly intoxicated with the imaginary beauty of this ideal ſyſtem, of which they have no experience, but which has been repreſented to them in all the moſt dazzling colours in which the eloquence of their leaders could paint it. Thoſe leaders themſelves, though they originally may have meant nothing but their own aggrandizement, become many of them in time the dupes of their own ſophiſtry, and are as eager for this great reformation as the weakeſt and fooliſheſt of their followers. Even though the leaders ſhould have preſerved their own heads, as indeed they commonly do, free from this fanaticiſm, yet they dare not always diſappoint the expectation of their followers; but are often obliged, though contrary to their principle and their conſcience, to act as if they were under the common deluſion. The violence of the party, refuſing all palliatives, all temperaments, all reaſonable accommodations, by requiring too much frequently obtains nothing;

nothing; and thofe inconveniences and diftreffes which, with a little moderation, might in a great meafure have been removed and relieved, are left altogether without the hope of a remedy.

The man whofe public fpirit is prompted altogether by humanity and benevolence, will refpect the eftablifhed powers and privileges even of individuals, and ftill more thofe of the great orders and focieties, into which the ftate is divided. Though he fhould confider fome of them as in fome meafure abúfive, he will content himfelf with moderating, what he often cannot annihilate without great violence. When he cannot conquer the rooted prejudices of the people by reafon and perfuafion, he will not attempt to fubdue them by force; but will religioufly obferve what, by Cicero, is juftly called the divine maxim of Plato, never to ufe violence to his country no more than to his parents. He will accommodate, as well as he can, his public arrangements to the confirmed habits and prejudices of the people; and will remedy, as well as he can, the inconveniences which may flow from the want of thofe regulations which the people are averfe to fubmit to. When he cannot eftablifh the right, he will not difdain to ameliorate the wrong;

but

but like Solon, when he cannot eſtabliſh the beſt ſyſtem of laws, he will endeavour to eſtabliſh the beſt that the people can bear.

The man of ſyſtem, on the contrary, is apt to be very wiſe in his own conceit; and is often ſo enamoured with the ſuppoſed beauty of his own ideal plan of government, that he cannot ſuffer the ſmalleſt deviation from any part of it. He goes on to eſtabliſh it completely and in all its parts, without any regard either to the great intereſts, or to the ſtrong prejudices which may oppoſe it. He ſeems to imagine that he can arrange the different members of a great ſociety with as much eaſe as the hand arranges the different pieces upon a cheſs-board. He does not conſider that the pieces upon the cheſs-board have no other principle of motion beſides that which the hand impreſſes upon them; but that, in the great cheſs-board of human ſociety, every ſingle piece has a principle of motion of its own, altogether different from that which the legiſlature might chooſe to impreſs upon it. If thoſe two principles coincide and act in the ſame direction, the game of human ſociety will go on eaſily and harmoniouſly, and is very likely to be happy and ſucceſsful. If they are oppoſite or different, the game will go on miſerably, and the

the ſociety muſt be at all times in the higheſt degree of diſorder.

Some general, and even ſyſtematical, idea of the perfection of policy and law, may no doubt be neceſſary for directing the views of the ſtateſman. But to inſiſt upon eſtabliſhing, and upon eſtabliſhing all at once, and in ſpite of all oppoſition, every thing which that idea may ſeem to require, muſt often be the higheſt degree of arrogance. It is to erect his own judgment into the ſupreme ſtandard of right and wrong. It is to fancy himſelf the only wiſe and worthy man in the commonwealth, and that his fellow-citizens ſhould accommodate themſelves to him and not he to them. It is upon this account, that of all political ſpeculators, ſovereign princes are by far the moſt dangerous. This arrogance is perfectly familiar to them. They entertain no doubt of the immenſe ſuperiority of their own judgment. When ſuch imperial and royal reformers, therefore, condeſcend to contemplate the conſtitution of the country which is committed to their government, they ſeldom ſee any thing ſo wrong in it as the obſtructions which it may ſometimes oppoſe to the execution of their own will. They hold in contempt the divine maxim of Plato, and conſider the ſtate as made for them-

themſelves, not themſelves for the ſtate. The great object of their reformation, therefore, is to remove thoſe obſtructions; to reduce the authority of the nobility; to take away the privileges of cities and provinces, and to render both the greateſt individuals and the greateſt orders of the ſtate, as incapable of oppoſing their commands, as the weakeſt and moſt inſignificant.

CHAP. III.

Of Univerſal Benevolence.

THOUGH our effectual good offices can very ſeldom be extended to any wider ſociety than that of our own country; our good-will is circumſcribed by no boundary, but may embrace the immenſity of the univerſe. We cannot form the idea of any innocent and ſenſible being, whoſe happineſs we ſhould not deſire, or to whoſe miſery, when diſtinctly brought home to the imagination, we ſhould not have ſome degree of averſion. The idea of a miſchievous, though ſenſible being, indeed, naturally provokes our hatred: but the ill-will which, in this caſe,

we bear to it, is really the effect of our universal benevolence. It is the effect of the sympathy which we feel with the misery and resentment of those other innocent and sensible beings, whose happiness is disturbed by its malice.

This universal benevolence, how noble and generous soever, can be the source of no solid happiness to any man who is not thoroughly convinced that all the inhabitants of the universe, the meanest as well as the greatest, are under the immediate care and protection of that great, benevolent, and all-wise Being, who directs all the movements of nature; and who is determined, by his own unalterable perfections, to maintain in it, at all times, the greatest possible quantity of happiness. To this universal benevolence, on the contrary, the very suspicion of a fatherless world, must be the most melancholy of all reflections; from the thought that all the unknown regions of infinite and incomprehensible space may be filled with nothing but endless misery and wretchedness. All the splendour of the highest prosperity can never enlighten the gloom with which so dreadful an idea must necessarily overshadow the imagination; nor, in a wise and virtuous man, can all the sorrow of the most afflicting adver-

adverſity ever dry up the joy which neceſſarily ſprings from the habitual and thorough conviction of the truth of the contrary ſyſtem.

The wiſe and virtuous man is at all times willing that his own private intereſt ſhould be ſacrificed to the public intereſt of his own particular order or ſociety. He is at all times willing, too, that the intereſt of this order or ſociety ſhould be ſacrificed to the greater intereſt of the ſtate or ſovereignty, of which it is only a ſubordinate part. He ſhould, therefore, be equally willing that all thoſe inferior intereſts ſhould be ſacrificed to the greater intereſt of the univerſe, to the intereſt of that great ſociety of all ſenſible and intelligent beings, of which God himſelf is the immediate adminiſtrator and director. If he is deeply impreſſed with the habitual and thorough conviction that this benevolent and all-wiſe Being can admit into the ſyſtem of his government, no partial evil which is not neceſſary for the univerſal good, he muſt conſider all the misfortunes which may befal himſelf, his friends, his ſociety, or his country, as neceſſary for the proſperity of the univerſe, and therefore as what he ought, not only to ſubmit to with reſignation, but as what he himſelf, if he had known all the

connexions and dependencies of things, ought sincerely and devoutly to have wished for.

Nor does this magnanimous resignation to the will of the great Director of the universe, seem in any respect beyond the reach of human nature. Good soldiers, who both love and trust their general, frequently march with more gaiety and alacrity to the forlorn station, from which they never expect to return, than they would to one where there was neither difficulty nor danger. In marching to the latter, they could feel no other sentiment than that of the dulness of ordinary duty: in marching to the former, they feel that they are making the noblest exertion which it is possible for man to make. They know that their general would not have ordered them upon this station, had it not been necessary for the safety of the army, for the success of the war. They cheerfully sacrifice their own little systems to the prosperity of a greater system. They take an affectionate leave of their comrades, to whom they wish all happiness and success; and march out, not only with submissive obedience, but often with shouts of the most joyful exultation, to that fatal, but splendid and honourable station to which they are appointed.

pointed. No conductor of an army can deſerve more unlimited truſt, more ardent and zealous affection, than the great Conductor of the univerſe. In the greateſt public as well as private diſaſters, a wiſe man ought to conſider that he himſelf, his friends and countrymen, have only been ordered upon the forlorn ſtation of the univerſe; that had it not been neceſſary for the good of the whole, they would not have been ſo ordered; and that it is their duty, not only with humble reſignation to ſubmit to this allotment, but to endeavour to embrace it with alacrity and joy. A wiſe man ſhould ſurely be capable of doing what a good ſoldier holds himſelf at all times in readineſs to do.

The idea of that divine Being, whoſe benevolence and wiſdom have, from all eternity, contrived and conducted the immenſe machine of the univerſe, ſo as at all times to produce the greateſt poſſible quantity of happineſs, is certainly of all the objects of human contemplation by far the moſt ſublime. Every other thought neceſſarily appears mean in the compariſon. The man whom we believe to be principally occupied in this ſublime contemplation, ſeldom fails to be the object of our highest veneration; and

though his life ſhould be altogether contemplative, we often regard him with a ſort of religious reſpect much ſuperior to that with which we look upon the moſt active and uſeful ſervant of the commonwealth. The Meditations of Marcus Antoninus, which turn principally upon this ſubject, have contributed more, perhaps, to the general admiration of his character, than all the different tranſactions of his juſt, merciful, and beneficent reign.

The adminiſtration of the great ſyſtem of the univerſe, however, the care of the univerſal happineſs of all rational and ſenſible beings, is the buſineſs of God and not of man. To man is allotted a much humbler department, but one much more ſuitable to the weakneſs of his powers, and to the narrowneſs of his comprehenſion; the care of his own happineſs, of that of his family, his friends, his country: that he is occupied in contemplating the more ſublime, can never be an excuſe for his neglecting the more humble department; and he muſt not expoſe himſelf to the charge which Avidius Caſſius is ſaid to have brought, perhaps unjuſtly, againſt Marcus Antoninus; that while he employed himſelf in philoſophical ſpeculations,

tions, and contemplated the prosperity of the universe, he neglected that of the Roman empire. The most sublime speculation of the contemplative philosopher can scarce compensate the neglect of the smallest active duty.

SECTION III.

Of Self-command.

THE man who acts according to the rules of perfect prudence, of ſtrict juſtice, and of proper benevolence, may be ſaid to be perfectly virtuous. But the moſt perfect knowledge of thoſe rules will not alone enable him to act in this manner: his own paſſions are very apt to miſlead him; ſometimes to drive him and ſometimes to ſeduce him to violate all the rules which he himſelf, in all his ſober and cool hours, approves of. The moſt perfect knowledge, if it is not ſupported by the moſt perfect ſelf-command, will not always enable him to do his duty.

Some of the beſt of the ancient moraliſts ſeem to have conſidered thoſe paſſions as divided into two different claſſes: firſt, into thoſe which it requires a conſiderable exertion of ſelf-command to reſtrain even for a ſingle moment; and ſecondly, into thoſe which it is eaſy to reſtrain for a ſingle moment, or even for a ſhort period of time; but which

which, by their continual and almoſt inceſſant ſolicitations, are, in the courſe of a life, very apt to miſlead into great deviations.

Fear and anger, together with ſome other paſſions which are mixed or connected with them, conſtitute the firſt claſs. The love of eaſe, of pleaſure, of applauſe, and of many other ſelfiſh gratifications, conſtitute the ſecond. Extravagant fear and furious anger, it is often difficult to reſtrain even for a ſingle moment. The love of eaſe, of pleaſure, of applauſe, and other ſelfiſh gratifications, it is always eaſy to reſtrain for a ſingle moment, or even for a ſhort period of time; but, by their continual ſolicitations, they often miſlead us into many weakneſſes which we have afterwards much reaſon to be aſhamed of. The former ſet of paſſions may often be ſaid to drive, the latter, to ſeduce us from our duty. The command of the former was, by the ancient moraliſts above alluded to, denominated fortitude, manhood, and ſtrength of mind; that of the latter, temperance, decency, modeſty, and moderation.

The command of each of theſe two ſets of paſſions, independent of the beauty which it derives from its utility; from its enabling us upon all occaſions to act according to the dic-

tates

tates of prudence, of juſtice, and of proper benevolence; has a beauty of its own, and ſeems to deſerve for its own ſake a certain degree of eſteem and admiration. In the one caſe, the ſtrength and greatneſs of the exertion excites ſome degree of that eſteem and admiration. In the other, the uniformity, the equality and unremitting ſteadineſs of that exertion.

The man who, in danger, in torture, upon the approach of death, preſerves his tranquillity unaltered, and ſuffers no word, no geſture to eſcape him which does not perfectly accord with the feelings of the moſt indifferent ſpectator, neceſſarily commands a very high degree of admiration. If he ſuffers in the cauſe of liberty and juſtice, for the ſake of humanity and the love of his country, the moſt tender compaſſion for his ſufferings, the ſtrongeſt indignation againſt the injuſtice of his perſecutors, the warmeſt ſympathetic gratitude for his beneficent intentions, the higheſt ſenſe of his merit, all join and mix themſelves with the admiration of his magnanimity, and often inflame that ſentiment into the moſt enthuſiaſtic and rapturous veneration. The heroes of ancient and modern hiſtory, who are remembered with the moſt peculiar favour and affection, are,

many

many of them, those who, in the cause of truth, liberty, and justice, have perished upon the scaffold, and who appeared there with that ease and dignity which became them. Had the enemies of Socrates suffered him to die quietly in his bed, the glory even of that great philosopher might possibly never have acquired that dazzling splendour in which it has been beheld in all succeeding ages. In the English history, when we look over the illustrious heads which have been engraven by Vertue and Howbraken, there is scarce any body, I imagine, who does not feel that the axe, the emblem of having been beheaded, which is engraved under some of the most illustrious of them; under those of the Sir Thomas Mores, of the Rhaleighs, the Russels, the Sydneys, &c. sheds a real dignity and interestingness over the characters to which it is affixed, much superior to what they can derive from all the futile ornaments of heraldry, with which they are sometimes accompanied.

Nor does this magnanimity give lustre only to the characters of innocent and virtuous men. It draws some degree of favourable regard even upon those of the greatest criminals; and when a robber or highwayman is brought to the scaffold, and behaves there

there with decency and firmneſs, though we perfectly approve of his puniſhment, we often cannot help regretting that a man who poſſeſſed ſuch great and noble powers ſhould have been capable of ſuch mean enormities.

War is the great ſchool both for acquiring and exerciſing this ſpecies of magnanimity. Death, as we ſay, is the king of terrors; and the man who has conquered the fear of death, is not likely to loſe his preſence of mind at the approach of any other natural evil. In war, men become familiar with death, and are thereby neceſſarily cured of that ſuperſtitious horror with which it is viewed by the weak and unexperienced. They conſider it merely as the loſs of life, and as no further the object of averſion than as life may happen to be that of deſire. They learn from experience, too, that many ſeemingly great dangers are not ſo great as they appear; and that, with courage, activity, and preſence of mind, there is often a good probability of extricating themſelves with honour from ſituations where at firſt they could ſee no hope. The dread of death is thus greatly diminiſhed; and the confidence or hope of eſcaping it, augmented. They learn to expoſe themſelves

to

to danger with less reluctance. They are less anxious to get out of it, and less apt to lose their presence of mind while they are in it. It is this habitual contempt of danger and death which ennobles the profession of a soldier, and bestows upon it, in the natural apprehensions of mankind, a rank and dignity superior to that of any other profession. The skilful and successful exercise of this profession, in the service of their country, seems to have constituted the most distinguishing feature in the character of the favourite heroes of all ages.

Great warlike exploit, though undertaken contrary to every principle of justice, and carried on without any regard to humanity, sometimes interests us, and commands even some degree of a certain sort of esteem for the very worthless characters which conduct it. We are interested even in the exploits of the Buccaneers; and read with some sort of esteem and admiration, the history of the most worthless men, who, in pursuit of the most criminal purposes, endured greater hardships, surmounted greater difficulties, and encountered greater dangers, than, perhaps, any which the ordinary course of history gives an account of.

The command of anger appears upon many occaſions not leſs generous and noble than that of fear. The proper expreſſion of juſt indignation compoſes many of the moſt ſplendid and admired paſſages both of ancient and modern eloquence. The Philippics of Demoſthenes, the Catalinarians of Cicero, derive their whole beauty from the noble propriety with which this paſſion is expreſſed. But this juſt indignation is nothing but anger reſtrained and properly attempered to what the impartial ſpectator can enter into. The bluſtering and noiſy paſſion which goes beyond this, is always odious and offenſive, and intereſts us, not for the angry man, but for the man with whom he is angry. The nobleneſs of pardoning appears, upon many occaſions, ſuperior even to the moſt perfect propriety of reſenting. When either proper acknowledgments have been made by the offending party; or, even without any ſuch acknowledgments, when the public intereſt requires that the moſt mortal enemies ſhould unite for the diſcharge of ſome important duty, the man who can caſt away all animoſity, and act with confidence and cordiality towards the perſon who had moſt grievouſly offended him,

him, seems justly to merit our highest admiration.

The command of anger, however, does not always appear in such splendid colours. Fear is contrary to anger, and is often the motive which restrains it; and in such cases the meanness of the motive takes away all the nobleness of the restraint. Anger prompts to attack, and the indulgence of it seems sometimes to shew a sort of courage and superiority to fear. The indulgence of anger is sometimes an object of vanity. That of fear never is. Vain and weak men, among their inferiors, or those who dare not resist them, often affect to be ostentatiously passionate, and fancy that they show, what is called, spirit in being so. A bully tells many stories of his own insolence, which are not true, and imagines that he thereby renders himself, if not more amiable and respectable, at least more formidable to his audience. Modern manners, which, by favouring the practice of duelling, may be said, in some cases, to encourage private revenge, contribute, perhaps, a good deal to render, in modern times, the restraint of anger by fear still more contemptible than it might otherwise appear to be. There is always something dignified in the command of fear, whatever

may

may be the motive upon which it is founded. It is not ſo with the command of anger. Unleſs it is founded altogether in the ſenſe of decency, of dignity, and propriety, it never is perfectly agreeable.

To act according to the dictates of prudence, of juſtice, and proper beneficence, ſeems to have no great merit where there is no temptation to do otherwiſe. But to act with cool deliberation in the midſt of the greateſt dangers and difficulties; to obſerve religiouſly the ſacred rules of juſtice in ſpite both of the greateſt intereſts which might tempt, and the greateſt injuries which might provoke us to violate them; never to ſuffer the benevolence of our temper to be damped or diſcouraged by the malignity and ingratitude of the individuals towards whom it may have been exerciſed; is the character of the moſt exalted wiſdom and virtue. Self-command is not only itſelf a great virtue, but from it all the other virtues ſeem to derive their principal luſtre.

The command of fear, the command of anger, are always great and noble powers. When they are directed by juſtice and benevolence, they are not only great virtues, but increaſe the ſplendour of thoſe other virtues. They may, however, ſometimes be directed by

by very different motives; and in this case, though still great and respectable, they may be excessively dangerous. The most intrepid valour may be employed in the cause of the greatest injustice. Amidst great provocations, apparent tranquillity and good humour may sometimes conceal the most determined and cruel resolution to revenge. The strength of mind requisite for such dissimulation, though always and necessarily contaminated by the baseness of falsehood, has, however, been often much admired by many people of no contemptible judgment. The dissimulation of Catharine of Medicis is often celebrated by the profound historian Davila; that of Lord Digby, afterwards Earl of Bristol, by the grave and conscientious Lord Clarendon; that of the first Ashley Earl of Shaftesbury, by the judicious Mr. Locke. Even Cicero seems to consider this deceitful character, not indeed as of the highest dignity, but as not unsuitable to a certain flexibility of manners, which, he thinks, may, notwithstanding, be, upon the whole, both agreeable and respectable. He exemplifies it by the characters of Homer's Ulysses, of the Athenian Themistocles, of the Spartan Lysander, and of the Roman Marcus Crassus. This character of dark and deep dissimulation

tion occurs moſt commonly in times of great public diſorder; amidſt the violence of faction and civil war. When law has become in a great meaſure impotent, when the moſt perfect innocence cannot alone inſure ſafety, regard to ſelf-defence obliges the greater part of men to have recourſe to dexterity, to addreſs, and to apparent accommodation to whatever happens to be, at the moment, the prevailing party. This falſe character, too, is frequently accompanied with the cooleſt and moſt determined courage. The proper exerciſe of it impoſes that courage, as death is commonly the certain conſequence of detection. It may be employed indifferently, either to exaſperate or to allay thoſe furious animoſities of adverſe factions which impoſe the neceſſity of aſſuming it; and though it may ſometimes be uſeful, it is at leaſt equally liable to be exceſſively pernicious.

The command of the leſs violent and turbulent paſſions ſeems much leſs liable to be abuſed to any pernicious purpoſe. Temperance, decency, modeſty, and moderation, are always amiable, and can ſeldom be directed to any bad end. It is from the unrelenting ſteadineſs of thoſe gentler exertions of ſelf-command, that the amiable virtue of

chastity, that the respectable virtues of industry and frugality, derive all that sober lustre which attends them. The conduct of all those who are contented to walk in the humble paths of private and peaceable life, derives from the same principle the greater part of the beauty and grace which belong to it; a beauty and grace which, though much less dazzling, is not always less pleasing than those which accompany the more splendid actions of the hero, the statesman, or the legislator.

After what has already been said, in several different parts of this discourse, concerning the nature of self-command, I judge it unnecessary to enter into any further detail concerning those virtues. I shall only observe at present, that the point of propriety, the degree of any passion which the impartial spectator approves of, is differently situated in different passions. In some passions the excess is less disagreeable than the defect; and in such passions the point of propriety seems to stand high, or nearer to the excess than to the defect. In other passions, the defect is less disagreeable than the excess; and in such passions the point of propriety seems to stand low, or nearer to the defect than to the excess. The former

are the paſſions which the ſpectator is moſt, the latter, thoſe which he is leaſt diſpoſed to ſympathize with. The former, too, are the paſſions of which the immediate feeling or ſenſation is agreeable to the perſon principally concerned; the latter, thoſe of which it is diſagreeable. It may be laid down as a general rule, that the paſſions which the ſpectator is moſt diſpoſed to ſympathize with, and in which, upon that account, the point of propriety may be ſaid to ſtand high, are thoſe of which the immediate feeling or ſenſation is more or leſs agreeable to the perſon principally concerned: and that, on the contrary, the paſſions which the ſpectator is leaſt diſpoſed to ſympathize with, and in which, upon that account, the point of propriety may be ſaid to ſtand low, are thoſe of which the immediate feeling or ſenſation is more or leſs diſagreeable, or even painful, to the perſon principally concerned. This general rule, ſo far as I have been able to obſerve, admits not of a ſingle exception. A few examples will at once both ſufficiently explain it and demonſtrate the truth of it.

The diſpoſition to the affections which tend to unite men in ſociety, to humanity, kindneſs, natural affection, friendſhip, eſteem, may ſometimes be exceſſive. Even the ex-

ceſs

ceſs of this diſpoſition, however, renders a man intereſting to every body. Though we blame it, we ſtill regard it with compaſſion, and even with kindneſs, and never with diſlike. We are more ſorry for it than angry at it. To the perſon himſelf, the indulgence even of ſuch exceſſive affections is, upon many occaſions, not only agreeable but delicious. Upon ſome occaſions, indeed, eſpecially when directed, as is too often the caſe, towards unworthy objects, it expoſes him to much real and heartfelt diſtreſs. Even upon ſuch occaſions, however, a well-diſpoſed mind regards him with the moſt exquiſite pity, and feels the higheſt indignation againſt thoſe who affect to deſpiſe him for his weakneſs and imprudence. The defect of this diſpoſition, on the contrary, what is called hardneſs of heart, while it renders a man inſenſible to the feelings and diſtreſſes of other people, renders other people equally inſenſible to him; and, by excluding him from the friendſhip of all the world, excludes him from the beſt and moſt comfortable of all ſocial enjoyments.

The diſpoſition to the affections which drive men from one another, and which tend, as it were, to break the bands of human ſociety; the diſpoſition to anger,

hatred, envy, malice, revenge; is, on the contrary, much more apt to offend by its excess than by its defect. The excess renders a man wretched and miserable in his own mind, and the object of hatred, and sometimes even of horror, to other people. The defect is very seldom complained of. It may, however, be defective. The want of proper indignation is a most essential defect in the manly character, and, upon many occasions, renders a man incapable of protecting either himself or his friends from insult and injustice. Even that principle, in the excess and improper direction of which consists the odious and detestable passion of envy, may be defective. Envy is that passion which views with malignant dislike the superiority of those who are really entitled to all the superiority they possess. The man, however, who, in matters of consequence, tamely suffers other people, who are entitled to no such superiority, to rise above him or get before him, is justly condemned as mean-spirited. This weakness is commonly founded in indolence, sometimes in good nature, in an aversion to opposition, to bustle and solicitation, and sometimes, too, in a sort of ill-judged magnanimity, which fancies that it can always continue to despise the advantage which

which it then despises, and, therefore, so easily gives up. Such weakness, however, is commonly followed by much regret and repentance; and what had some appearance of magnanimity in the beginning, frequently gives place to a most malignant envy in the end, and to a hatred of that superiority, which those who have once attained it, may often become really entitled to, by the very circumstance of having attained it. In order to live comfortably in the world, it is, upon all occasions, as necessary to defend our dignity and rank, as it is to defend our life or our fortune.

Our sensibility to personal danger and distress, like that to personal provocation, is much more apt to offend by its excess than by its defect. No character is more contemptible than that of a coward; no character is more admired than that of the man who faces death with intrepidity, and maintains his tranquillity and presence of mind amidst the most dreadful dangers. We esteem the man who supports pain and even torture with manhood and firmness; and we can have little regard for him who sinks under them, and abandons himself to useless outcries and womanish lamentations. A fretful temper, which feels, with too much

fenfibility, every little crofs accident, renders a man miferable in himfelf and offenfive to other people. A calm one, which does not allow its tranquillity to be difturbed, either by the fmall injuries, or by the little difafters incident to the ufual courfe of human affairs; but which, amidft the natural and moral evils infefting the world, lays its account, and is contented to fuffer a little from both, is a bleffing to the man himfelf, and gives eafe and fecurity to all his companions.

Our fenfibility, however, both to our own injuries and to our own misfortunes, though generally too ftrong, may likewife be too weak. The man who feels little for his own misfortunes muft always feel lefs for thofe of other people, and be lefs difpofed to relieve them. The man who has little refentment for the injuries which are done to himfelf, muft always have lefs for thofe which are done to other people, and be lefs difpofed either to protect or to avenge them. A ftupid infenfibility to the events of human life neceffarily extinguifhes all that keen and earneft attention to the propriety of our own conduct, which conftitutes the real effence of virtue. We can feel little anxiety about the propriety of our own actions, when we are indifferent about the events which may refult

sult from them. The man who feels the full distress of the calamity which has befallen him, who feels the whole baseness of the injustice which has been done to him, but who feels still more strongly what the dignity of his own character requires; who does not abandon himself to the guidance of the undisciplined passions which his situation might naturally inspire; but who governs his whole behaviour and conduct according to those restrained and corrected emotions which the great inmate, the great demi-god within the breast prescribes and approves of; is alone the real man of virtue, the only real and proper object of love, respect, and admiration. Insensibility and that noble firmness, that exalted self-command, which is founded in the sense of dignity and propriety, are so far from being altogether the same, that in proportion as the former takes place, the merit of the latter is, in many cases, entirely taken away.

But though the total want of sensibility to personal injury, to personal danger and distress, would, in such situations, take away the whole merit of self-command, that sensibility, however, may very easily be too exquisite, and it frequently is so. When the sense of propriety, when the authority of the judge within the breast, can control this ex-

treme sensibility, that authority must no doubt appear very noble and very great. But the exertion of it may be too fatiguing; it may have too much to do. The individual, by a great effort, may behave perfectly well. But the contest between the two principles, the warfare within the breast, may be too violent to be at all consistent with internal tranquillity and happiness. The wise man whom nature has endowed with this too exquisite sensibility, and whose too lively feelings have not been sufficiently blunted and hardened by early education and proper exercise, will avoid, as much as duty and propriety will permit, the situations for which he is not perfectly fitted. The man whose feeble and delicate constitution renders him too sensible to pain, to hardship, and to every sort of bodily distress, should not wantonly embrace the profession of a soldier. The man of too much sensibility to injury, should not rashly engage in the contests of faction. Though the sense of propriety should be strong enough to command all those sensibilities, the composure of the mind must always be disturbed in the struggle. In this disorder the judgment cannot always maintain its ordinary acuteness and precision; and though he may always mean

to act properly, he may often act rashly and imprudently and in a manner which he himself will, in the succeeding part of his life, be for ever ashamed of. A certain intrepidity, a certain firmness of nerves and hardiness of constitution, whether natural or acquired, are undoubtedly the best preparatives for all the great exertions of self-command.

Though war and faction are certainly the best schools for forming every man to this hardiness and firmness of temper, though they are the best remedies for curing him of the opposite weaknesses, yet, if the day of trial should happen to come before he has completely learned his lesson, before the remedy has had time to produce its proper effect, the consequences might not be agreeable.

Our sensibility to the pleasures, to the amusements and enjoyments of human life, may offend, in the same manner, either by its excess or by its defect. Of the two, however, the excess seems less disagreeable than the defect. Both to the spectator and to the person principally concerned, a strong propensity to joy is certainly more pleasing than a dull insensibility to the objects of amusement and diversion. We are charmed with the gaiety of youth, and even with the playfulness

fulneſs of childhood: but we ſoon grow weary of the flat and taſteleſs gravity which too frequently accompanies old age. When this propenſity, indeed, is not reſtrained by the ſenſe of propriety, when it is unſuitable to the time or to the place, to the age or to the ſituation of the perſon, when to indulge it, he neglects either his intereſt or his duty; it is juſtly blamed as exceſſive, and as hurtful both to the individual and to the ſociety. In the greater part of ſuch caſes, however, what is chiefly to be found fault with is, not ſo much the ſtrength of the propenſity to joy, as the weakneſs of the ſenſe of propriety and duty. A young man who has no reliſh for the diverſions and amuſements that are natural and ſuitable to his age, who talks of nothing but his book or his buſineſs, is diſliked as formal and pedantic; and we give him no credit for his abſtinence even from improper indulgencies, to which he ſeems to have ſo little inclination.

The principle of ſelf-eſtimation may be too high, and it may likewiſe be too low. It is ſo very agreeable to think highly, and ſo very diſagreeable to think meanly of ourſelves, that, to the perſon himſelf, it cannot well be doubted, but that ſome degree of exceſs muſt be much leſs diſagreeable than any

degree

degree of defect. But to the impartial spectator, it may perhaps be thought, things must appear quite differently, and that to him the defect must always be less disagreeable than the excess. And in our companions, no doubt, we much more frequently complain of the latter than of the former. When they assume upon us, or set themselves before us, their self-estimation mortifies our own. Our own pride and vanity prompt us to accuse them of pride and vanity, and we cease to be the impartial spectators of their conduct. When the same companions, however, suffer any other man to assume over them a superiority which does not belong to him, we not only blame them, but often despise them as mean spirited. When, on the contrary, among other people, they push themselves a little more forward, and scramble to an elevation disproportioned, as we think, to their merit, though we may not perfectly approve of their conduct, we are often, upon the whole, diverted with it; and, where there is no envy in the case, we are almost always much less displeased with them, than we should have been, had they suffered themselves to sink below their proper station.

In estimating our own merit, in judging of

our own character and conduct, there are two different ſtandards to which we naturally compare them. The one is the idea of exact propriety and perfection, ſo far as we are each of us capable of comprehending that idea. The other is that degree of approximation to this idea which is commonly attained in the world, and which the greater part of our friends and companions, of our rivals and competitors, may have actually arrived at. We very ſeldom (I am diſpoſed to think, we never) attempt to judge of ourſelves without giving more or leſs attention to both theſe different ſtandards. But the attention of different men, and even of the ſame man at different times, is often very unequally divided between them; and is ſometimes principally directed towards the one, and ſometimes towards the other.

So far as our attention is directed towards the firſt ſtandard, the wiſeſt and beſt of us all, can, in his own character and conduct, ſee nothing but weakneſs and imperfection; can diſcover no ground for arrogance and preſumption, but a great deal for humility, regret, and repentance. So far as our attention is directed towards the ſecond, we may be affected either in the one way or in the other,

other, and feel ourselves, either really above, or really below, the standard to which we compare ourselves.

The wise and virtuous man directs his principal attention to the first standard; the idea of exact propriety and perfection. There exists in the mind of every man an idea of this kind, gradually formed from his observations upon the character and conduct both of himself and of other people. It is the slow, gradual, and progressive work of the great demigod within the breast, the great judge and arbiter of conduct. This idea is in every man more or less accurately drawn, its colouring is more or less just, its outlines are more or less exactly designed, according to the delicacy and acuteness of that sensibility, with which those observations were made, and according to the care and attention employed in making them. In the wise and virtuous man they have been made with the most acute and delicate sensibility, and the utmost care and attention have been employed in making them. Every day some feature is improved; every day some blemish is corrected. He has studied this idea more than other people, he comprehends it more distinctly, he has formed a much more correct image of it, and is much

more deeply enamoured of its exquisite and divine beauty. He endeavours, as well as he can, to assimilate his own character to this archetype of perfection. But he imitates the work of a divine artist, which can never be equalled. He feels the imperfect success of all his best endeavours, and sees, with grief and affliction, in how many different features the mortal copy falls short of the immortal original. He remembers, with concern and humiliation, how often, from want of attention, from want of judgment, from want of temper, he has, both in words and actions, both in conduct and conversation, violated the exact rules of perfect propriety; and has so far departed from that model, according to which he wished to fashion his own character and conduct. When he directs his attention towards the second standard, indeed, that degree of excellence which his friends and acquaintances have commonly arrived at, he may be sensible of his own superiority. But, as his principal attention is always directed towards the first standard, he is necessarily much more humbled by the one comparison than he ever can be elevated by the other. He is never so elated as to look down with insolence even upon those who are really below him.

him. He feels so well his own imperfection, he knows so well the difficulty with which he attained his own distant approximation to rectitude, that he cannot regard with contempt the still greater imperfection of other people. Far from insulting over their inferiority, he views it with the most indulgent commiseration, and, by his advice as well as example, is at all times willing to promote their further advancement. If, in any particular qualification, they happen to be superior to him, (for who is so perfect as not to have many superiors in many different qualifications?) far from envying their superiority, he, who knows how difficult it is to excel, esteems and honours their excellence, and never fails to bestow upon it the full measure of applause which it deserves. His whole mind, in short, is deeply impressed, his whole behaviour and deportment are distinctly stamped with the character of real modesty; with that of a very moderate estimation of his own merit, and, at the same time, of a full sense of the merit of other people.

In all the liberal and ingenious arts, in painting, in poetry, in music, in eloquence, in philosophy, the great artist feels always the real imperfection of his own best works, and

and is more sensible than any man how much they fall short of that ideal perfection of which he has formed some conception, which he imitates as well as he can, but which he despairs of ever equalling. It is the inferior artist only, who is ever perfectly satisfied with his own performances. He has little conception of this ideal perfection, about which he has little employed his thoughts; and it is chiefly to the works of other artists, of, perhaps, a still lower order, that he deigns to compare his own works. Boileau, the great French poet, (in some of his works, perhaps not inferior to the greatest poet of the same kind, either ancient or modern) used to say that no great man was ever completely satisfied with his own works. His acquaintance Santeuil (a writer of Latin verses, and who, on account of that school-boy accomplishment, had the weakness to fancy himself a poet) assured him that he himself was always completely satisfied with his own. Boileau replied, with, perhaps, an arch ambiguity, That he certainly was the only great man that ever was so. Boileau, in judging of his own works, compared them with the standard of ideal perfection, which, in his own particular branch of the poetic art, he had, I presume, meditated

as deeply, and conceived as distinctly, as it is possible for man to conceive it. Santeuil, in judging of his own works, compared them, I suppose, chiefly to those of the other Latin poets of his own time, to the greater part of whom he was certainly very far from being inferior. But to support and finish off, if I may say so, the conduct and conversation of a whole life to some resemblance of this ideal perfection, is surely much more difficult than to work up to an equal resemblance any of the productions of any of the ingenious arts. The artist sits down to his work undisturbed, at leisure, in the full possession and recollection of all his skill, experience, and knowledge. The wise man must support the propriety of his own conduct in health and in sickness, in success and in disappointment, in the hour of fatigue and drowsy indolence, as well as in that of the most awakened attention. The most sudden and unexpected assaults of difficulty and distress must never surprise him. The injustice of other people must never provoke him to injustice. The violence of faction must never confound him. All the hardships and hazards of war must never either dishearten or appal him.

Of the persons who, in estimating their own merit, in judging of their own charac-

ter,

ter and conduct, direct by far the greater part of their attention to the second standard, to that ordinary degree of excellence which is commonly attained by other people, there are some who really and justly feel themselves very much above it, and who, by every intelligent and impartial spectator, are acknowledged to be so. The attention of such persons, however, being always principally directed, not to the standard of ideal, but to that of ordinary perfection, they have little sense of their own weaknesses and imperfections; they have little modesty; are often assuming, arrogant, and presumptuous; great admirers of themselves, and great contemners of other people. Though their characters are in general much less correct, and their merit much inferior to that of the man of real and modest virtue; yet their excessive presumption, founded upon their own excessive self-admiration, dazzles the multitude, and often imposes even upon those who are much superior to the multitude. The frequent, and often wonderful, success of the most ignorant quacks and impostors, both civil and religious, sufficiently demonstrate how easily the multitude are imposed upon by the most extravagant and groundless pretensions. But when those preten-

sions

sions are supported by a very high degree of real and solid merit, when they are displayed with all the splendour which ostentation can bestow upon them, when they are supported by high rank and great power, when they have often been successfully exerted, and are, upon that account, attended by the loud acclamations of the multitude; even the man of sober judgment often abandons himself to the general admiration. The very noise of those foolish acclamations often contributes to confound his understanding, and while he sees those great men only at a certain distance, he is often disposed to worship them with a sincere admiration, superior even to that with which they appear to worship themselves. When there is no envy in the case, we all take pleasure in admiring, and are, upon this account, naturally disposed, in our own fancies, to render complete and perfect in every respect the characters which, in many respects, are so very worthy of admiration. The excessive self-admiration of those great men is well understood, perhaps, and even seen through, with some degree of derision, by those wise men who are much in their familiarity, and who secretly smile at those lofty pretensions, which, by people at a distance, are often regarded with reverence,

and almost with adoration. Such, however, have been, in all ages, the greater part of those men who have procured to themselves the most noisy fame, the most extensive reputation; a fame and reputation, too, which have often descended to the remotest posterity.

Great success in the world, great authority over the sentiments and opinions of mankind, have very seldom been acquired without some degree of this excessive self-admiration. The most splendid characters, the men who have performed the most illustrious actions, who have brought about the greatest revolutions, both in the situations and opinions of mankind; the most successful warriors, the greatest statesmen and legislators, the eloquent founders and leaders of the most numerous and most successful sects and parties; have many of them been, not more distinguished for their very great merit, than for a degree of presumption and self-admiration altogether disproportioned even to that very great merit. This presumption was, perhaps, necessary, not only to prompt them to undertakings which a more sober mind would never have thought of, but to command the submission and obedience of their followers to support them in such undertak-

ings. When crowned with success, accordingly, this presumption has often betrayed them into a vanity that approached almost to insanity and folly. Alexander the Great appears, not only to have wished that other people should think him a god, but to have been at least very well disposed to fancy himself such. Upon his death-bed, the most ungodlike of all situations, he requested of his friends that, to the respectable list of deities, into which himself had long before been inserted, his old mother Olympia might likewise have the honour of being added. Amidst the respectful admiration of his followers and disciples, amidst the universal applause of the public, after the oracle, which probably had followed the voice of that applause, had pronounced him the wisest of men, the great wisdom of Socrates, though it did not suffer him to fancy himself a god, yet was not great enough to hinder him from fancying that he had secret and frequent intimations from some invisible and divine Being. The sound head of Cæsar was not so perfectly sound as to hinder him from being much pleased with his divine genealogy from the goddess Venus; and, before the temple of this pretended great-grandmother, to receive, without rising from his seat, the Roman Senate, when that

illustrious body came to present him with some decrees conferring upon him the most extravagant honours. This insolence, joined to some other acts of an almost childish vanity, little to be expected from an understanding at once so very acute and comprehensive, seems, by exasperating the public jealousy, to have emboldened his assassins, and to have hastened the execution of their conspiracy. The religion and manners of modern times give our great men little encouragement to fancy themselves either gods or even prophets. Success, however, joined to great popular favour, has often so far turned the heads of the greatest of them, as to make them ascribe to themselves both an importance and an ability much beyond what they really possessed; and, by this presumption, to precipitate themselves into many rash and sometimes ruinous adventures. It is a characteristic almost peculiar to the great Duke of Marlborough, that ten years of such uninterrupted and such splendid success as scarce any other general could boast of, never betrayed him into a single rash action, scarce into a single rash word or expression. The same temperate coolness and self-command cannot, I think, be ascribed to any other great warrior of later times; not to Prince Eugene,

Eugene, not to the late King of Prussia, not to the great Prince of Condé, not even to Gustavus Adolphus. Turenne seems to have approached the nearest to it; but several different transactions of his life sufficiently demonstrate that it was in him by no means so perfect as in the great Duke of Marlborough.

In the humble projects of private life, as well as in the ambitious and proud pursuits of high stations, great abilities and successful enterprise, in the beginning, have frequently encouraged to undertakings which necessarily led to bankruptcy and ruin in the end.

The esteem and admiration which every impartial spectator conceives for the real merit of those spirited, magnanimous, and high-minded persons, as it is a just and well-founded sentiment, so it is a steady and permanent one, and altogether independent of their good or bad fortune. It is otherwise with that admiration which he is apt to conceive for their excessive self-estimation and presumption. While they are successful, indeed, he is often perfectly conquered and overborne by them. Success covers from his eyes, not only the great imprudence, but frequently the great injustice of many of their enterprises; and, far from blaming this defective part of their character, he often views it

with the most enthusiastic admiration. When they are unfortunate, however, things change their colours and their names. What was before heroic magnanimity, resumes its proper appellation of extravagant rashness and folly; and the blackness of that avidity and injustice, which was before hid under the splendour of prosperity, comes full into view, and blots the whole lustre of their enterprise. Had Cæsar, instead of gaining, lost the battle of Pharsalia, his character would, at this hour, have ranked a little above that of Cataline, and the weakest man would have viewed his enterprise against the laws of his country in blacker colours, than, perhaps, even Cato, with all the animosity of a party-man, ever viewed it at the time. His real merit, the justness of his taste, the simplicity and elegance of his writings, the propriety of his eloquence, his skill in war, his resources in distress, his cool and sedate judgment in danger, his faithful attachment to his friends, his unexampled generosity to his enemies, would all have been acknowledged; as the real merit of Cataline, who had many great qualities, is acknowledged at this day. But the insolence and injustice of his all-grasping ambition would have darkened and extinguished the glory of all that real merit. For-

tune

tune has in this, as well as in some other respects already mentioned, great influence over the moral sentiments of mankind, and, according as she is either favourable or adverse, can render the same character the object, either of general love and admiration, or of universal hatred and contempt. This great disorder in our moral sentiments is by no means, however, without its utility; and we may on this, as well as on many other occasions, admire the wisdom of God even in the weakness and folly of man. Our admiration of success is founded upon the same principle with our respect for wealth and greatness, and is equally necessary for establishing the distinction of ranks and the order of society. By this admiration of success we are taught to submit more easily to those superiors, whom the course of human affairs may assign to us; to regard with reverence, and sometimes even with a sort of respectful affection, that fortunate violence which we are no longer capable of resisting; not only the violence of such splendid characters as those of a Cæsar or an Alexander, but often that of the most brutal and savage barbarians, of an Attila, a Gengis, or a Tamerlane. To all such mighty conquerors the great mob of mankind are naturally disposed to look up

with a

with a wondering, though, no doubt, with a very imperfect and foolish admiration. By this admiration, however, they are taught to acquiesce with less reluctance under that government which an irresistible force imposes upon them, and from which no reluctance could deliver them.

Though in prosperity, however, the man of excessive self-estimation may sometimes appear to have some advantage over the man of correct and modest virtue; though the applause of the multitude, and of those who see them both only at a distance, is often much louder in favour of the one than it ever is in favour of the other; yet, all things fairly computed, the real balance of advantage is, perhaps in all cases, greatly in favour of the latter and against the former. The man who neither ascribes to himself, nor wishes that other people should ascribe to him, any other merit besides that which really belongs to him, fears no humiliation, dreads no detection, but rests contented and secure upon the genuine truth and solidity of his own character. His admirers may neither be very numerous nor very loud in their applauses; but the wisest man who sees him the nearest and who knows him the best, admires him the most. To a real wise man the judicious and

and well-weighed appre[illegible] of a single [illegible] man, gives more [illegible] satisfaction than all the noisy [illegible] of ten thousand [illegible] [illegible] with [illegible] [illegible] Athe[illegible] [illegible] the whole [illegible] notwith[illegible] [illegible] [illegible]

It is other[illegible] with [illegible] self-estima[illegible] [illegible] the [illegible] the [illegible] of pro[illegible] just [illegible] gance [illegible] that [illegible] regard[illegible] suspect [illegible] becom[illegible] [illegible] [illegible] pendence to [illegible] to idolize [illegible] [illegible]

killed Clytus, for having preferred the exploits of his father Philip to his own; put Callisthenes to death in torture, for having refused to adore him in the Persian manner; and murdered the great friend of his father, the venerable old Parmenio, after having, upon the most groundless suspicions, sent first to the torture and afterwards to the scaffold the only remaining son of that old man, the rest having all before died in his own service. This was that Parmenio of whom Philip used to say, that the Athenians were very fortunate who could find ten generals every year, while he himself, in the whole course of his life, could never find one but Parmenio. It was upon the vigilance and attention of this Parmenio that he reposed at all times with confidence and security; and, in his hours of mirth and jollity, used to say, Let us drink, my friends, we may do it with safety, for Parmenio never drinks. It was this same Parmenio, with whose presence and counsel, it had been said, Alexander had gained all his victories; and without whose presence and counsel, he had never gained a single victory. The humble, admiring, and flattering friends, whom Alexander left in power and authority behind him, divided his empire among themselves, and

and after having thus robbed his family and kindred of their inheritance, put, one after another, every single surviving individual of them, whether male or female, to death.

We frequently not only pardon, but thoroughly enter into and sympathize with the excessive self-estimation of those splendid characters in which we observe a great and distinguished superiority above the common level of mankind. We call them spirited, magnanimous, and high-minded; words which all involve in their meaning a considerable degree of praise and admiration. But we cannot enter into and sympathize with the excessive self-estimation of those characters in which we can discern no such distinguished superiority. We are disgusted and revolted by it; and it is with some difficulty that we can either pardon or suffer it. We call it pride or vanity; two words, of which the latter always, and the former for the greater part, involve in their meaning a considerable degree of blame.

[illegible]

The proud man is sincere, and, in the bottom of his heart, is convinced of his own superiority; though it may sometimes be difficult to guess upon what that conviction is founded. He wishes you to view him in no other light than that in which, when he places himself in your situation, he really views himself. He demands no more of you than what he thinks justice. If you appear not to respect him as he respects himself, he is more offended than mortified, and feels the same indignant resentment as if he had suffered a real injury. He does not even then, however, deign to explain the grounds of his own pretensions. He disdains to court your esteem. He affects even to despise it, and endeavours to maintain his assumed station, not so much by making you sensible of his superiority, as of your own meanness. He seems to wish, not so much to excite your esteem for *himself*, as to mortify that for *yourself*.

The vain man is not sincere, and, in the bottom of his heart, is very seldom convinced of that superiority which he wishes you to ascribe to him. He wishes you to view him in much more splendid colours than those in which, when he places himself

in

in your situation, and supposes you to know all that he knows, he can really view himself. When you appear to view him, therefore, in different colours, perhaps in his proper colours, he is much more mortified than offended. The grounds of his claim to that character which he wishes you to ascribe to him, he takes every opportunity of displaying, both by the most ostentatious and unnecessary exhibition of the good qualities and accomplishments which he possesses in some tolerable degree, and sometimes even by false pretensions to those which he either possesses in no degree, or in so very slender a degree that he may well enough be said to possess them in no degree. Far from despising your esteem, he courts it with the most anxious assiduity. Far from wishing to mortify your self-estimation, he is happy to cherish it, in hopes that in return you will cherish his own. He flatters in order to be flattered. He studies to please, and endeavours to bribe you into a good opinion of him by politeness and complaisance, and sometimes even by real and essential good offices, though often displayed, perhaps, with unnecessary ostentation.

The vain man sees the respect which is paid to rank and fortune, and wishes to

usurp this respect, as well as that for talents and virtues. His dress, his equipage, his way of living, accordingly, all announce both a higher rank and a greater fortune than really belongs to him; and in order to support this foolish imposition for a few years in the beginning of his life, he often reduces himself to poverty and distress long before the end of it. As long as he can continue his expence, however, his vanity is delighted with viewing himself, not in the light in which you would view him if you knew all that he knows; but in that in which, he imagines, he has, by his own address, induced you actually to view him. Of all the illusions of vanity this is, perhaps, the most common. Obscure strangers who visit foreign countries, or who, from a remote province, come to visit, for a short time, the capital of their own country, most frequently attempt to practise it. The folly of the attempt, though always very great and most unworthy of a man of sense, may not be altogether so great upon such as upon most other occasions. If their stay is short, they may escape any disgraceful detection; and, after indulging their vanity for a few months or a few years, they may return to their

own

own homes, and repair, by future parsimony, the waste of their past profusion.

The proud man can very seldom be accused of this folly. His sense of his own dignity renders him careful to preserve his independency, and, when his fortune happens not to be large, though he wishes to be decent, he studies to be frugal and attentive in all his expences. The ostentatious expence of the vain man is highly offensive to him. It outshines, perhaps, his own. It provokes his indignation as an insolent assumption of a rank which is by no means due; and he never talks of it without loading it with the harshest and severest reproaches.

The proud man does not always feel himself at his ease in the company of his equals, and still less in that of his superiors. He cannot lay down his lofty pretensions, and the countenance and conversation of such company overawe him so much that he dare not display them. He has recourse to humbler company, for which he has little respect, which he would not willingly chuse, and which is by no means agreeable to him; that of his inferiors, his flatterers, and dependants. He seldom visits his superiors, or, if he does, it is rather to shew that he is en-

titled to live in such company, than for any real satisfaction that he enjoys in it. It is as Lord Clarendon says of the Earl of Arundel, that he sometimes went to court, because he could there only find a greater man than himself; but that he went very seldom, because he found there a greater man than himself.

It is quite otherwise with the vain man. He courts the company of his superiors as much as the proud man shuns it. Their splendour, he seems to think, reflects a splendour upon those who are much about them. He haunts the courts of kings and the levees of ministers, and gives himself the air of being a candidate for fortune and preferment, when in reality he possesses the much more precious happiness, if he knew how to enjoy it, of not being one. He is fond of being admitted to the tables of the great, and still more fond of magnifying to other people the familiarity with which he is honoured there. He associates himself, as much as he can, with fashionable people, with those who are supposed to direct the public opinion, with the witty, with the learned, with the popular; and he shuns the company of his best friends whenever the very uncertain current of

of public favour happens to run in any respect against them. With the people to whom he wishes to recommend himself, he is not always very delicate about the means which he employs for that purpose; unnecessary ostentation, groundless pretensions, constant assentation, frequently flattery, though for the most part a pleasant and sprightly flattery, and very seldom the gross and fulsome flattery of a parasite. The proud man, on the contrary, never flatters, and is frequently scarce civil to any body.

Notwithstanding all its groundless pretensions, however, vanity is almost always a sprightly and a gay, and very often a good-natured passion. Pride is always a grave, a sullen, and a severe one. Even the falsehoods of the vain man are all innocent falsehoods, meant to raise himself, not to lower other people. To do the proud man justice, he very seldom stoops to the baseness of falsehood. When he does, however, his falsehoods are by no means so innocent. They are all mischievous, and meant to lower other people. He is full of indignation at the unjust superiority, as he thinks it, which is given to them. He views them with malignity and envy, and, in talking of them, often en-

vours, as much as he can, to extenuate and leſſen whatever are the grounds upon which their ſuperiority is ſuppoſed to be founded. Whatever tales are circulated to their diſadvantage, though he ſeldom forges them himſelf, yet he often takes pleaſure in believing them, is by no means unwilling to repeat them, and even ſometimes with ſome degree of exaggeration. The worſt falſehoods of vanity are all what we call white lies: thoſe of pride, whenever it condeſcends to falſehood, are all of the oppoſite complexion.

Our diſlike to pride and vanity generally diſpoſes us to rank the perſons whom we accuſe of thoſe vices rather below than above the common level. In this judgment however, I think, we are moſt frequently in the wrong, and that both the proud and the vain man are often (perhaps for the moſt part) a good deal above it; though not near ſo much as either the one really thinks himſelf, or as the other wiſhes you to think him. If we compare them with their own pretenſions, they may appear the juſt objects of contempt. But when we compare them with what the greater part of their rivals and competitors really are, they may appear quite otherwiſe, and very much above the common

mon level. Where there is this real superiority, pride is frequently attended with many respectable virtues; with truth, with integrity, with a high sense of honour, with cordial and steady friendship, with the most inflexible firmness and resolution. Vanity, with many amiable ones; with humanity, with politeness, with a desire to oblige in all little matters, and sometimes with a real generosity in great ones; a generosity, however, which it often wishes to display in the most splendid colours that it can. By their rivals and enemies, the French, in the last century, were accused of vanity; the Spaniards, of pride; and foreign nations were disposed to consider the one as the more amiable; the other, as the more respectable people.

The words *vain* and *vanity* are never taken in a good sense. We sometimes say of a man, when we are talking of him in good-humour, that he is the better for his vanity, or that his vanity is more diverting than offensive; but we still consider it as a foible and a ridicule in his character.

The words *proud* and *pride*, on the contrary, are sometimes taken in a good sense. We frequently say of a man, that he is too

proud, or that he has too much noble pride, ever to suffer himself to do a mean thing. Pride is, in this case, confounded with magnanimity. Aristotle, a philosopher who certainly knew the world, in drawing the character of the magnanimous man, paints him with many features which, in the two last centuries, were commonly ascribed to the Spanish character: that he was deliberate in all his resolutions; slow, and even tardy, in all his actions; that his voice was grave, his speech deliberate, his step and motion slow; that he appeared indolent and even slothful, not at all disposed to bustle about little matters, but to act with the most determined and vigorous resolution upon all great and illustrious occasions; that he was not a lover of danger, or forward to expose himself to little dangers, but to great dangers; and that, when he exposed himself to danger, he was altogether regardless of his life.

The proud man is commonly too well contented with himself to think that his character requires any amendment. The man who feels himself all-perfect, naturally enough despises all further improvement. His self-sufficiency and absurd conceit of his own superiority commonly attend him from his youth to his

his most advanced age; and he dies, as Hamlet says, with all his sins upon his head, unanointed, unanealed.

It is frequently quite otherwise with the vain man. The desire of the esteem and admiration of other people, when for qualities and talents which are the natural and proper objects of esteem and admiration, is the real love of true glory; a passion which, if not the very best passion of human nature, is certainly one of the best. Vanity is very frequently no more than an attempt prematurely to usurp that glory before it is due. Though your son, under five-and-twenty years of age, should be but a coxcomb; do not, upon that account, despair of his becoming, before he is forty, a very wise and worthy man, and a real proficient in all those talents and virtues to which, at present, he may only be an ostentatious and empty pretender. The great secret of education is to direct vanity to proper objects. Never suffer him to value himself upon trivial accomplishments. But do not always discourage his pretensions to those that are of real importance. He would not pretend to them if he did not earnestly desire to possess them. Encourage this desire; afford him every means to facilitate the acquisition; and do not

not take too much offence, although he ſhould ſometimes aſſume the air of having attained it a little before the time.

Such, I ſay, are the diſtinguiſhing characteriſtics of pride and vanity, when each of them acts according to its proper character. But the proud man is often vain; and the vain man is often proud. Nothing can be more natural than that the man, who thinks much more highly of himſelf than he deſerves, ſhould wiſh that other people ſhould think ſtill more highly of him: or that the man, who wiſhes that other people ſhould think more highly of him than he thinks of himſelf, ſhould, at the ſame time, think much more highly of himſelf than he deſerves. Thoſe two vices being frequently blended in the ſame character, the characteriſtics of both are neceſſarily confounded; and we ſometimes find the ſuperficial and impertinent oſtentation of vanity joined to the moſt malignant and deriſive inſolence of pride. We are ſometimes, upon that account, at a loſs how to rank a particular character, or whether to place it among the proud or among the vain.

Men of merit conſiderably above the common level, ſometimes under-rate as well as over-rate themſelves. Such characters, though

though not very dignified, are often, in private society, far from being disagreeable. His companions all feel themselves much at their ease in the society of a man so perfectly modest and unassuming. If those companions, however, have not both more discernment and more generosity than ordinary, though they may have some kindness for him, they have seldom much respect; and the warmth of their kindness is very seldom sufficient to compensate the coldness of their respect. Men of no more than ordinary discernment never rate any person higher than he appears to rate himself. He seems doubtful himself, they say, whether he is perfectly fit for such a situation or such an office; and immediately give the preference to some impudent blockhead who entertains no doubt about his own qualifications. Though they should have discernment, yet, if they want generosity, they never fail to take advantage of his simplicity, and to assume over him an impertinent superiority which they are by no means entitled to. His good-nature may enable him to bear this for some time; but he grows weary at last, and frequently when it is too late, and when that rank, which he ought to have assumed, is lost irrecoverably, and usurped, in consequence of his own backwardness,

wardness, by some of his more forward, though much less meritorious companions. A man of this character must have been very fortunate in the early choice of his companions, if, in going through the world, he meets always with complete justice, even from those whom, from his own liberality, he might have some reason to consider as his best friends; and a youth, too unassuming and too unambitious, is frequently followed by an insignificant, complaining, and discontented old age.

Those unfortunate persons whom nature has formed a good deal below the common level, seem sometimes to rate themselves still more below it than they really are. This humility appears sometimes to sink them into idiotism. Whoever has taken the trouble to examine idiots with attention, will find that, in many of them, the faculties of the understanding are by no means weaker than in several other people, who, though acknowledged to be dull and stupid, are not, by any body, accounted idiots. Many idiots, with no more than ordinary education, have been taught to read, write, and account tolerably well. Many persons, never accounted idiots, notwithstanding the most careful education, and notwithstanding that, in their ad-

vanced age, they have had ſpirit enough to attempt to learn what their early education had not taught them, have never been able to acquire in any tolerable degree, any one of thoſe three accompliſhments. By an inſtinct of pride, however, they ſet themſelves upon a level with their equals in age and ſituation; and, with courage and firmneſs, maintain their proper ſtation among their companions. By an oppoſite inſtinct, the idiot feels himſelf below every company into which you can introduce him. Ill-uſage, to which he is extremely liable, is capable of throwing him into the moſt violent fits of rage and fury. But no good uſage, no kindneſs or indulgence, can ever raiſe him to converſe with you as your equal. If you can bring him to converſe with you at all, however, you will frequently find his anſwers ſufficiently pertinent, and even ſenſible. But they are always ſtamped with a diſtinct conſciouſneſs of his own great inferiority. He ſeems to ſhrink and, as it were, to retire from your look and converſation; and to feel, when he places himſelf in your ſituation, that, notwithſtanding your apparent condeſcenſion, you cannot help conſidering him as immenſely below you. Some idiots, perhaps the greater part, ſeem to be ſo,

chiefly or altogether, from a certain numbness or torpidity in the faculties of the understanding. But there are others, in whom those faculties do not appear more torpid or benumbed than in many other people who are not accounted idiots. But that instinct of pride, necessary to support them upon an equality with their brethren, seems totally wanting in the former and not in the latter.

That degree of self-estimation, therefore, which contributes most to the happiness and contentment of the person himself, seems likewise most agreeable to the impartial spectator. The man who esteems himself as he ought, and no more than he ought, seldom fails to obtain from other people all the esteem that he himself thinks due. He desires no more than is due to him, and he rests upon it with complete satisfaction.

The proud and the vain man, on the contrary, are constantly dissatisfied. The one is tormented with indignation at the unjust superiority, as he thinks it, of other people. The other is in continual dread of the shame which, he foresees, would attend upon the detection of his groundless pretensions. Even the extravagant pretensions of the man of real magnanimity, though, when supported

by

by ſplendid abilities and virtues, and, above all, by good fortune, they impoſe upon the multitude, whoſe applauſes he little regards, do not impoſe upon thoſe wiſe men whoſe approbation he can only value, and whoſe eſteem he is moſt anxious to acquire. He feels that they ſee through, and ſuſpects that they deſpiſe his exceſſive preſumption; and he often ſuffers the cruel misfortune of becoming, firſt the jealous and ſecret, and at laſt the open, furious, and vindictive enemy of thoſe very perſons, whoſe friendſhip it would have given him the greateſt happineſs to enjoy with unſuſpicious ſecurity.

Though our diſlike to the proud and the vain often diſpoſes us to rank them rather below than above their proper ſtation, yet, unleſs we are provoked by ſome particular and perſonal impertinence, we very ſeldom venture to uſe them ill. In common caſes, we endeavour for our own eaſe, rather to acquieſce, and, as well as we can, to accommodate ourſelves to their folly. But, to the man who under-rates himſelf, unleſs we have both more diſcernment and more generoſity than belong to the greater part of men, we ſeldom fail to do, at leaſt, all the injuſtice which he does to himſelf, and frequently a great deal more. He is not only more un-

happy

happy in his own feelings than either the proud or the vain, but he is much more liable to every sort of ill-usage from other people. In almost all cases, it is better to be a little too proud, than, in any respect, too humble; and, in the sentiment of self estimation, some degree of excess seems, both to the person himself and to the impartial spectator, to be less disagreeable than any degree of defect.

In this, therefore, as well as in every other emotion, passion, and habit, the degree that is most agreeable to the impartial spectator is likewise most agreeable to the person himself; and according as either the excess or the defect is least offensive to the former, so, either the one or the other is in proportion least disagreeable [illegible]

CONCLUSION of the SIXTH PART.

CONCERN for our own happiness recommends to us the virtue of prudence: concern for that of other people, the virtues of justice and beneficence; of which, the one restrains us from hurting, the other prompts us to promote that happiness. Independent of any regard either to what are, or to what ought to be, or to what upon a certain condition would be, the sentiments of other people, the first of those three virtues is originally recommended to us by our selfish, the other two by our benevolent affections. Regard to the sentiments of other people, however, comes afterwards both to enforce and to direct the practice of all those virtues; and no man during, either the whole course of his life, or that of any considerable part of it, ever trod steadily and uniformly in the paths of prudence, of justice, or of proper beneficence, whose conduct was not principally directed by a regard to the sentiments of the supposed impartial spectator, of the great inmate of the breast, the great judge and arbiter

of conduct. If in the courſe of the day we have ſwerved in any reſpect from the rules which he preſcribes to us; if we have either exceeded or relaxed in our frugality; if we have either exceeded or relaxed in our induſtry; if, through paſſion or inadvertency, we have hurt in any reſpect the intereſt or happineſs of our neighbour; if we have neglected a plain and proper opportunity of promoting that intereſt and happineſs; it is this inmate who, in the evening, calls us to an account for all thoſe omiſſions and violations, and his reproaches often make us bluſh inwardly both for our folly and inattention to our own happineſs, and for our ſtill greater indifference and inattention, perhaps, to that of other people.

But though the virtues of prudence, juſtice, and beneficence, may, upon different occaſions, be recommended to us almoſt equally by two different principles; thoſe of ſelf-command are, upon moſt occaſions, principally and almoſt entirely recommended to us by one; by the ſenſe of propriety, by regard to the ſentiments of the ſuppoſed impartial ſpectator. Without the reſtraint which this principle impoſes, every paſſion would, upon moſt occaſions, ruſh headlong, if I may ſay ſo, to its own gratification. Anger would follow

follow the suggestions of its own fury; fear those of its own violent agitations. Regard to no time or place would induce vanity to refrain from the loudest and most impertinent ostentation; or voluptuousness from the most open, indecent, and scandalous indulgence. Respect for what are, or for what ought to be, or for what upon a certain condition would be, the sentiments of other people, is the sole principle which, upon most occasions, overawes all those mutinous and turbulent passions into that tone and temper which the impartial spectator can enter into and sympathize with.

Upon some occasions, indeed, these passions are restrained, not so much by a sense of their impropriety, as by prudential considerations of the bad consequences which might follow from their indulgence. In such cases, the passions, though restrained, are not always subdued, but often remain lurking in the breast with all their original fury. The man whose anger is restrained by fear, does not always lay aside his anger, but only reserves its gratification for a more safe opportunity. But the man who, in relating to some other person the injury which has been done to him, feels at once the fury of his passion cooled and becalmed by

by ſympathy with the more moderate ſentiments of his companion, who at once adopts thoſe more moderate ſentiments, and comes to view that injury, not in the black and atrocious colours in which he had originally beheld it, but in the much milder and fairer light, in which his companion naturally views it; not only reſtrains, but in ſome meaſure ſubdues, his anger. The paſſion becomes really leſs than it was before, and leſs capable of exciting him to the violent and bloody revenge which at firſt, perhaps, he might have thought of inflicting.

Thoſe paſſions which are reſtrained by the ſenſe of propriety, are all in ſome degree moderated and ſubdued by it. But thoſe which are reſtrained only by prudential conſiderations of any kind, are, on the contrary, frequently inflamed by the reſtraint, and ſometimes (long after the provocation given, and when nobody is thinking about it) burſt out abſurdly and unexpectedly, and with tenfold fury and violence.

Anger, however, as well as every other paſſion, may, upon many occaſions, be very properly reſtrained by prudential conſiderations. Some exertion of manhood and

and ſelf-command is even neceſſary for this ſort of reſtraint; and the impartial ſpectator may ſometimes view it with that ſort of cold eſteem due to that ſpecies of conduct which he conſiders as a mere matter of vulgar prudence; but never with that affectionate admiration with which he ſurveys the ſame paſſions, when, by the ſenſe of propriety, they are moderated and ſubdued to what he himſelf can readily enter into. In the former ſpecies of reſtraint, he may frequently diſcern ſome degree of propriety, and, if you will, even of virtue; but it is a propriety and virtue of a much inferior order to thoſe which he always feels with tranſport and admiration in the latter.

The virtues of prudence, juſtice, and beneficence, have no tendency to produce any but the moſt agreeable effects. Regard to thoſe effects, as it originally recommends them to the actor, ſo does it afterwards to the impartial ſpectator. In our approbation of the character of the prudent man, we feel, with peculiar complacency, the ſecurity which he muſt enjoy while he walks under the ſafeguard of that ſedate and deliberate virtue. In our approbation of the character of the juſt man, we feel, with equal complacency, the ſecurity which all thoſe connected with

him whether in neighbourhood, ſociety, or buſineſs, muſt derive from his ſcrupulous anxiety never either to hurt or offend. In our approbation of the character of the beneficent man, we enter into the gratitude of all thoſe who are within the ſphere of his good offices, and conceive with them the higheſt ſenſe of his merit. In our approbation of all thoſe virtues, our ſenſe of their agreeable effects, of their utility, either to the perſon who exerciſes them, or to ſome other perſons, joins with our ſenſe of their propriety, and conſtitutes always a conſiderable, frequently the greater, part of that approbation.

But in our approbation of the virtues of ſelf-command, complacency with their effects ſometimes conſtitutes no part, and frequently but a ſmall part of that approbation. Thoſe effects may ſometimes be agreeable, and ſometimes diſagreeable; and though our approbation is no doubt ſtronger in the former caſe, it is by no means altogether deſtroyed in the latter. The moſt heroic valour may be employed indifferently in the cauſe either of juſtice or of injuſtice; and though it is no doubt much more loved and admired in the former caſe, it ſtill appears a great and reſpectable quality even in the latter. In that, and in all the other virtues of ſelf-command, the

the splendid and dazzling quality seems always to be the greatness and steadiness of the exertion, and the strong sense of propriety which is necessary in order to make and to maintain that exertion. The effects are too often but too little regarded.

THE THEORY OF MORAL SENTIMENTS.

PART VII.

Of Syſtems of MORAL PHILOSOPHY.

Conſiſting of Four Sections.

SECTION I.

Of the Queſtions which ought to be examined in a Theory of Moral Sentiments.

IF we examine the moſt celebrated and remarkable of the different theories which have been given concerning the nature and origin of our moral ſentiments, we ſhall find that almoſt all of them coincide with ſome part or other

other of that which I have been endeavouring to give an account of; and that if every thing which has already been said be fully considered, we shall be at no loss to explain what was the view or aspect of nature which led each particular author to form his particular system. From some one or other of those principles which I have been endeavouring to unfold, every system of morality that ever had any reputation in the world has, perhaps, ultimately been derived. As they are all of them, in this respect, founded upon natural principles, they are all of them in some measure in the right. But as many of them are derived from a partial and imperfect view of nature, there are many of them too in some respects in the wrong.

In treating of the principles of morals there are two questions to be considered. First, wherein does virtue consist? Or what is the tone of temper, and tenour of conduct, which constitutes the excellent and praiseworthy character, the character which is the natural object of esteem, honour, and approbation? And, secondly, by what power or faculty in the mind is it, that this character, whatever it be, is recommended to us? Or in other words, how and by what means does it come to pass, that the mind

prefers

prefers one tenour of conduct to another, denominates the one right and the other wrong; considers the one as the object of approbation, honour, and reward, and the other of blame, censure, and punishment?

We examine the first question when we consider whether virtue consists in benevolence, as Dr. Hutcheson imagines; or in acting suitably to the different relations we stand in, as Dr. Clarke supposes; or in the wise and prudent pursuit of our own real and solid happiness, as has been the opinion of others.

We examine the second question, when we consider, whether the virtuous character, whatever it consists in, be recommended to us by self-love, which makes us perceive that this character, both in ourselves and others, tends most to promote our own private interest; or by reason, which points out to us the difference between one character and another, in the same manner as it does that between truth and falsehood; or by a peculiar power of perception, called a moral sense, which this virtuous character gratifies and pleases, as the contrary disgusts and displeases it; or last of all, by some other principle in human nature, such as a modification of sympathy, or the like.

I shall

I ſhall begin with conſidering the ſyſtems which have been formed concerning the firſt of theſe queſtions, and ſhall proceed afterwards to examine thoſe concerning the ſecond.

SECTION II.

Of the different Accounts which have been given of the Nature of Virtue.

INTRODUCTION.

THE different accounts which have been given of the nature of virtue, or of the temper of mind which constitutes the excellent and praise-worthy character, may be reduced to three different classes. According to some, the virtuous temper of mind does not consist in any one species of affections, but in the proper government and direction of all our affections, which may be either virtuous or vicious according to the objects which they pursue, and the degree of vehemence with which they pursue them. According to these authors, therefore, virtue consists in propriety.

According to others, virtue consists in the judicious pursuit of our own private interest and happiness, or in the proper government and direction of those selfish affections

affections which aim solely at this end. In the opinion of these authors, therefore, virtue consists in prudence.

Another set of authors make virtue consist in those affections only which aim at the happiness of others, not in those which aim at our own. According to them, therefore, disinterested benevolence is the only motive which can stamp upon any action the character of virtue.

The character of virtue, it is evident, must either be ascribed indifferently to all our affections, when under proper government and direction; or it must be confined to some one class or division of them. The great division of our affections is into the selfish and the benevolent. If the character of virtue, therefore, cannot be ascribed indifferently to all our affections, when under proper government and direction, it must be confined either to those which aim directly at our own private happiness, or to those which aim directly at that of others. If virtue, therefore, does not consist in propriety, it must consist either in prudence or in benevolence. Besides these three, it is scarce possible to imagine that any other account can be given of the nature of virtue. I shall endeavour to show hereafter how all the

the other accounts, which are ſeemingly different from any of theſe, coincide at bottom with ſome one or other of them.

CHAP. I.

Of thoſe Syſtems which make Virtue conſiſt in Propriety.

ACCORDING to Plato, to Ariſtotle, and to Zeno, virtue conſiſts in the propriety of conduct, or in the ſuitableneſs of the affection from which we act to the object which excites it.

I. In the ſyſtem of Plato* the ſoul is conſidered as ſomething like a little ſtate or republic, compoſed of three different faculties or orders.

The firſt is the judging faculty, the faculty which determines not only what are the proper means for attaining any end, but alſo what ends are fit to be purſued, and what degree of relative value we ought to put upon each. This faculty Plato called, as it is very properly called, reaſon, and conſi-

* See Plato de Rep. lib. iv.

considered it as what had a right to be the governing principle of the whole. Under this appellation, it is evident, he comprehended not only that faculty by which we judge of truth and falsehood, but that by which we judge of the propriety or impropriety of desires and affections.

The different passions and appetites, the natural subjects of this ruling principle, but which are so apt to rebel against their master, he reduced to two different classes or orders. The first consisted of those passions, which are founded in pride and resentment, or in what the schoolmen call the irascible part of the soul; ambition, animosity, the love of honour and the dread of shame, the desire of victory, superiority, and revenge; all those passions, in short, which are supposed either to rise from, or to denote what, by a metaphor in our language, we commonly call spirit or natural fire. The second consisted of those passions which are founded in the love of pleasure, or in what the schoolmen call the concupiscible part of the soul. It comprehended all the appetites of the body, the love of ease and security, and of all sensual gratifications.

It rarely happens that we break in upon that plan of conduct, which the governing

principle prescribes, and which in all our cool hours we had laid down to ourselves as what was most proper for us to pursue, but when prompted by one or other of those two different sets of passions; either by ungovernable ambition and resentment, or by the importunate solicitations of present ease and pleasure. But though these two orders of passions are so apt to mislead us, they are still considered as necessary parts of human nature: the first having been given to defend us against injuries, to assert our rank and dignity in the world, to make us aim at what is noble and honourable, and to make us distinguish those who act in the same manner; the second, to provide for the support and necessities of the body.

In the strength, acuteness, and perfection of the governing principle was placed the essential virtue of prudence, which, according to Plato, consisted in a just and clear discernment, founded upon general and scientific ideas, of the ends which were proper to be pursued, and of the means which were proper for attaining them.

When the first set of passions, those of the irascible part of the soul, had that degree of strength and firmness which enabled them, under the direction of reason, to de-

ſpiſe all dangers in the purſuit of what was honourable and noble; it conſtituted the virtue of fortitude and magnanimity. This order of paſſions, according to this ſyſtem, was of a more generous and noble nature than the other. They were conſidered upon many occaſions as the auxiliaries of reaſon, to check and reſtrain the inferior and brutal appetites. We are often angry at ourſelves, it was obſerved, we often become the objects of our own reſentment and indignation, when the love of pleaſure prompts to do what we diſapprove of, and the iraſcible part of our nature is in this manner called in to aſſiſt the rational againſt the concupiſcible.

When all thoſe three different parts of our nature were in perfect concord with one another, when neither the iraſcible nor concupiſcible paſſions ever aimed at any gratification which reaſon did not approve of, and when reaſon never commanded any thing, but what theſe of their own accord were willing to perform: this happy compoſure, this perfect and complete harmony of ſoul, conſtituted that virtue which in their language is expreſſed by a word which we commonly tranſlate temperance, but which might more properly be tranſlated

good

good temper, or sobriety and moderation of mind.

Justice, the last and greatest of the four cardinal virtues, took place according to this system, when each of those three faculties of the mind confined itself to its proper office, without attempting to encroach upon that of any other; when reason directed and passion obeyed, and when each passion performed its proper duty, and exerted itself towards its proper object easily and without reluctance, and with that degree of force and energy, which was suitable to the value of what it pursued. In this consisted that complete virtue, that perfect propriety of conduct, which Plato, after some of the ancient Pythagoreans, denominated Justice.

The word, it is to be observed, which expresses justice in the Greek language, has several different meanings; and as the correspondent word in all other languages, so far as I know, has the same, there must be some natural affinity among those various significations. In one sense we are said to do justice to our neighbour when we abstain from doing him any positive harm, and do not directly hurt him, either in his person, or in his estate, or in his reputation. This

is that juftice which I have treated of above, the obfervance of which may be extorted by force, and the violation of which expofes to punifhment. In another fenfe we are faid not to do juftice to our neighbour unlefs we conceive for him all that love, refpect, and efteem, which his character, his fituation, and his connexion with ourfelves, render fuitable and proper for us to feel, and unlefs we act accordingly. It is in this fenfe that we are faid to do injuftice to a man of merit who is connected with us, though we abftain from hurting him in every refpect, if we do not exert ourfelves to ferve him, and to place him in that fituation in which the impartial fpectator would be pleafed to fee him. The firft fenfe of the word coincides with what Ariftotle and the Schoolmen call commutative juftice, and with what Grotius calls the *juftitia expletrix*, which confifts in abftaining from what is another's, and in doing voluntarily whatever we can with propriety be forced to do. The fecond fenfe of the word coincides with what fome have called diftributive juftice [*], and with the *juftitia attri-*

[*] The diftributive juftice of Ariftotle is fomewhat different. It confifts in the proper diftribution of rewards from the public ftock of a community. See Ariftotle Ethic. Nic. l. [illegible]

butrix of Grotius, which consists in proper beneficence, in the becoming use of what is our own, and in the applying it to those purposes either of charity or generosity, to which it is most suitable, in our situation, that it should be applied. In this sense justice comprehends all the social virtues. There is yet another sense in which the word justice is sometimes taken, still more extensive than either of the former, though very much a-kin to the last; and which runs too, so far as I know, through all languages. It is in this last sense that we are said to be unjust, when we do not seem to value any particular object with that degree of esteem, or to pursue it with that degree of ardour which to the impartial spectator it may appear to deserve or to be naturally fitted for exciting. Thus we are said to do injustice to a poem or a picture, when we do not admire them enough, and we are said to do them more than justice when we admire them too much. In the same manner we are said to do injustice to ourselves when we appear not to give sufficient attention to any particular object of self-interest. In this last sense, what is called justice means the same thing with exact and perfect propriety of conduct and be-

haviour, and comprehends in it, not only the offices of both commutative and diſtributive juſtice, but of every other virtue, of prudence, of fortitude, of temperance. It is in this laſt ſenſe that Plato evidently underſtands what he calls juſtice, and which, therefore, according to him, comprehends in it the perfection of every ſort of virtue.

Such is the account given by Plato of the nature of virtue, or of that temper of mind which is the proper object of praiſe and approbation. It conſiſts, according to him, in that ſtate of mind in which every faculty confines itſelf within its proper ſphere without encroaching upon that of any other, and performs its proper office with that preciſe degree of ſtrength and vigour which belongs to it. His account, it is evident, coincides in every reſpect with what we have ſaid above concerning the propriety of conduct.

II. Virtue, according to Ariſtotle*, conſiſts in the habit of mediocrity according to right reaſon. Every particular virtue, according to him, lies in a kind of middle between two oppoſite vices, of which the

* See Ariſtotle, Ethic. Nic. l. ii. c. 5. et ſeq. et l. iii. c. 5. et ſeq.

one

one offends from being too much, the other from being too little affected by a particular species of objects. Thus the virtue of fortitude or courage lies in the middle between the opposite vices of cowardice and of presumptuous rashness, of which the one offends from being too much, and the other from being too little affected by the objects of fear. Thus too the virtue of frugality lies in a middle between avarice and profusion, of which the one consists in an excess, the other in a defect of the proper attention to the objects of self-interest. Magnanimity, in the same manner, lies in a middle between the excess of arrogance and the defect of pusillanimity, of which the one consists in too extravagant, the other in too weak a sentiment of our own worth and dignity. It is unnecessary to observe that this account of virtue corresponds too pretty exactly with what has been said above concerning the propriety and impropriety of conduct.

According to Aristotle*, indeed, virtue did not so much consist in those moderate and right affections, as in the habit of this moderation. In order to understand this,

* See Aristot. Ethic. Nic. lib. ii. ch. 1, 2, 3, and 4.

it is to be obſerved, that virtue may be conſidered either as the quality of an action, or as the quality of a perſon. Conſidered as the quality of an action, it conſiſts, even according to Ariſtotle, in the reaſonable moderation of the affection from which the action proceeds, whether this diſpoſition be habitual to the perſon or not. Conſidered as the quality of a perſon, it conſiſts, in the habit of this reaſonable moderation, in its having become the cuſtomary and uſual diſpoſition of the mind. Thus the action which proceeds from an occaſional fit of generoſity is undoubtedly a generous action, but the man who performs it, is not neceſſarily a generous perſon, becauſe it may be the ſingle action of the kind which he ever performed. The motive and diſpoſition of heart, from which this action was performed, may have been quite juſt and proper: but as this happy mood ſeems to have been the effect rather of accidental humour than of any thing ſteady or permanent in the character, it can reflect no great honour on the performer. When we denominate a character generous or charitable, or virtuous in any reſpect, we mean to ſignify that the diſpoſition expreſſed by each of thoſe appellations is the uſual and cuſtomary

ary diſpoſition of the perſon. But ſingle actions of any kind, how proper and ſuitable ſoever, are of little conſequence to ſhow that this is the caſe. If a ſingle action was ſufficient to ſtamp the character of any virtue upon the perſon who performed it, the moſt worthleſs of mankind might lay claim to all the virtues; ſince there is no man who has not, upon ſome occaſions, acted with prudence, juſtice, temperance, and fortitude. But though ſingle actions, how laudable ſoever, reflect very little praiſe upon the perſon who performs them, a ſingle vicious action performed by one whoſe conduct is uſually very regular, greatly diminiſhes and ſometimes deſtroys altogether our opinion of his virtue. A ſingle action of this kind ſufficiently ſhows that his habits are not perfect, and that he is leſs to be depended upon, than, from the uſual train of his behaviour, we might have ben apt to imagine.

Ariſtotle too *, when he made virtue to conſiſt in practical habits, had it probably in his view to oppoſe the doctrine of Plato, who ſeems to have been of opinion that juſt ſentiments and reaſonable judgments

* See Ariſtotle, Mag. Mor. lib. i. ch. 1.

concern-

concerning what was fit to be done or to be avoided, were alone ſufficient to conſtitute the moſt perfect virtue. Virtue, according to Plato, might be conſidered as a ſpecies of ſcience, and no man, he thought, could ſee clearly and demonſtratively what was right and what was wrong, and not act accordingly. Paſſion might make us act contrary to doubtful and uncertain opinions, not to plain and evident judgments. Ariſtotle, on the contrary, was of opinion, that no conviction of the underſtanding was capable of getting the better of inveterate habits, and that good morals aroſe not from knowledge but from action.

III. According to Zeno *, the founder of the Stoical doctrine, every animal was by nature recommended to its own care, and was endowed with the principle of ſelf-love, that it might endeavour to preſerve, not only its exiſtence, but all the different parts of its nature, in the beſt and moſt perfect ſtate of which they were capable.

The ſelf-love of man embraced, if I may ſay ſo, his body and all its different members, his mind and all its different faculties

* See Cicero de finibus, lib. iii.; alſo Diogenes Laertius in Zenone, lib. vii. ſegment 84.

and

and powers, and desired the preservation and maintenance of them all in their best and most perfect condition. Whatever tended to support this state of existence was, therefore, by nature pointed out to him as fit to be chosen; and whatever tended to destroy it, as fit to be rejected. Thus health, strength, agility and ease of body as well as the external conveniences which could promote these; wealth, power, honours, the respect and esteem of those we live with; were naturally pointed out to us as things eligible, and of which the possession was preferable to the want. On the other hand, sickness, infirmity, unwieldiness, pain of body as well as all the external inconveniences which tend to occasion or bring on any of them; poverty, the want of authority, the contempt or hatred of those we live with; were in the same manner, pointed out to us as things to be shunned and avoided. In each of those two opposite classes of objects, there were some which appeared to be more the objects either of choice or rejection, than others in the same class. Thus, in the first class, health appeared evidently preferable to strength, and strength to agility; reputation to power,

and power to riches. And thus too, in the ſecond claſs, ſickneſs was more to be avoided than unwieldineſs of body, ignominy than poverty, and poverty than the loſs of power. Virtue and the propriety of conduct conſiſted in chooſing and rejecting all different objects and circumſtances according as they were by nature rendered more or leſs the objects of choice or rejection; in ſelecting always from among the ſeveral objects of choice preſented to us, that which was moſt to be choſen, when we could not obtain them all; and in ſelecting too, out of the ſeveral objects of rejection offered to us, that which was leaſt to be avoided, when it was not in our power to avoid them all. By chooſing and rejecting with this juſt and accurate diſcernment, by thus beſtowing upon every object the preciſe degree of attention it deſerved, according to the place which it held in this natural ſcale of things, we maintained, according to the Stoics, that perfect rectitude of conduct which conſtituted the eſſence of virtue. This was what they called to live conſiſtently, to live according to nature, and to obey thoſe laws and directions which nature, or the Author of nature, had preſcribed for our conduct.

So far the Stoical idea of propriety and virtue is not very different from that of Aristotle and the ancient Peripatetics.

Among those primary objects which nature had recommended to us as eligible, was the prosperity of our family, of our relations, of our friends, of our country, of mankind, and of the universe in general. Nature, too, had taught us, that as the prosperity of two was preferable to that of one, that of many, or of all, must be infinitely more so. That we ourselves were but one, and that consequently wherever our prosperity was inconsistent with that, either of the whole, or of any considerable part of the whole, it ought, even in our own choice, to yield to what was so vastly preferable. As all the events in this world were conducted by the providence of a wise, powerful, and good God, we might be assured that whatever happened tended to the prosperity and perfection of the whole. If we ourselves, therefore, were in poverty, in sickness, or in any other calamity, we ought, first of all, to use our utmost endeavours, so far as justice and our duty to others would allow, to rescue ourselves from this disagreeable circumstance. But if after all we could do, we found this impossible, we ought

to reſt ſatisfied that the order and perfection of the univerſe required that we ſhould in the mean time continue in this ſituation. And as the proſperity of the whole ſhould, even to us, appear preferable to ſo inſignificant a part as ourſelves, our ſituation, whatever it was, ought from that moment to become the object of our liking, if we would maintain that complete propriety and rectitude of ſentiment and conduct in which conſiſted the perfection of our nature. If, indeed, any opportunity of extricating ourſelves ſhould offer, it became our duty to embrace it. The order of the univerſe, it was evident, no longer required our continuance in this ſituation, and the great Director of the world plainly called upon us to leave it, by ſo clearly pointing out the road which we were to follow. It was the ſame caſe with the adverſity of our relations, our friends, our country. If, without violating any more ſacred obligation, it was in our power to prevent or put an end to their calamity, it undoubtedly was our duty to do ſo. The propriety of action, the rule which Jupiter had given us for the direction of our conduct, evidently required this of us. But if it was altogether out of our power to do either, we ought then to conſi-

consider this event as the most fortunate which could possibly have happened; because we might be assured that it tended most to the prosperity and order of the whole, which was what we ourselves, if we were wise and equitable, ought most of all to desire. It was our own final interest considered as a part of that whole, of which the prosperity ought to be, not only the principal, but the sole object of our desire.

"In what sense," says Epictetus, "are "some things said to be according to our "nature, and others contrary to it? It is "in that sense in which we consider our-"selves as separated and detached from all "other things. For thus it may be said "to be according to the nature of the foot "to be always clean. But if you consider "it as a foot, and not as something de-"tached from the rest of the body, it must "behove it sometimes to trample in the "dirt, and sometimes to tread upon thorns, "and sometimes, too, to be cut off for "the sake of the whole body; and if it re-"fuses this, it is no longer a foot. Thus "too, ought we to conceive with regard "to ourselves. What are you? A man. "If you consider yourself as something

"sep-

" ſeparated and detached, it is agreeable to " your nature to live to old age, to be rich, " to be in health. But if you conſider your- " ſelf as a man, and as a part of a whole, " upon account of that whole, it will behove " you ſometimes to be in ſickneſs, ſometimes " to be expoſed to the inconveniency of a " ſea voyage, ſometimes to be in want; and " at laſt, perhaps, to die before your time. " Why then do you complain? Do not " you know that by doing ſo, as the foot " ceaſes to be a foot, ſo you ceaſe to be a " man?"

A wiſe man never complains of the deſtiny of Providence, nor thinks the univerſe in confuſion when he is out of order. He does not look upon himſelf as a whole, ſeparated and detached from every other part of nature, to be taken care of by itſelf and for itſelf. He regards himſelf in the light in which he imagines the great genius of human nature, and of the world, regards him. He enters, if I may ſay ſo, into the ſentiments of that divine Being, and conſiders himſelf as an atom, a particle, of an immenſe and infinite ſyſtem, which muſt and ought to be diſpoſed of, according to the conveniency of the whole. Aſſured of the wiſdom which directs all the events of hu-

man

man life, whatever lot befals him, he accepts it with joy, satisfied that, if he had known all the connections and dependencies of the different parts of the universe, it is the very lot which he himself would have wished for. If it is life, he is contented to live; and if it is death, as nature must have no further occasion for his presence here, he willingly goes where he is appointed. I accept, said a cynical philosopher, whose doctrines were in this respect the same as those of the Stoics, I accept with equal joy and satisfaction, whatever fortune can befal me. Riches or poverty, pleasure or pain, health or sickness, all is alike: nor would I desire that the Gods should in any respect change my destination. If I was to ask of them any thing beyond what their bounty has already bestowed, it should be that they would inform me beforehand what it was their pleasure should be done with me, that I might of my own accord place myself in this situation, and demonstrate the chearfulness with which I embraced their allotment. If I am going to sail, says Epictetus, I chuse the best ship and the best pilot, and I wait for the fairest weather that my circumstances and duty will allow. Prudence and propriety, the princi-

principles which the Gods have given me for the direction of my conduct, require this of me; but they require no more: and if, notwithstanding, a storm arises, which neither the strength of the vessel nor the skill of the pilot are likely to withstand, I give myself no trouble about the consequence. All that I had to do is done already. The directors of my conduct never command me to be miserable, to be anxious, desponding, or afraid. Whether we are to be drowned, or to come to a harbour, is the business of Jupiter, not mine. I leave it entirely to his determination, nor ever break my rest with considering which way he is likely to decide it. I receive whatever comes with equal indifference and security.

From this perfect confidence in that benevolent wisdom which governs the universe, and from this entire resignation to whatever order that wisdom might think proper to establish, it necessarily followed, that, to the Stoical wise man, all the events of human life must be in a great measure indifferent. His happiness consisted altogether, first, in the contemplation of the happiness and perfection of the great system of the universe, of the good government of the great republic of Gods and men, of all rational

tional and sensible beings; and, secondly, in discharging his duty, in acting properly in the affairs of this great republic whatever little part that wisdom had assigned to him. The propriety or impropriety of his endeavours might be of great consequence to him. Their success or disappointment could be of none at all; could excite no passionate joy or sorrow, no passionate desire or aversion. If he preferred some events to others, if some situations were the objects of his choice and others of his rejection, it was not because he regarded the one as in themselves in any respect better than the other, or thought that his own happiness would be more complete in what is called the fortunate than in what is regarded as the distressful situation; but because the propriety of action, the rule which the Gods had given him for the direction of his conduct, required him to chuse and reject in this manner. All his affections were absorbed and swallowed up in two great affections; in that for the discharge of his own duty, and in that for the greatest possible happiness of all rational and sensible beings. For the gratification of this latter affection, he relied with the most perfect security upon the wisdom and power of the great

Superintendant of the universe. His sole anxiety was about the gratification of the former; not about the event, but about the propriety of his own endeavours. Whatever the event might be, he trusted to a superior power and wisdom for turning it to promote that great end which he himself was most desirous of promoting.

This propriety of choosing and rejecting, though originally pointed out to us, and as it were recommended and introduced to our acquaintance by the things, and for the sake of the things chosen and rejected; yet when we had once become thoroughly acquainted with it, the order, the grace, the beauty which we discerned in this conduct, the happiness which we felt resulted from it, necessarily appeared to us of much greater value than the actual obtaining of all the different objects of choice, or the actual avoiding of all those of rejection. From the observation of this propriety arose the happiness and the glory; from the neglect of it, the misery and the disgrace of human nature.

But to a wise man, to one whose passions were brought under perfect subjection to the ruling principles of his nature, the exact

act observation of this propriety was equally easy upon all occasions. Was he in prosperity, he returned thanks to Jupiter for having joined him with circumstances which were easily mastered, and in which there was little temptation to do wrong. Was he in adversity, he equally returned thanks to the director of this spectacle of human life, for having opposed to him a vigorous athlete, over whom, though the contest was likely to be more violent, the victory was more glorious, and equally certain. Can there be any shame in that distress which is brought upon us without any fault of our own, and in which we behave with perfect propriety? There can, therefore, be no evil, but, on the contrary, the greatest good and advantage. A brave man exults in those dangers in which, from [illegible] his [illegible] of [illegible] flows from [illegible] propriety [illegible] One who is [illegible] aversion to [illegible] with the [illegible] per, one who is [illegible]

does not dread any circumstance in which the Superintendant of the universe may think proper to place him. The bounty of that divine Being has provided him with virtues which render him superior to every situation. If it is pleasure, he has temperance to refrain from it; if it is pain, he has constancy to bear it; if it is danger or death, he has magnanimity and fortitude to despise it. The events of human life can never find him unprepared, or at a loss how to maintain that propriety of sentiment and conduct which, in his own apprehension, constitutes at once his glory and his happiness.

Human life the Stoics appear to have considered as a game of great skill; in which, however, there was a mixture of chance, or of what is vulgarly understood to be chance. In such games the stake is commonly a trifle, and the whole pleasure of the game arises from playing well, from playing fairly, and playing skilfully. If notwithstanding all his skill, however, the good player should, by the influence of chance, happen to lose, the loss ought to be a matter, rather of merriment, than of serious sorrow. He has made no false stroke; he has done nothing which he

ought

ought to be ashamed of; he has enjoyed completely the whole pleasure of the game. If, on the contrary, the bad player, notwithstanding all his blunders, should, in the same manner, happen to win, his success can give him but little satisfaction. He is mortified by the remembrance of all the faults which he committed. Even during the play he can enjoy no part of the pleasure which it is capable of affording. From ignorance of the rules of the game, fear and doubt and hesitation are the disagreeable sentiments that precede almost every stroke which he plays; and when he has played it, the mortification of finding it a gross blunder, commonly completes the unpleasing circle of his sensations. Human life, with all the advantages which can possibly attend it, ought, according to the Stoics, to be [illegible] as a mere two-penny stake; a [illegible] to merit any [illegible] [illegible] the stake, [illegible] playing. [illegible] winning the [illegible] depended upon [illegible] and out of o[illegible] exposed ourselves to [illegible]

uneaſineſs, and frequently to grievous and mortifying diſappointments. If we placed it in playing well, in playing fairly, in playing wiſely and ſkilfully; in the propriety of our own conduct in ſhort; we placed it in what, by proper diſcipline, education, and attention, might be altogether in our own power, and under our own direction. Our happineſs was perfectly ſecure, and beyond the reach of fortune. The event of our actions, if it was out of our power, was equally out of our concern, and we could never feel either fear or anxiety about it; nor ever ſuffer any grievous, or even any ſerious diſappointment.

Human life itſelf, as well as every different advantage or diſadvantage which can attend it, might, they ſaid, according to different circumſtances, be the proper object either of our choice or of our rejection. If, in our actual ſituation, there were more circumſtances agreeable to nature than contrary to it; more circumſtances which were the objects of choice than of rejection; life, in this caſe, was, upon the whole, the proper object of choice, and the propriety of conduct required that we ſhould remain in it. If, on the other hand, there were, in our actual ſituation, without any probable hope

hope of amendment, more circumstances contrary to nature than agreeable to it; more circumstances which were the objects of rejection than of choice; life itself, in this case, became, to a wise man, the object of rejection, and he was not only at liberty to remove out of it, but the propriety of conduct, the rule which the Gods had given him for the direction of his conduct, required him to do so. I am ordered, says Epictetus, not to dwell at Nicopolis. I do not dwell there. I am ordered not to dwell at Athens. I do not dwell at Athens. I am ordered not to dwell in Rome. I do not dwell in Rome. I am ordered to dwell in the little and rocky island of Gyaræ. I go and dwell there. But the house smokes in Gyaræ. If the smoke is moderate I will bear it, and stay there. If it is excessive, I will go to a house from whence no tyrant can remove me. I keep in mind always that the door is open, that I can walk out when I please, and retire to that hospitable house which is at all times open to all the world; for beyond my undermost garment, beyond my body, no man living has any power over me. If your situation is upon the whole disagreeable; if your house smokes too much for you,

you, ſaid the Stoics, walk forth by all means. But walk forth without repining; without murmuring or complaining. Walk forth calm, contented, rejoicing, returning thanks to the Gods, who, from their infinite bounty, have opened the ſafe and quiet harbour of death, at all times ready to receive us from the ſtormy ocean of human life; who have prepared this ſacred, this inviolable, this great aſylum, always open, always acceſſible; altogether beyond the reach of human rage and injuſtice; and large enough to contain both all thoſe who wiſh, and all thoſe who do not wiſh to retire to it: an aſylum which takes away from every man every pretence of complaining, or even of fancying that there can be any evil in human life, except ſuch as he may ſuffer from his own folly and weakneſs.

The Stoics, in the few fragments of their philoſophy which have come down to us, ſometimes talk of leaving life with a gaiety, and even with a levity, which, were we to conſider thoſe paſſages by themſelves, might induce us to believe that they imagined we could with propriety leave it whenever we had a mind, wantonly and capriciouſly, upon the ſlighteſt diſguſt or uneaſi-

uneasiness. "When you sup with such a "person," says Epictetus, "you complain "of the long stories which he tells you "about his Mysian wars. 'Now my "friend, says he, having told you how I "took possession of an eminence at such a "place, I will tell you how I was besieged "in such another place.' But if you have "a mind not to be troubled with his long "stories, do not accept of his supper. If "you accept of his supper, you have not "the least pretence to complain of his long "stories. It is the same case with what "you call the evils of human life. Never "complain of that of which it is at all "times in your power to rid yourself." Notwithstanding this gaiety and even levity of expression, however, the alternative of leaving life, or of remaining in it, was, according to the Stoics, a matter of the most serious and important deliberation. We ought never to leave it till we were distinctly called upon to do so by that superintending Power which had originally placed us in it. But we were to consider ourselves as called upon to do so, not merely at the appointed and unavoidable term of human life. Whenever the providence of that superintending Power had [illegible] our

con-

condition in life upon the whole the proper object rather of rejection than of choice; the great rule which he had given us for the direction of our conduct, then required us to leave it. We might then be said to hear the awful and benevolent voice of that divine Being distinctly calling upon us to do so.

It was upon this account that, according to the Stoics, it might be the duty of a wise man to remove out of life though he was perfectly happy; while, on the contrary, it might be the duty of a weak man to remain in it, though he was necessarily miserable. If, in the situation of the wise man, there were more circumstances which were the natural objects of rejection than of choice, the whole situation became the object of rejection, and the rule which the Gods had given him for the direction of his conduct, required that he should remove out of it as [illegible] particular circumstances might [illegible] was, however, perfectly happy [illegible] the time that he [illegible] to remain in it. He had [illegible], not in obtaining the [illegible], or in avoiding those [illegible] and [illegible]; not in the success,

success, but in the fitness of his endeavours and exertions. If in the situation of the weak man, on the contrary, there were more circumstances which were the natural objects of choice than of rejection; his whole situation became the proper object of choice, and it was his duty to remain in it. He was unhappy, however, from not knowing how to use those circumstances. Let his cards be ever so good, he did not know how to play them, and could enjoy no sort of real satisfaction, either in the progress, or in the event of the game, in whatever manner it might happen to turn out*.

The propriety, upon some occasions, of voluntary death, though it was, perhaps, more insisted upon by the Stoics, than by any other sect of ancient philosophers, was, however, a doctrine common to them all, even to the peaceable and indolent Epicureans. During the age in which flourished the founders of all the principal sects of ancient philosophy; during the Peloponnesian war, and for many years after its conclusion, all the different republics of Greece were, at home, almost always distracted by the most furious factions; and abroad, involved in the

* See Cicero de finibus, lib. 3. c. 13. Olivet's edition.

most

moſt ſanguinary wars, in which each fought, not merely ſuperiority or dominion, but either completely to extirpate all its enemies, or, what was not leſs cruel, to reduce them to the vileſt of all ſtates, that of domeſtic ſlavery, and to ſell them, man, woman, and child, like ſo many herds of cattle, to the higheſt bidder in the market. The ſmallneſs of the greater part of thoſe ſtates, too, rendered it, to each of them, no very improbable event, that it might itſelf fall into that very calamity which it had ſo frequently, either, perhaps, actually inflicted, or at leaſt attempted to inflict upon ſome of its neighbours. In this diſorderly ſtate of things, the moſt perfect innocence, joined to both the higheſt rank and the greateſt public ſervices, could give no ſecurity to any man that, even at home and among his own relations and fellow-citizens, he was not, at ſome time or another, from the prevalence of ſome hoſtile and furious faction, to be condemned to the moſt cruel and ignominious puniſhment. If he was taken priſoner in war, or if the city of which he was a member was conquered, he was expoſed, if poſſible, to ſtill greater injuries and inſults. But every man naturally, or rather neceſſarily, familiarizes his imagination with the diſtreſſes to which

which he foreſees that his ſituation may frequently expoſe him. It is impoſſible that a ſailor ſhould not frequently think of ſtorms and ſhipwrecks, and foundering at ſea, and of how he himſelf is likely both to feel and to act upon ſuch occaſions. It was impoſſible, in the ſame manner, that a Grecian patriot or hero ſhould not familiarize his imagination with all the different calamities to which he was ſenſible his ſituation muſt frequently, or rather conſtantly expoſe him. As an American ſavage prepares his death-ſong, and conſiders how he ſhould act when he has fallen into the hands of his enemies, and is by them put to death in the moſt lingering tortures, and amidſt the inſults and deriſion of all the ſpectators; ſo a Grecian patriot or hero could not avoid frequently employing his thoughts in conſidering what he ought both to ſuffer and to do in baniſhment, in captivity, when reduced to ſlavery, when put to the torture, when brought to the ſcaffold. But the philoſophers of all the different ſects very juſtly repreſented virtue; that is, wiſe, juſt, firm, and temperate conduct; not only as the moſt probable, but as the certain and infallible road to happineſs even in this life. This conduct, however, could not always exempt, and might even ſometimes ex-

poſe

poſe the perſon who followed it to all the calamities which were incident to that unſettled ſituation of public affairs. They endeavoured, therefore, to ſhow that happineſs was either altogether, or at leaſt in a great meaſure, independent of fortune; the Stoics, that it was ſo altogether; the Academic and Peripatetic philoſophers, that it was ſo in a great meaſure. Wiſe, prudent, and good conduct was, in the firſt place, the conduct moſt likely to enſure ſucceſs in every ſpecies of undertaking; and ſecondly, though it ſhould fail of ſucceſs, yet the mind was not left without conſolation. The virtuous man might ſtill enjoy the complete approbation of his own breaſt; and might ſtill feel that, how untoward ſoever things might be without, all was calm, and peace, and harmony within. He might generally comfort himſelf, too, with the aſſurance that he poſſeſſed the love and eſteem of every intelligent and impartial ſpectator, who could not fail both to admire his conduct, and to regret his misfortune.

Thoſe philoſophers endeavoured, at the ſame time, to ſhow, that the greateſt misfortunes to which human life was liable, might be ſupported more eaſily than was commonly imagined. They endeavoured to

point out the comforts which a man might still enjoy when reduced to poverty, when driven into banishment, when exposed to the injustice of popular clamour, when labouring under blindness, under deafness, in the extremity of old age, upon the approach of death. They pointed out, too, the considerations which might contribute to support his constancy under the agonies of pain and even of torture, in sickness, in sorrow for the loss of children, for the death of friends and relations, &c. The few fragments which have come down to us of what the ancient philosophers had written upon these subjects, form, perhaps, one of the most instructive, as well as one of the most interesting remains of antiquity. The spirit and manhood of their doctrines make a wonderful contrast with the desponding, plaintive, and whining tone of some modern systems.

But while these ancient philosophers endeavoured in this manner to suggest every consideration which could, as Milton says, arm the obdurate breast with stubborn patience, as with triple steel; they, at the same time, laboured above all to convince their followers that there neither was nor could be any evil in death, and that, if their situation

became at any time too hard for their constancy to support, the remedy was at hand, the door was open, and they might, without fear, walk out when they pleased. If there was no world beyond the present, death, they said, could be no evil; and if there was another world, the Gods must likewise be in that other, and a just man could fear no evil while under their protection. Those philosophers in short, prepared a death-song, if I may say so, which the Grecian patriots and heroes might make use of upon the proper occasions; and, of all the different sects, the Stoics, I think it must be acknowledged, had prepared by far the most animated and spirited song.

Suicide, however, never seems to have been very common among the Greeks. Excepting Cleomenes, I cannot at present recollect any very illustrious, either patriot or hero of Greece, who died by his own hand. The death of Aristomenes is as much beyond the period of true history as that of Ajax. The common story of the death of Themistocles, though within that period, bears upon its face all the marks of a most romantic fable. Of all the Greek heroes whose lives have been written by Plutarch, Cleomenes appears to have been the only one who

who periſhed in this manner. Theramines, Socrates, and Phocion, who certainly did not want courage, ſuffered themſelves to be ſent to priſon, and ſubmitted patiently to that death to which the injuſtice of their fellow-citizens had condemned them. The brave Eumenes allowed himſelf to be delivered up, by his own mutinous ſoldiers, to his enemy Antigonus, and was ſtarved to death, without attempting any violence. The gallant Philopœmen ſuffered himſelf to be taken priſoner by the Meſſenians, was thrown into a dungeon, and was ſuppoſed to have been privately poiſoned. Several of the philoſophers, indeed, are ſaid to have died in this manner; but their lives have been ſo very fooliſhly written, that very little credit is due to the greater part of the tales which are told of them. Three different accounts have been given of the death of Zeno the Stoic. One is, that after enjoying, for ninety-eight years, the moſt perfect ſtate of health, he happened, in going out of his ſchool, to fall, and though he ſuffered no other damage than that of breaking or diſlocating one of his fingers, he ſtruck the ground with his hand, and in the words of the Niobe of Euripides, ſaid, *I come, why doſt thou call me?* and immediately went home and hanged himſelf. At

that great age, one should think, he might have had a little more patience. Another account is, that, at the same age, and in consequence of a like accident, he starved himself to death. The third account is, that, at seventy-two years of age, he died in the natural way; by far the most probable account of the three, and supported too by the authority of a cotemporary, who must have had every opportunity of being well informed; of Persæus, originally the slave, and afterwards the friend and disciple of Zeno. The first account is given by Apollonius of Tyre, who flourished about the time of Augustus Cæsar, between two and three hundred years after the death of Zeno. I know not who is the author of the second account. Apollonius, who was himself a Stoic, had probably thought it would do honour to the founder of a sect which talked so much about voluntary death, to die in this manner by his own hand. Men of letters, though, after their death, they are frequently more talked of than the greatest princes or statesmen of their times, are generally, during their life, so obscure and insignificant that their adventures are seldom recorded by cotemporary historians. Those of after-ages, in order to satisfy the public curiosity,

ósity, and having no authentic documents either to ſupport or to contradict their narratives, ſeem frequently to have faſhioned them according to their own fancy; and almoſt always with a great mixture of the marvellous. In this particular caſe the marvellous, though ſupported by no authority, ſeems to have prevailed over the probable, though ſupported by the beſt. Diogenes Laertius plainly gives the preference to the ſtory of Apollonius. Lucian and Lactantius appear both to have given credit to that of the great age and of the violent death.

This faſhion of voluntary death appears to have been much more prevalent among the proud Romans, than it ever was among the lively, ingenious, and accommodating Geeks. Even among the Romans, the faſhion ſeems not to have been eſtabliſhed in the early, and, what are called, the virtuous ages of the republic. The common ſtory of the death of Regulus, though probably a fable, could never have been invented, had it been ſuppoſed that any diſhonour could fall upon that hero, from patiently ſubmitting to the tortures which the Carthaginians are ſaid to have inflicted upon him. In the later ages of the republic ſome diſhonour, I apprehend, would have attended this ſubmiſſion. In the

different civil wars which preceded the fall of the commonwealth, many of the eminent men of all the contending parties chose rather to perish by their own hands, than to fall into those of their enemies. The death of Cato, celebrated by Cicero, and censured by Cæsar, and become the subject of a very serious controversy between, perhaps, the two most illustrious advocates that the world had ever beheld, stamped a character of splendour upon this method of dying which it seems to have retained for several ages after. The eloquence of Cicero was superior to that of Cæsar. The admiring prevailed greatly over the censuring party, and the lovers of liberty, for many ages afterwards, looked up to Cato as to the most venerable martyr of the republican party. The head of a party, the Cardinal de Retz observes, may do what he pleases; as long as he retains the confidence of his own friends, he can never do wrong; a maxim of which his Eminence had himself, upon several occasions, an opportunity of experiencing the truth. Cato, it seems, joined to his other virtues that of an excellent bottle companion. His enemies accused him of drunkenness, but, says Seneca, whoever objected this vice to Cato, will find it much easier to prove that drunkenness

ennefs is a virtue, than that Cato could be addicted to any vice.

Under the Emperors this method of dying feems to have been, for a long time, perfectly fafhionable. In the epiftles of Pliny we find an account of feveral perfons who chofe to die in this manner, rather from vanity and oftentation, it would feem, than from what would appear, even to a fober and judicious Stoic, any proper or neceffary reafon. Even the ladies, who are feldom behind in following the fafhion, feem frequently to have chofen, moft unneceffarily, to die in this manner; and like the ladies in Bengal, to accompany, upon fome occafions, their hufbands to the tomb. The prevalence of this fafhion certainly occafioned many deaths which would not otherwife have happened. All the havock, however, which this, perhaps the higheft exertion of human vanity and impertinence, could occafion, would, probably, at no time, be very great.

The principle of fuicide, the principle which would teach us, upon fome occafions, to confider that violent action as an object of applaufe and approbation, feems to be altogether a refinement of philofophy. Nature, in her found and healthful ftate, feems never to prompt us to fuicide. There is indeed, a

species of melancholy (a disease to which human nature, among its other calamities, is unhappily subject) which seems to be accompanied with, what one may call, an irresistible appetite for self-destruction. In circumstances often of the highest external prosperity, and sometimes too, in spite even of the most serious and deeply impressed sentiments of religion, this disease has frequently been known to drive its wretched victims to this fatal extremity. The unfortunate persons who perish in this miserable manner are the proper objects, not of censure, but of commiseration. To attempt to punish them, when they are beyond the reach of all human punishment, is not more absurd than it is unjust. That punishment can fall only on their surviving friends and relations, who are always perfectly innocent, and to whom the loss of their friend, in this disgraceful manner, must always be alone a very heavy calamity. Nature, in her sound and healthful state, prompts us to avoid distress upon all occasions; upon many occasions to defend ourselves against it, though at the hazard, or even at the certainty of perishing in that defence. But, when we have neither been able to defend ourselves from it, nor have perished in that defence, no natural principle, no regard

gard to the approbation of the supposed impartial spectator, to the judgment of the man within the breast, seems to call upon us to escape from it by destroying ourselves. It is only the consciousness of our own weakness, of our own incapacity to support the calamity with proper manhood and firmness, which can drive us to this resolution. I do not remember to have either read or heard of any American savage, who, upon being taken prisoner by some hostile tribe, put himself to death, in order to avoid being afterwards put to death in torture, and amidst the insults and mockery of his enemies. He places his glory in supporting those torments with manhood, and in retorting those insults with tenfold contempt and derision.

This contempt of life and death, however, and, at the same time, the most entire submission to the order of Providence; the most complete contentment with every event which the current of human affairs could possibly cast up, may be considered as the two fundamental doctrines upon which rested the whole fabric of Stoical morality. The independent and spirited, but often harsh Epictetus, may be considered as the great apostle of the first of those doctrines: the mild, the

the humane, the benevolent Antoninus, of the ſecond.

The emancipated ſlave of Epaphroditus, who, in his youth, had been ſubjected to the inſolence of a brutal maſter, who, in his riper years, was, by the jealouſy and caprice of Domitian, baniſhed from Rome and Athens, and obliged to dwell at Nicopolis, and who, by the ſame tyrant, might expect every moment to be ſent to Gyaræ, or, perhaps, to be put to death; could preſerve his tranquillity only by foſtering in his mind the moſt ſovereign contempt of human life. He never exults ſo much, accordingly his eloquence is never ſo animated, as when he repreſents the futility and nothingneſs of all its pleaſures and all its pains.

The good-natured Emperor, the abſolute ſovereign of the whole civilized part of the world, who certainly had no peculiar reaſon to complain of his own allotment, delights in expreſſing his contentment with the ordinary courſe of things, and in pointing out beauties even in thoſe parts of it where vulgar obſervers are not apt to ſee any. There is a propriety and even an engaging grace, he obſerves, in old age as well as in youth; and the weakneſs and decrepitude of the one ſtate

are as suitable to nature as the bloom and vigour of the other. Death, too, is just as proper a termination of old age, as youth is of childhood, or manhood of youth. As we frequently say, he remarks upon another occasion, that the physician has ordered to such a man to ride on horseback, or to use the cold bath, or to walk barefooted; so ought we to say, that Nature, the great conductor and physician of the universe, has ordered to such a man a disease, or the amputation of a limb, or the loss of a child. By the prescriptions of ordinary physicians the patient swallows many a bitter potion; undergoes many a painful operation. From the very uncertain hope, however, that health may be the consequence, he gladly submits to all. The harshest prescriptions of the great Physician of nature, the patient may, in the same manner, hope will contribute to his own health, to his own final prosperity and happiness: and he may be perfectly assured that they not only contribute, but are indispensably necessary to the health, to the prosperity and happiness of the universe, to the furtherance and advancement of the great plan of Jupiter. Had they not been so, the universe would never have produced them; its all-wise Architect and Conductor would never have

have suffered them to happen. As all, even the smallest of the co-existent parts of the universe, are exactly fitted to one another, and all contribute to compose one immense and connected system; so all, even apparently the most insignificant of the successive events which follow one another, make parts, and necessary parts, of that great chain of causes and effects which had no beginning, and which will have no end: and which, as they all necessarily result from the original arrangement and contrivance of the whole; so they are all essentially necessary not only to its prosperity, but to its continuance and preservation. Whoever does not cordially embrace whatever befalls him, whoever is sorry that it has befallen him, whoever wishes that it had not befallen him, wishes, so far as in him lies, to stop the motion of the universe, to break that great chain of succession, by the progress of which that system can alone be continued and preserved, and, for some little conveniency of his own, to disorder and discompose the whole machine of the world. "O world!" says he, in another place, "all things are suitable to me
"which are suitable to thee. Nothing is too
"early or too late to me which is seasonable
"for thee. All is fruit to me which thy

"ſeaſons bring forth. From thee are all "things; in thee are all things; for thee are "all things. One man ſays, O beloved city "of Cecrops. Wilt not thou ſay, O beloved "city of God?"

From theſe very ſublime doctrines the Stoics, or at leaſt ſome of the Stoics, attempted to deduce all their paradoxes.

The Stoical wiſe man endeavoured to enter into the views of the great Superintendant of the univerſe, and to ſee things in the ſame light in which that divine Being beheld them. But to the great Superintendant of the univerſe, all the different events which the courſe of his providence may bring forth, what to us appear the ſmalleſt and the greateſt, the burſting of a bubble, as Mr. Pope ſays, and that of a world, for example, were perfectly equal, were equally parts of that great chain which he had predeſtined from all eternity, were equally the effects of the ſame unerring wiſdom, of the ſame univerſal and boundleſs benevolence. To the Stoical wiſe man, in the ſame manner, all thoſe different events were perfectly equal. In the courſe of thoſe events, indeed, a little department, in which he had himſelf ſome little management and direction, had been aſſigned to him. In this department he endeavoured to act as pro-

perly

perly as he could, and to conduct himself according to those orders which, he understood, had been prescribed to him. But he took no anxious or passionate concern either in the success or in the disappointment of his own most faithful endeavours. The highest prosperity and the total destruction of that little department, of that little system which had been in some measure committed to his charge, were perfectly indifferent to him. If those events had depended upon him, he would have chosen the one and he would have rejected the other. But as they did not depend upon him, he trusted to a superior wisdom, and was perfectly satisfied that the event which happened, whatever it might be, was the very event which he himself, had he known all the connections and dependencies of things, would most earnestly and devoutly have wished for. Whatever he did under the influence and direction of those principles was equally perfect; and when he stretched out his finger, to give the example which they commonly made use of, he performed an action in every respect as meritorious, as worthy of praise and admiration, as when he laid down his life for the service of his country. As, to the great Superintendant of the universe, the greatest and

and the ſmalleſt exertions of his power, the formation and diſſolution of a world, the formation and diſſolution of a bubble, were equally eaſy, were equally admirable, and equally the effects of the ſame divine wiſdom and benevolence; ſo, to the Stoical wiſe man, what we would call the great action, required no more exertion than the little one, was equally eaſy, proceeded from exactly the ſame principles, was in no reſpect more meritorious, nor worthy of any higher degree of praiſe and admiration.

As all thoſe who had arrived at this ſtate of perfection, were equally happy; ſo all thoſe who fell in the ſmalleſt degree ſhort of it, how nearly ſoever they might approach to it, were equally miſerable. As the man, they ſaid, who was but an inch below the ſurface of the water, could no more breathe than he who was an hundred yards below it; ſo the man who had not completely ſubdued all his private, partial, and ſelfiſh paſſions, who had any other earneſt deſire but that for the univerſal happineſs, who had not completely emerged from that abyſs of miſery and diſorder into which his anxiety for the gratification of thoſe private, partial, and ſelfiſh paſſions had involved him, could no more breathe the free air of liberty and inde-

pendency;

pendency, could no more enjoy the ſecurity and happineſs of the wiſe man, than he who was moſt remote from that ſituation. As all the actions of the wiſe man were perfect, and equally perfect; ſo all thoſe of the man who had not arrived at this ſupreme wiſdom were faulty, and, as ſome Stoics pretended, equally faulty. As one truth, they ſaid, could not be more true, nor one falſehood more falſe than another; ſo an honourable action could not be more honourable, nor a ſhameful one more ſhameful than another. As in ſhooting at a mark, the man who miſſed it by an inch had equally miſſed it with him who had done ſo by a hundred yards: ſo the man who, in what to us appears the moſt inſignificant action, had acted improperly and without a ſufficient reaſon, was equally faulty with him who had done ſo in, what to us appears, the moſt important; the man who has killed a cock, for example, improperly and without a ſufficient reaſon, with him who had murdered his father.

If the firſt of thoſe two paradoxes ſhould appear ſufficiently violent, the ſecond is evidently too abſurd to deſerve any ſerious conſideration. It is, indeed, ſo very abſurd, that one can ſcarce help ſuſpecting that it muſt

muſt have been in ſome meaſure miſunderſtood or miſrepreſented. At any rate, I cannot allow myſelf to believe that ſuch men as Zeno or Cleanthes, men, it is ſaid, of the moſt ſimple as well as of the moſt ſublime eloquence, could be the authors, either of theſe, or of the greater part of the other Stoical paradoxes, which are in general mere impertinent quibbles, and do ſo little honour to their ſyſtem that I ſhall give no further account of them. I am diſpoſed to impute them rather to Chryſippus, the diſciple and follower, indeed, of Zeno and Cleanthes, but who, from all that has been delivered down to us concerning him, ſeems to have been a mere dialectical pedant, without taſte or elegance of any kind. He may have been the firſt who reduced their doctrines into a ſcholaſtic or technical ſyſtem of artificial definitions, diviſions, and ſubdiviſions; one of the moſt effectual expedients, perhaps, for extinguiſhing whatever degree of good ſenſe there may be in any moral or metaphyſical doctrine. Such a man may very eaſily be ſuppoſed to have underſtood too literally ſome animated expreſſions of his maſters in deſcribing the happineſs of the man of perfect virtue, and the unhappineſs of whoever fell ſhort of that character.

The Stoics in general seem to have admitted that there might be a degree of proficiency in those who had not advanced to perfect virtue and happiness. They distributed those proficients into different classes, according to the degree of their advancement; and they called the imperfect virtues which they supposed them capable of exercising, not rectitudes, but proprieties, fitnesses, decent and becoming actions, for which a plausible or probable reason could be assigned, what Cicero expresses by the Latin word *officia*, and Seneca I think more exactly, by that of *convenientia*. The doctrine of those imperfect, but attainable virtues, seems to have constituted what we may call the practical morality of the Stoics. It is the subject of Cicero's Offices; and is said to have been that of another book written by Marcus Brutus, but which is now lost.

The plan and system which Nature has sketched out for our conduct, seems to be altogether different from that of the Stoical philosophy.

By Nature the events which immediately affect that little department in which we ourselves have some little management and direction, which immediately affect ourselves, our friends, our country, are the events which

intereſt us the moſt, and which chiefly excite our deſires and averſions, our hopes and fears, our joys and ſorrows. Should thoſe paſſions be, what they are very apt to be, too vehement, Nature has provided a proper remedy and correction. The real or even the imaginary preſence of the impartial ſpectator, the authority of the man within the breaſt, is always at hand to overawe them into the proper tone and temper of moderation.

If notwithſtanding our moſt faithful exertions, all the events which can affect this little department, ſhould turn out the moſt unfortunate and diſaſtrous, Nature has by no means left us without conſolation. That conſolation may be drawn, not only from the complete approbation of the man within the breaſt, but, if poſſible, from a ſtill nobler and more generous principle, from a firm reliance upon, and a reverential ſubmiſſion to, that benevolent wiſdom which directs all the events of human life, and which, we may be aſſured, would never have ſuffered thoſe miſfortunes to happen, had they not been indiſpenſably neceſſary for the good of the whole.

Nature has not preſcribed to us this ſublime contemplation as the great buſineſs and occupation of our lives. She only points it out

to us as the consolation of our misfortunes. The Stoical philosophy prescribes it as the great business and occupation of our lives. That philosophy teaches us to interest ourselves earnestly and anxiously in no events, external to the good order of our own minds, to the propriety of our own choosing and rejecting, except in those which concern a department where we neither have nor ought to have any sort of management or direction, the department of the great Superintendant of the universe. By the perfect apathy which it prescribes to us, by endeavouring, not merely to moderate, but to eradicate all our private, partial, and selfish affections, by suffering us to feel for whatever can befal ourselves, our friends, our country, not even the sympathetic and reduced passions of the impartial spectator, it endeavours to render us altogether indifferent and unconcerned in the success or miscarriage of every thing which Nature has prescribed to us as the proper business and occupation of our lives.

The reasonings of philosophy, it may be said, though they may confound and perplex the understanding, can never break down the necessary connection which Nature has established between causes and their effects. The causes which naturally excite our desires

and averſions, our hopes and fears, our joys and ſorrows, would no doubt, notwithſtanding all the reaſonings of Stoiciſm, produce upon each individual, according to the degree of his actual ſenſibility, their proper and neceſſary effects. The judgments of the man within the breaſt, however, might be a good deal affected by thoſe reaſonings, and that great inmate might be taught by them to attempt to overawe all our private, partial, and ſelfiſh affections into a more or leſs perfect tranquillity. To direct the judgments of this inmate is the great purpoſe of all ſyſtems of morality. That the Stoical philoſophy had very great influence upon the character and conduct of its followers, cannot be doubted; and that though it might ſometimes incite them to unneceſſary violence, its general tendency was to animate them to actions of the moſt heroic magnanimity and moſt extenſive benevolence.

IV Beſides theſe ancient, there are ſome modern ſyſtems, according to which virtue conſiſts in propriety; or in the ſuitableneſs of the affection from which we act, to the cauſe or object which excites it. The ſyſtem of Dr Clark, which places virtue in acting according to the relations of things, in regulating our conduct according to the fitneſs or

incongruity which there may be in the application of certain actions to certain things, or to certain relations: that of Mr. Woollaſton, which places it in acting according to the truth of things, according to their proper nature and eſſence, or in treating them as what they really are, and not as what they are not: that of my Lord Shafteſbury, which places it in maintaining a proper balance of the affections, and in allowing no paſſion to go beyond its proper ſphere; are all of them more or leſs inaccurate deſcriptions of the ſame fundamental idea.

None of thoſe ſyſtems either give, or even pretend to give, any preciſe or diſtinct meaſure by which this fitneſs or propriety of affection can be aſcertained or judged of. That preciſe and diſtinct meaſure can be found nowhere but in the ſympathetic feelings of the impartial and well informed ſpectator.

The deſcription of virtue, beſides, which is either given, or at leaſt meant and intended to be given, in each of thoſe ſyſtems, for ſome of the modern authors are not very fortunate in their manner of expreſſing themſelves, is no doubt quite juſt, ſo far as it goes. There is no virtue without propriety, and wherever there is propriety ſome degree of approbation is due. But ſtill this deſcription is

is imperfect. For though propriety is an essential ingredient in every virtuous action, it is not always the sole ingredient. Beneficent actions have in them another quality by which they appear not only to deserve approbation but recompense. None of those systems account either easily or sufficiently for that superior degree of esteem which seems due to such actions, or for that diversity of sentiment which they naturally excite. Neither is the description of vice more complete. For, in the same manner, though impropriety is a necessary ingredient in every vicious action, it is not always the sole ingredient; and there is often the highest degree of absurdity and impropriety in very harmless and insignificant actions. Deliberate actions, of a pernicious tendency to those we live with, have, besides their impropriety, a peculiar quality of their own, by which they appear to deserve, not only disapprobation, but punishment; and to be the objects, not of dislike merely, but of resentment and revenge: and none of those systems easily and sufficiently account for that superior degree of detestation which we feel for such actions.

CHAP. II.

Of those Systems which make Virtue consist in Prudence.

THE most ancient of those systems which make virtue consist in prudence, and of which any considerable remains have come down to us, is that of Epicurus, who is said, however, to have borrowed all the leading principles of his philosophy from some of those who had gone before him, particularly from Aristippus; though it is very probable, notwithstanding this allegation of his enemies, that at least his manner of applying those principles was altogether his own.

According to Epicurus *, bodily pleasure and pain were the sole ultimate objects of natural desire and aversion. That they were always the natural objects of those passions, he thought required no proof. Pleasure might, indeed, appear sometimes to be avoided; not, however, because it was pleasure, but because, by the enjoyment of it, we should either forfeit some greater pleasure, or expose ourselves to some pain that was

* See Cicero de finibus, lib. i. Diogenes Laert. l. x.

more

more to be avoided than this pleasure was to be desired. Pain, in the same manner, might appear sometimes to be eligible; not, however, because it was pain, but because by enduring it we might either avoid a still greater pain, or acquire some pleasure of much more importance. That bodily pain and pleasure, therefore, were always the natural objects of desire and aversion, was, he thought, abundantly evident. Nor was it less so, he imagined, that they were the sole ultimate objects of those passions. Whatever else was either desired or avoided, was so, according to him, upon account of its tendency to produce one or other of those sensations. The tendency to procure pleasure rendered power and riches desirable, as the contrary tendency to produce pain made poverty and insignificancy the objects of aversion. Honour and reputation were valued, because the esteem and love of those we live with were of the greatest consequence both to procure pleasure and defend us from pain. Ignominy and bad fame, on the contrary, were to be avoided, because the hatred, contempt, and resentment of those we lived with, destroyed all security, and necessarily exposed us to the greatest bodily evils.

All

All the pleaſures and pains of the mind were, according to Epicurus, ultimately derived from thoſe of the body. The mind was happy when it thought of the paſt pleaſures of the body, and hoped for others to come: and it was miſerable when it thought of the pains which the body had formerly endured, and dreaded the ſame or greater thereafter.

But the pleaſures and pains of the mind, though ultimately derived from thoſe of the body, were vaſtly greater than their originals. The body felt only the ſenſation of the preſent inſtant, whereas the mind felt alſo the paſt and the future, the one by remembrance, the other by anticipation, and conſequently both ſuffered and enjoyed much more. When we are under the greateſt bodily pain, he obſerved, we ſhall always find, if we attend to it, that it is not the ſuffering of the preſent inſtant which chiefly torments us, but either the agonizing remembrance of the paſt, or the yet more horrible dread of the future. The pain of each inſtant, conſidered by itſelf, and cut off from all that goes before and all that comes after it, is a trifle not worth the regarding. Yet this is all which the body can ever be ſaid to ſuffer. In the ſame

ſame manner, when we enjoy the greateſt pleaſure, we ſhall always find that the bodily ſenſation, the ſenſation of the preſent inſtant, makes but a ſmall part of our happineſs, that our enjoyment chiefly ariſes either from the cheerful recollection of the paſt, or the ſtill more joyous anticipation of the future, and that the mind always contributes by much the largeſt ſhare of the entertainment.

Since our happineſs and miſery, therefore, depended chiefly on the mind, if this part of our nature was well diſpoſed, if our thoughts and opinions were as they ſhould be, it was of little importance in what manner our body was affected. Though under great bodily pain, we might ſtill enjoy a conſiderable ſhare of happineſs, if our reaſon and judgment maintained their ſuperiority. We might entertain ourſelves with the remembrance of paſt, and with the hopes of future pleaſure; we might ſoften the rigour of our pains, by recollecting what it was which, even in this ſituation, we were under any neceſſity of ſuffering. That this was merely the bodily ſenſation, the pain of the preſent inſtant, which by itſelf could never be very great. That whatever agony we ſuffered from the dread of its continuance, was the effect of an opinion of the mind which might be corrected

rected by juster sentiments; by considering that, if our pains were violent, they would probably be of short duration; and that if they were of long continuance, they would probably be moderate, and admit of many intervals of ease; and that, at any rate, death was always at hand and within call to deliver us, which as, according to him, it put an end to all sensation, either of pain or pleasure, could not be regarded as an evil. When we are, said he, death is not; and when death is, we are not; death therefore can be nothing to us.

If the actual sensation of positive pain was in itself so little to be feared, that of pleasure was still less to be desired. Naturally the sensation of pleasure was much less pungent than that of pain. If, therefore, this last could take so very little from the happiness of a well-disposed mind, the other could add scarce any thing to it. When the body was free from pain and the mind from fear and anxiety, the superadded sensation of bodily pleasure could be of very little importance; and though it might diversify, could not properly be said to increase the happiness of this situation.

In ease of body, therefore, and in security or tranquillity of mind, consisted, according

to Epicurus, the most perfect state of human nature, the most complete happiness which man was capable of enjoying. To obtain this great end of natural desire was the sole object of all the virtues, which, according to him, were not desirable upon their own account, but upon account of their tendency to bring about this situation.

Prudence, for example, though, according to this philosophy, the source and principle of all the virtues, was not desirable upon its own account. That careful and laborious and circumspect state of mind, ever watchful and ever attentive to the most distant consequences of every action, could not be a thing pleasant or agreeable for its own sake, but upon account of its tendency to procure the greatest goods and to keep off the greatest evils.

To abstain from pleasure too, to curb and restrain our natural passions for enjoyment, which was the office of temperance, could never be desirable for its own sake. The whole value of this virtue arose from its utility, from its enabling us to postpone the present enjoyment for the sake of a greater to come, or to avoid a greater pain that might ensue from it. Temperance, in short, was nothing but prudence with regard to pleasure.

To fupport labour, to endure pain, to be expofed to danger or to death, the fituations which fortitude would often lead us into, were furely ftill lefs the objects of natural defire. They were chofen only to avoid greater evils. We fubmitted to labour, in order to avoid the greater fhame and pain of poverty, and we expofed ourfelves to danger and to death in defence of our liberty and property, the means and inftruments of pleafure and happinefs; or in defence of our country, in the fafety of which our own was neceffarily comprehended. Fortitude enabled us to do all this cheerfully, as the beft which, in our prefent fituation, could poffibly be done, and was in reality no more than prudence, good judgment, and prefence of mind in properly appreciating pain, labour, and danger, always choofing the lefs in order to avoid the greater.

It is the fame cafe with juftice. To abftain from what is another's was not defirable on its own account, and it could not furely be better for you, that I fhould poffefs what is my own, than that you fhould poffefs it. You ought, however, to abftain from whatever belongs to me, becaufe by doing otherwife you will provoke the refentment and indignation of mankind. The fecurity and tranquil-

tranquillity of your mind will be entirely destroyed. You will be filled with fear and consternation at the thought of that punishment which you will imagine that men are at all times ready to inflict upon you, and from which no power, no art, no concealment, will ever, in your own fancy, be sufficient to protect you. That other species of justice which consists in doing proper good offices to different persons, according to the various relations of neighbours, kinsmen, friends, benefactors, superiors, or equals, which they may stand in to us, is recommended by the same reasons. To act properly in all these different relations procures us the esteem and love of those we live with; as to do otherwise excites their contempt and hatred. By the one we naturally secure, by the other we necessarily endanger our own ease and tranquillity, the great and ultimate objects of all our desires. The whole virtue of justice, therefore, the most important of all the virtues, is no more than discreet and prudent conduct with regard to our neighbours.

Such is the doctrine of Epicurus concerning the nature of virtue. It may seem extraordinary that this philosopher, who is described as a person of the most amiable manners, should never have observed, that, whatever may

may be the tendency of thoſe virtues, or of the contrary vices, with regard to our bodily eaſe and ſecurity, the ſentiments which they naturally excite in others are the objects of a much more paſſionate deſire or averſion than all their other conſequences; that to be amiable, to be reſpectable, to be the proper object of eſteem, is by every well-diſpoſed mind more valued than all the eaſe and ſecurity which love, reſpect, and eſteem can procure us; that, on the contrary, to be odious, to be contemptible, to be the proper object of indignation, is more dreadful than all that we can ſuffer in our body from hatred, contempt, or indignation; and that conſequently our deſire of the one character, and our averſion to the other, cannot ariſe from any regard to the effects which either of them is likely to produce upon the body.

This ſyſtem is, no doubt, altogether inconſiſtent with that which I have been endeavouring to eſtabliſh. It is not difficult, however, to diſcover from what phaſis, if I may ſay ſo, from what particular view or aſpect of nature, this account of things derives its probability. By the wiſe contrivance of the Author of nature, virtue is upon all ordinary occaſions, even with regard to this life, real wiſdom, and the ſureſt and readieſt means of obtain-

obtaining both safety and advantage. Our success or disappointment in our undertakings must very much depend upon the good or bad opinion which is commonly entertained of us, and upon the general disposition of those we live with, either to assist or to oppose us. But the best, the surest, the easiest, and the readiest way of obtaining the advantageous and of avoiding the unfavourable judgments of others, is undoubtedly to render ourselves the proper objects of the former and not of the latter. "Do you desire," said Socrates, "the reputation of a good musician?
"The only sure way of obtaining it, is to
"become a good musician. Would you de-
"sire in the same manner to be thought ca-
"pable of serving your country either as a
"general or as a statesman? The best way
"in this case too is really to acquire the art
"and experience of war and government,
"and to become really fit to be a general or a
"statesman. And in the same manner if
"you would be reckoned sober, temperate,
"just, and equitable, the best way of ac-
"quiring this reputation is to become sober,
"temperate, just, and equitable. If you can
"really render yourself amiable, respectable,
"and the proper object of esteem, there is
"no fear of your not soon acquiring the

"love, the respect, and esteem of those you "live with." Since the practice of virtue, therefore is in general so advantageous, and that of vice so contrary to our interest, the consideration of these opposite tendencies undoubtedly stamps an additional beauty and propriety upon the one, and a new deformity and impropriety upon the other. Temperance, magnanimity, justice, and beneficence, come thus to be approved of, not only under their proper characters, but under the additional character of the highest wisdom and most real prudence. And in the same manner, the contrary vices of intemperance, pusillanimity, injustice, and either malevolence or sordid selfishness, come to be disapproved of, not only under their proper characters, but under the additional character of the most short-sighted folly and weakness. Epicurus appears in every virtue to have attended to this species of propriety only. It is that which is most apt to occur to those who are endeavouring to persuade others to regularity of conduct. When men by their practice, and perhaps too by their maxims, manifestly show that the natural beauty of virtue is not likely to have much effect upon them, how is it possible to move them but by representing the folly of their conduct, and how much

they

they themselves are in the end likely to suffer by it?

By running up all the different virtues too to this one species of propriety, Epicurus indulged a propensity, which is natural to all men, but which philosophers in particular are apt to cultivate with a peculiar fondness, as the great means of displaying their ingenuity, the propensity to account for all appearances from as few principles as possible. And he, no doubt, indulged this propensity still further, when he referred all the primary objects of natural desire and aversion to the pleasures and pains of the body. The great patron of the atomical philosophy, who took so much pleasure in deducing all the powers and qualities of bodies from the most obvious and familiar, the figure, motion, and arrangement of the small parts of matter, felt no doubt a similar satisfaction, when he accounted, in the same manner, for all the sentiments and passions of the mind from those which are most obvious and familiar.

The system of Epicurus agreed with those of Plato, Aristotle, and Zeno, in making virtue consist in acting in the most suitable manner to obtain the primary objects of natural

deſire. It differed from all of them in two other reſpects; firſt, in the account which it gave of thoſe primary objects of natural deſire; and ſecondly, in the account which it gave of the excellence of virtue, or of the reaſon why that quality ought to be eſteemed.

The primary objects of natural deſire conſiſted, according to Epicurus, in bodily pleaſure and pain, and in nothing elſe: whereas, according to the other three philoſophers, there were many other objects, ſuch as knowledge, ſuch as the happineſs of our relations, of our friends, of our country, which were ultimately deſirable for their own ſakes.

Virtue too, according to Epicurus, did not deſerve to be purſued for its own ſake, nor was itſelf one of the ultimate objects of natural appetite, but was eligible only upon account of its tendency to prevent pain and to procure eaſe and pleaſure. In the opinion of the other three, on the contrary, it was deſirable not merely as the means of procuring the other primary objects of natural deſire, but as ſomething which was in itſelf more valuable than them all. Man, they thought, being born for action, his happineſs muſt conſiſt, not merely in the agreeableneſs of his paſſive ſenſations, but alſo in the propriety of his active exertions.

CHAP. III.

Of thoſe Syſtems which make Virtue conſiſt in Benevolence.

THE ſyſtem which makes virtue conſiſt in benevolence, though I think not ſo ancient as all of thoſe which I have already given an account of, is, however, of very great antiquity. It ſeems to have been the doctrine of the greater part of thoſe philoſophers who, about and after the age of Auguſtus, called themſelves Eclectics, who pretended to follow chiefly the opinions of Plato and Pythagoras, and who, upon that account are commonly known by the name of the later Platoniſts.

In the divine nature, according to theſe authors, benevolence or love was the ſole principle of action, and directed the exertion of all the other attributes. The wiſdom of the Deity was employed in finding out the means for bringing about thoſe ends which his goodneſs ſuggeſted, as his infinite power was exerted to execute them. Benevolence, however, was ſtill the ſupreme and governing

 attribute,

attribute, to which the others were subservient, and from which the whole excellency, or the whole morality, if I may be allowed such an expression, of the divine operations, was ultimately derived. The whole perfection and virtue of the human mind consisted in some resemblance or participation of the divine perfections, and, consequently, in being filled with the same principle of benevolence and love which influenced all the actions of the Deity. The actions of men which flowed from this motive were alone truly praise-worthy, or could claim any merit in the sight of the Deity. It was by actions of charity and love only that we could imitate, as became us, the conduct of God, that we could express our humble and devout admiration of his infinite perfections, that by fostering in our own minds the same divine principle, we could bring our own affections to a greater resemblance with his holy attributes, and thereby become more proper objects of his love and esteem; till at last we arrived at that immediate converse and communication with the Deity to which it was the great object of this philosophy to raise us.

This system, as it was much esteemed by many ancient fathers of the Christian church, so

ſo after the Reformation it was adopted by ſeveral divines of the moſt eminent piety and learning and of the moſt amiable manners; particularly, by Dr. Ralph Cudworth, by Dr. Henry More, and by Mr. John Smith of Cambridge. But of all the patrons of this ſyſtem, ancient or modern, the late Dr. Hutcheſon was undoubtedly, beyond all compariſon, the moſt acute, the moſt diſtinct, the moſt philoſophical, and, what is of the greateſt conſequence of all, the ſobereſt and moſt judicious.

That virtue conſiſts in benevolence is a notion ſupported by many appearances in human nature. It has been obſerved already, that proper benevolence is the moſt graceful and agreeable of all the affections, that it is recommended to us by a double ſympathy, that as its tendency is neceſſarily beneficent, it is the proper object of gratitude and reward, and that upon all theſe accounts it appears to our natural ſentiments to poſſeſs a merit ſuperior to any other. It has been obſerved too, that even the weakneſſes of benevolence are not very diſagreeable to us, whereas thoſe of every other paſſion are always extremely diſguſting. Who does not abhor exceſſive malice, exceſſive ſelfiſhneſs, or exceſſive reſentment? But the moſt ex-

ceſſive indulgence even of partial friendſhip is not ſo offenſive. It is the benevolent paſſions only which can exert themſelves without any regard or attention to propriety, and yet retain ſomething about them which is engaging. There is ſomething pleaſing even in mere inſtinctive good-will which goes on to do good offices without once reflecting whether by this conduct it is the proper object either of blame or approbation. It is not ſo with the other paſſions. The moment they are deſerted, the moment they are unaccompanied by the ſenſe of propriety, they ceaſe to be agreeable.

As benevolence beſtows upon thoſe actions which proceed from it, a beauty ſuperior to all others, ſo the want of it, and much more the contrary inclination, communicates a peculiar deformity to whatever evidences ſuch a diſpoſition. Pernicious actions are often puniſhable for no other reaſon than becauſe they ſhew a want of ſufficient attention to the happineſs of our neighbour.

Beſides all this, Dr. Hutcheſon* obſerved, that whenever in any action, ſuppoſed to proceed from benevolent affections, ſome other motive had been diſcovered, our ſenſe of the merit of this action was juſt ſo far di-

* See Inquiry concerning Virtue, ſect. 1 and 2.

minished

minished as this motive was believed to have influenced it. If an action, supposed to proceed from gratitude, should be discovered to have arisen from an expectation of some new favour, or if what was apprehended to proceed from public spirit, should be found out to have taken its origin from the hope of a pecuniary reward, such a discovery would entirely destroy all notion of merit or praiseworthiness in either of these actions. Since, therefore, the mixture of any selfish motive, like that of a baser alloy, diminished or took away altogether the merit which would otherwise have belonged to any action, it was evident, he imagined, that virtue must consist in pure and disinterested benevolence alone.

When those actions, on the contrary, which are commonly supposed to proceed from a selfish motive, are discovered to have arisen from a benevolent one, it greatly enhances our sense of their merit. If we believed of any person that he endeavoured to advance his fortune from no other view but that of doing friendly offices, and of making proper returns to his benefactors, we should only love and esteem him the more. And this observation seemed still more to confirm the conclusion, that it was benevolence only which

which could stamp upon any action the character of virtue.

Last of all, what, he imagined, was an evident proof of the justness of this account of virtue, in all the disputes of casuists concerning the rectitude of conduct, the public good, he observed, was the standard to which they constantly referred; thereby universally acknowledging that whatever tended to promote the happiness of mankind was right, and laudable, and virtuous, and the contrary, wrong, blameable, and vicious. In the late debates about passive obedience and the right of resistance, the sole point in controversy among men of sense was, whether universal submission would probably be attended with greater evils than temporary insurrections when privileges were invaded. Whether what, upon the whole, tended most to the happiness of mankind, was not also morally good, was never once, he said, made a question.

Since benevolence, therefore, was the only motive which could bestow upon any action the character of virtue, the greater the benevolence which was evidenced by any action, the greater the praise which must belong to it.

Those

Those actions which aimed at the happiness of a great community, as they demonstrated a more enlarged benevolence than those which aimed only at that of a smaller system, so were they, likewise, proportionally the more virtuous. The most virtuous of all affections, therefore, was that which embraced as its objects the happiness of all intelligent beings. The least virtuous, on the contrary, of those to which the character of virtue could in any respect belong, was that which aimed no further than at the happiness of an individual, such as a son, a brother, a friend.

In directing all our actions to promote the greatest possible good, in submitting all inferior affections to the desire of the general happiness of mankind, in regarding one's self but as one of the many, whose prosperity was to be pursued no further than it was consistent with, or conducive to that of the whole, consisted the perfection of virtue.

Self-love was a principle which could never be virtuous in any degree or in any direction. It was vicious whenever it obstructed the general good. When it had no other effect than to make the individual take care of his own happiness, it was merely innocent, and though it deserved no praise, neither ought it

it to incur any blame. Thoſe benevolent actions which were performed, notwithſtanding ſome ſtrong motive from ſelf-intereſt, were the more virtuous upon that account. They demonſtrated the ſtrength and vigour of the benevolent principle.

Dr. Hutcheſon * was ſo far from allowing ſelf-love to be in any caſe a motive of virtuous actions, that even a regard to the pleaſure of ſelf-approbation, to the comfortable applauſe of our own conſciences, according to him, diminiſhed the merit of a benevolent action. This was a ſelfiſh motive, he thought, which, ſo far as it contributed to any action, demonſtrated the weakneſs of that pure and diſintereſted benevolence which could alone ſtamp upon the conduct of man the character of virtue. In the common judgments of mankind, however, this regard to the approbation of our own minds is ſo far from being conſidered as what can in any reſpect diminiſh the virtue of any action, that it is rather looked upon as the ſole motive which deſerves the appellation of virtuous.

Such is the account given of the nature of virtue in this amiable ſyſtem, a ſyſtem which has a peculiar tendency to nouriſh and ſup-

* Inquiry concerning virtue, ſect. 2. art. 4. alſo Illuſtrations on the moral ſenſe, ſect. 5. laſt paragraph.

port

port in the human heart the noblest and the most agreeable of all affections, and not only to check the injustice of self-love, but in some measure to discourage that principle altogether, by representing it as what could never reflect any honour upon those who were influenced by it.

As some of the other systems which I have already given an account of, do not sufficiently explain from whence arises the peculiar excellency of the supreme virtue of beneficence, so this system seems to have the contrary defect, of not sufficiently explaining from whence arises our approbation of the inferior virtues of prudence, vigilance, circumspection, temperance, constancy, firmness. The view and aim of our affections, the beneficent and hurtful effects which they tend to produce, are the only qualities at all attended to in this system. Their propriety and impropriety, their suitableness and unsuitableness, to the cause which excites them, are disregarded altogether.

Regard to our own private happiness and interest, too, appear upon many occasions very laudable principles of action. The habits of œconomy, industry, discretion, attention and application of thought, are generally supposed to be cultivated from self-interested

motives,

motives, and at the ſame time are apprehended to be very praiſe-worthy qualities, which deſerve the eſteem and approbation of every body. The mixture of a ſelfiſh motive, it is true, ſeems often to ſully the beauty of thoſe actions which ought to ariſe from a benevolent affection. The cauſe of this, however, is not that ſelf-love can never be the motive of a virtuous action, but that the benevolent principle appears in this particular caſe to want its due degree of ſtrength, and to be altogether unſuitable to its object. The character, therefore, ſeems evidently imperfect, and upon the whole to deſerve blame rather than praiſe. The mixture of a benevolent motive in an action to which ſelf-love alone ought to be ſufficient to prompt us, is not ſo apt indeed to diminiſh our ſenſe of its propriety, or of the virtue of the perſon who performs it. We are not ready to ſuſpect any perſon of being defective in ſelfiſhneſs. This is by no means the weak ſide of human nature, or the failing of which we are apt to be ſuſpicious. If we could really believe, however, of any man, that, was it not from a regard to his family and friends, he would not take that proper care of his health, his life, or his fortune, to which ſelf-preſervation alone ought to be ſufficient to prompt him, it would undoubtedly

doubtedly be a failing, though one of those amiable failings which render a person rather the object of pity than of contempt or hatred. It would still, however, somewhat diminish the dignity and respectableness of his character. Carelessness and want of œconomy are universally disapproved of, not, however, as proceeding from a want of benevolence, but from a want of the proper attention to the objects of self-interest.

Though the standard by which casuists frequently determine what is right or wrong in human conduct, be its tendency to the welfare or disorder of society, it does not follow that a regard to the welfare of society should be the sole virtuous motive of action, but only that, in any competition, it ought to cast the balance against all other motives.

Benevolence may, perhaps, be the sole principle of action in the Deity, and there are several, not improbable, arguments which tend to persuade us that it is so. It is not easy to conceive what other motive an independent and all-perfect Being, who stands in need of nothing external, and whose happiness is complete in himself, can act from. But whatever may be the case with the Deity, so imperfect a creature as man, the support of whose existence requires so many things external

ternal to him, muſt often act from many other motives. The condition of human nature were peculiarly hard, if thoſe affections, which, by the very nature of our being, ought frequently to influence our conduct, could upon no occaſion appear virtuous, or deſerve eſteem and commendation from any body.

Thoſe three ſyſtems, that which places virtue in propriety, that which places it in prudence, and that which makes it conſiſt in benevolence, are the principal accounts which have been given of the nature of virtue. To one or other of them, all the other deſcriptions of virtue, how different ſoever they may appear, are eaſily reducible.

That ſyſtem which places virtue in obedience to the will of the Deity, may be counted either among thoſe which make it conſiſt in prudence, or among thoſe which make it conſiſt in propriety. When it is aſked, why we ought to obey the will of the Deity, this queſtion, which would be impious and abſurd in the higheſt degree if aſked from any doubt that we ought to obey him, can admit but of two different anſwers. It muſt either be ſaid that we ought to obey the will of the Deity becauſe he is a Being of infinite power, who will reward us eternally if we do ſo, and puniſh

puniſh us eternally if we do otherwiſe: or it muſt be ſaid, that independent of any regard to our own happineſs, or to rewards and puniſhments of any kind, there is a congruity and fitneſs that a creature ſhould obey its creator, that a limited and imperfect being ſhould ſubmit to one of infinite and incomprehenſible perfections. Beſides one or other of theſe two, it is impoſſible to conceive that any other anſwer can be given to this queſtion. If the firſt anſwer be the proper one, virtue conſiſts in prudence, or in the proper purſuit of our own final intereſt and happineſs; ſince it is upon this account that we are obliged to obey the will of the Deity. If the ſecond anſwer be the proper one, virtue muſt conſiſt in propriety, ſince the ground of our obligation to obedience is the ſuitableneſs or congruity of the ſentiments of humility and ſubmiſſion to the ſuperiority of the object which excites them.

That ſyſtem which places virtue in utility, coincides too with that which makes it conſiſt in propriety. According to this ſyſtem, all thoſe qualities of the mind which are agreeable or advantageous, either to the perſon himſelf or to others, are approved of as virtuous, and the contrary diſapproved of as vicious. But the agreeableneſs or utility

of any affection depends upon the degree which it is allowed to subsist in. Every affection is useful when it is confined to a certain degree of moderation; and every affection is disadvantageous when it exceeds the proper bounds. According to this system therefore, virtue consists not in any one affection, but in the proper degree of all the affections. The only difference between it and that which I have been endeavouring to establish, is, that it makes utility, and not sympathy, or the correspondent affection of the spectator, the natural and original measure of this proper degree.

CHAP. IV.

Of licentious Systems.

ALL those systems, which I have hitherto given an account of, suppose that there is a real and essential distinction between vice and virtue, whatever these qualities may consist in. There is a real and essential difference between the propriety and impropriety of any affection, between benevolence and any other principle of action, between real prudence and short-sighted folly or precipi-

tate

tate rafhnefs. In the main too all of them contribute to encourage the praife-worthy, and to difcourage the blameable difpofition.

It may be true, perhaps, of fome of them, that they tend, in fome meafure, to break the balance of the affections, and to give the mind a particular bias to fome principles of action, beyond the proportion that is due to them. The ancient fyftems which place virtue in propriety, feem chiefly to recommend the great, the awful, and the refpectable virtues, the virtues of felf-government, and felf-command; fortitude, magnanimity, independency upon fortune, the contempt of all outward accidents, of pain, poverty, exile, and death. It is in thefe great exertions that the nobleft propriety of conduct is difplayed. The foft, the amiable, the gentle virtues, all the virtues of indulgent humanity, are, in comparifon, but little infifted upon, and feem, on the contrary, by the Stoics in particular, to have been often regarded as mere weakneffes which it behoved a wife man not to harbour in his breaft.

The benevolent fyftem, on the other hand, while it fofters and encourages all thofe milder virtues in the higheft degree, feems entirely to neglect the more awful and refpectable qualities of the mind. It even de-

nies them the appellation of virtues. It calls them moral abilities, and treats them as qualities which do not deſerve the ſame ſort of eſteem and approbation that is due to what is properly denominated virtue. All thoſe principles of action which aim only at our own intereſt, it treats, if that be poſſible, ſtill worſe. So far from having any merit of their own, they diminiſh, it pretends, the merit of benevolence, when they co-operate with it: and prudence, it is aſſerted, when employed only in promoting private intereſt, can never even be imagined a virtue.

That ſyſtem, again, which makes virtue conſiſt in prudence only, while it gives the higheſt encouragement to the habits of caution, vigilance, ſobriety, and judicious moderation, ſeems to degrade equally both the amiable and reſpectable virtues, and to ſtrip the former of all their beauty, and the latter of all their grandeur.

But notwithſtanding theſe defects, the general tendency of each of thoſe three ſyſtems is to encourage the beſt and moſt laudable habits of the human mind: and it were well for ſociety, if, either mankind in general, or even thoſe few who pretend to live according to any philoſophical rule, were to regulate their conduct by the precepts of any one of them.

We may learn from each of them fomething that is both valuable and peculiar. If it was poffible, by precept and exhortation, to infpire the mind with fortitude and magnanimity, the ancient fyftems of propriety would feem fufficient to do this. Or if it was poffible, by the fame means, to foften it into humanity, and to awaken the affections of kindnefs and general love towards thofe we live with, fome of the pictures with which the benevolent fyftem prefents us, might feem capable of producing this effect. We may learn from the fyftem of Epicurus, though undoubtedly the moft imperfect of all the three, how much the practice of both the amiable and refpectable virtues is conducive to our own intereft, to our own eafe and fafety and quiet even in this life. As Epicurus placed happinefs in the attainment of eafe and fecurity, he exerted himfelf in a particular manner to fhow that virtue was, not merely the beft and the fureft, but the only means of acquiring thofe invaluable poffeffions. The good effects of virtue, upon our inward tranquillity and peace of mind, are what other philofophers have chiefly celebrated. Epicurus, without neglecting this topic, has chiefly infifted upon the influence of that amiable quality on our outward profperity

and ſafety. It was upon this account that his writings were ſo much ſtudied in the ancient world by men of all different philoſophical parties. It is from him that Cicero, the great enemy of the Epicurean ſyſtem, borrows his moſt agreeable proofs that virtue alone is ſufficient to ſecure happineſs. Seneca, though a Stoic, the ſect moſt oppoſite to that of Epicurus, yet quotes this philoſopher more frequently than any other.

There is, however, another ſyſtem which ſeems to take away altogether the diſtinction between vice and virtue, and of which the tendency is, upon that account, wholly pernicious; I mean the ſyſtem of Dr. Mandeville. Though the notions of this author are in almoſt every reſpect erroneous, there are, however, ſome appearances in human nature, which, when viewed in a certain manner, ſeem at firſt ſight to favour them. Theſe, deſcribed and exaggerated by the lively and humorous, though coarſe and ruſtic eloquence of Dr. Mandeville, have thrown upon his doctrines an air of truth and probability which is very apt to impoſe upon the unſkilful.

Dr. Mandeville conſiders whatever is done from a ſenſe of propriety, from a regard to what is commendable and praiſe-worthy, as being

being done from a love of praiſe and commendation, or as he calls it from vanity. Man, he obſerves, is naturally much more intereſted in his own happineſs than in that of others, and it is impoſſible that in his heart he can ever really prefer their proſperity to his own. Whenever he appears to do ſo, we may be aſſured that he impoſes upon us, and that he is then acting from the ſame ſelfiſh motives as at all other times. Among his other ſelfiſh paſſions, vanity is one of the ſtrongeſt, and he is always eaſily flattered and greatly delighted with the applauſes of thoſe about him. When he appears to ſacrifice his own intereſt to that of his companions, he knows that this conduct will be highly agreeable to their ſelf-love, and that they will not fail to expreſs their ſatisfaction by beſtowing upon him the moſt extravagant praiſes. The pleaſure which he expects from this, over-balances, in his opinion, the intereſt which he abandons in order to procure it. His conduct, therefore, upon this occaſion, is in reality juſt as ſelfiſh, and ariſes from juſt as mean a motive as upon any other. He is flattered, however, and he flatters himſelf with the belief that it is entirely diſintereſted; ſince, unleſs this was ſuppoſed, it would not ſeem to merit any commenda-

tion either in his own eyes or in thoſe of others. All public ſpirit, therefore, all preference of public to private intereſt, is, according to him, a mere cheat and impoſition upon mankind; and that human virtue which is ſo much boaſted of, and which is the occaſion of ſo much emulation among men, is the mere offspring of flattery begot upon pride.

Whether the moſt generous and public-ſpirited actions may not, in ſome ſenſe, be regarded as proceeding from ſelf-love, I ſhall not at preſent examine. The deciſion of this queſtion is not, I apprehend, of any importance towards eſtabliſhing the reality of virtue, ſince ſelf-love may frequently be a virtuous motive of action. I ſhall only endeavour to ſhow that the deſire of doing what is honourable and noble, of rendering ourſelves the proper objects of eſteem and approbation, cannot with any propriety be called vanity. Even the love of well-grounded fame and reputation, the deſire of acquiring eſteem by what is really eſtimable, does not deſerve that name. The firſt is the love of virtue, the nobleſt and the beſt paſſion of human nature. The ſecond is the love of true glory, a paſſion inferior no doubt to the former, but which in dignity appears to come immediately after it. He is guilty of

of vanity who desires praise for qualities which are either not praise-worthy in any degree, or not in that degree in which he expects to be praised for them; who sets his character upon the frivolous ornaments of dress and equipage, or upon the equally frivolous accomplishments of ordinary behaviour. He is guilty of vanity who desires praise for what indeed very well deserves it, but what he perfectly knows does not belong to him. The empty coxcomb who gives himself airs of importance which he has no title to, the silly liar who assumes the merit of adventures which never happened, the foolish plagiary who gives himself out for the author of what he has no pretensions to, are properly accused of this passion. He too is said to be guilty of vanity who is not contented with the silent sentiments of esteem and approbation, who seems to be fonder of their noisy expressions and acclamations than of the sentiments themselves, who is never satisfied but when his own praises are ringing in his ears, and who solicits with the most anxious importunity all external marks of respect, is fond of titles, of compliments, of being visited, of being attended, of being taken notice of in public places with the appearance of deference and attention. This frivolous passion

is

is altogether different from either of the two former, and is the paſſion of the loweſt and the leaſt of mankind, as they are of the nobleſt and the greateſt.

But though theſe three paſſions, the deſire of rendering ourſelves the proper objects of honour and eſteem, or of becoming what is honourable and eſtimable; the deſire of acquiring honour and eſteem by really deſerving thoſe ſentiments; and the frivolous deſire of praiſe at any rate, are widely different; though the two former are always approved of, while the latter never fails to be deſpiſed; there is, however, a certain remote affinity among them, which, exaggerated by the humorous and diverting eloquence of this lively author, has enabled him to impoſe upon his readers. There is an affinity between vanity and the love of true glory, as both theſe paſſions aim at acquiring eſteem and approbation. But they are different in this, that the one is a juſt, reaſonable, and equitable paſſion, while the other is unjuſt, abſurd, and ridiculous. The man who deſires eſteem for what is really eſtimable, deſires nothing but what he is juſtly entitled to, and what cannot be refuſed him without ſome ſort of injury. He, on the contrary, who deſires it upon any other terms, demands what he has no

no juſt claim to. The firſt is eaſily ſatisfied, is not apt to be jealous or ſuſpicious that we do not eſteem him enough, and is ſeldom ſolicitous about receiving many external marks of our regard. The other on the contrary, is never to be ſatisfied, is full of jealouſy and ſuſpicion that we do not eſteem him ſo much as he deſires, becauſe he has ſome ſecret conſciouſneſs that he deſires more than he deſerves. The leaſt neglect of ceremony, he conſiders as a mortal affront, and as an expreſſion of the moſt determined contempt. He is reſtleſs and impatient, and perpetually afraid that we have loſt all reſpect for him, and is upon this account always anxious to obtain new expreſſions of eſteem, and cannot be kept in temper but by continual attendance and adulation.

There is an affinity too between the deſire of becoming what is honourable and eſtimable, and the deſire of honour and eſteem, between the love of virtue and the love of true glory. They reſemble one another not only in this reſpect, that both aim at really being what is honourable and noble, but even in that reſpect in which the love of true glory reſembles what is properly called vanity, ſome reference to the ſentiments of others. The man of the greateſt magnanimity,

nimity, who deſires virtue for its own ſake, and is moſt indifferent about what actually are the opinions of mankind with regard to him, is ſtill, however, delighted with the thoughts of what they ſhould be, with the conſciouſneſs that though he may neither be honoured nor applauded, he is ſtill the proper object of honour and applauſe, and that if mankind, were cool and candid and conſiſtent with themſelves, and properly informed of the motives and circumſtances of his conduct, they would not fail to honour and applaud him. Though he deſpiſes the opinions which are actually entertained of him, he has the higheſt value for thoſe which ought to be entertained of him. That he might think himſelf worthy of thoſe honourable ſentiments, and, whatever was the idea which other men might conceive of his character, that when he ſhould put himſelf in their ſituation, and conſider, not what was, but what ought to be their opinion, he ſhould always have the higheſt idea of it himſelf, was the great and exalted motive of his conduct. As even in the love of virtue, therefore, there is ſtill ſome reference, though not to what is, yet to what in reaſon and propriety ought to be the opinion of others, there is even in this reſpect ſome affinity between it, and the love of

of true glory. There is however, at the same time, very great difference between them. The man who acts solely from a regard to what is right and fit to be done, from a regard to what is the proper object of esteem and approbation, though these sentiments should never be bestowed upon him, acts from the most sublime and godlike motive which human nature is even capable of conceiving. The man, on the other hand, who while he desires to merit approbation is at the same time anxious to obtain it, though he too is laudable in the main, yet his motives have a greater mixture of human infirmity. He is in danger of being mortified by the ignorance and injustice of mankind, and his happiness is exposed to the envy of his rivals and the folly of the public. The happiness of the other, on the contrary, is altogether secure and independent of fortune, and of the caprice of those he lives with. The contempt and hatred which may be thrown upon him by the ignorance of mankind, he considers as not belonging to him, and is not at all mortified by it. Mankind despise and hate him from a false notion of his character and conduct. If they knew him better, they would esteem and love him. It is not him whom, properly speaking, they hate and despise,

despise, but another person whom they mistake him to be. Our friend, whom we should meet at a masquerade in the garb of our enemy, would be more diverted than mortified, if under that disguise we should vent our indignation against him. Such are the sentiments of a man of real magnanimity, when exposed to unjust censure. It seldom happens, however, that human nature arrives at this degree of firmness. Though none but the weakest and most worthless of mankind are much delighted with false glory, yet, by a strange inconsistency, false ignominy is often capable of mortifying those who appear the most resolute and determined.

Dr. Mandeville is not satisfied with representing the frivolous motive of vanity, as the source of all those actions which are commonly accounted virtuous. He endeavours to point out the imperfection of human virtue in many other respects. In every case, he pretends, it falls short of that complete self-denial which it pretends to, and, instead of a conquest, is commonly no more than a concealed indulgence of our passions. Wherever our reserve with regard to pleasure falls short of the most ascetic abstinence, he treats it as gross luxury and sensuality. Every thing, according to him, is luxury which

exceeds what is abſolutely neceſſary for the ſupport of human nature, ſo that there is vice even in the uſe of a clean ſhirt, or of a convenient habitation. The indulgence of the inclination to ſex, in the moſt lawful union, he conſiders as the ſame ſenſuality with the moſt hurtful gratification of that paſſion, and derides that temperance and that chaſtity which can be practiſed at ſo cheap a rate. The ingenious ſophiſtry of his reaſoning, is here, as upon many other occaſions, covered by the ambiguity of language. There are ſome of our paſſions which have no other names except thoſe which mark the diſagreeable and offenſive degree. The ſpectator is more apt to take notice of them in this degree than in any other. When they ſhock his own ſentiments, when they give him ſome ſort of antipathy and uneaſineſs, he is neceſſarily obliged to attend to them, and is from thence naturally led to give them a name. When they fall in with the natural ſtate of his own mind, he is very apt to overlook them altogether, and either gives them no name at all, or, if he give them any, it is one which marks rather the ſubjection and reſtraint of the paſſion, than the degree which it ſtill is allowed to ſubſiſt in, after it is ſo ſubjected and reſtrained. Thus the common

mon names* of the love of pleasure, and of the love of sex, denote a vicious and offensive degree of those passions. The words temperance and chastity, on the other hand, seem to mark rather the restraint and subjection which they are kept under, than the degree which they are still allowed to subsist in. When he can show, therefore, that they still subsist in some degree, he imagines, he has entirely demolished the reality of the virtues of temperance and chastity, and shown them to be mere impositions upon the inattention and simplicity of mankind. These virtues, however, do not require an entire insensibility to the objects of the passions which they mean to govern. They only aim at restraining the violence of those passions, so far as not to hurt the individual, and neither disturb nor offend the society.

It is the great fallacy of Dr. Mandeville's book† to represent every passion as wholly vicious, which is so in any degree and in any direction. It is thus that he treats every thing as vanity which has any reference, either to what are, or to what ought to be the sentiments of others: and it is by means of this sophistry, that he establishes his favourite conclusion, that private vices are public benefits.

* [illegible]

† Fable of the Bees.

fits If the love of magnificence, a taste for the elegant arts and improvements of human life, for whatever is agreeable in dress, furniture, or equipage, for architecture, statuary, painting, and music, is to be regarded as luxury, sensuality, and ostentation, even in those whose situation allows, without any inconveniency, the indulgence of those passions, it is certain that luxury, sensuality, and ostentation, are public benefits: since without the qualities upon which he thinks proper to bestow such opprobrious names, the arts of refinement could never find encouragement, and must languish for want of employment. Some popular ascetic doctrines, which had been current before his time, and which placed virtue in the entire extirpation and annihilation of all our passions, were the real foundation of this licentious system. It was easy for Dr. Mandeville to prove, first, that this entire conquest never actually took place among men, and secondly, that, if it was to take place universally, it would be pernicious to society, by putting an end to all industry and commerce, and in a manner to the whole business of human life. By the first of these propositions he seemed to prove that there was no real virtue, and that what pretended to be such, was a mere cheat and imposition

upon mankind; and by the ſecond, that private vices were public benefits, ſince without them no ſociety could proſper or flouriſh.

Such is the ſyſtem of Dr. Mandeville, which once made ſo much noiſe in the world, and which, though, perhaps, it never gave occaſion to more vice than what would have been without it, at leaſt taught that vice, which aroſe from other cauſes, to appear with more effrontery, and to avow the corruption of its motives with a profligate audacioufneſs, which had never been heard of before.

But how deſtructive ſoever this ſyſtem may appear, it could never have impoſed upon ſo great a number of perſons, nor have occaſioned ſo general an alarm among thoſe who are the friends of better principles, had it not in ſome reſpects bordered upon the truth. A ſyſtem of natural philoſophy may appear very plauſible, and be for a long time very generally received in the world, and yet have no foundation in nature, nor any ſort of reſemblance to the truth. The vortices of Des Cartes were regarded by a very ingenious nation, for near a century together, as a moſt ſatisfactory account of the revolutions of the heavenly bodies. Yet it has been demonſtrated, to the conviction of all mankind, that

that these pretended causes of those wonderful effects, not only do not actually exist, but are utterly impossible, and if they did exist could produce no such effects as are ascribed to them. But it is otherwise with systems of moral philosophy, and an author who pretends to account for the origin of our moral sentiments, cannot deceive us so grossly, nor depart so very far from all resemblance to the truth. When a traveller gives an account of some distant country, he may impose upon our credulity the most groundless and absurd fictions as the most certain matters of fact. But when a person pretends to inform us of what passes in our neigbourhood, and of the affairs of the very parish which we live in, though here too, if we are so careless as not to examine things with our own eyes, he may deceive us in many respects, yet the greatest falsehoods which he imposes upon us must bear some resemblance to the truth, and must even have a considerable mixture of truth in them. An author who treats of natural philosophy, and pretends to assign the causes of the great phenomena of the universe, pretends to give an account of the affairs of a very distant country, concerning which he may tell us what he pleases, and as long as his narration keeps within the bounds

of ſeeming poſſibility he need not deſpair of gaining our belief. But when he propoſes to explain the origin of our deſires and affections, of our ſentiments of approbation and diſapprobation, he pretends to give an account, not only of the affairs of the very pariſh that we live in, but of our own domeſtic concerns. Though here too, like indolent maſters who put their truſt in a ſteward who deceives them, we are very liable to be impoſed upon, yet we are incapable of paſſing any account which does not preſerve ſome little regard to the truth. Some of the articles, at leaſt, muſt be juſt, and even thoſe which are moſt overcharged muſt have had ſome foundation, otherwiſe the fraud would be detected even by that careleſs inſpection which we are diſpoſed to give. The author who ſhould aſſign, as the cauſe of any natural ſentiment, ſome principle which neither had any connexion with it, nor reſembled any other principle which had ſome ſuch connexion, would appear abſurd and ridiculous to the moſt injudicious and unexperienced reader.

SECTION III.

Of the different Syſtems which have been formed concerning the Principle of Approbation.

INTRODUCTION

AFTER the inquiry concerning the nature of virtue, the next queſtion of importance in Moral Philoſophy is concerning the principle of approbation, concerning the power or faculty of the mind which renders certain characters agreeable or diſagreeable to us, makes us prefer one tenour of conduct to another, denominate the one right and the other wrong, and conſider the one as the object of approbation, honour, and reward; the other as that of blame, cenſure, and puniſhment.

Three different accounts have been given of this principle of approbation. According to ſome, we approve and diſapprove both of our own actions and of thoſe of others, from ſelf-love only, or from ſome view of their

tendency to our own happineſs or diſadvantage: according to others, reaſon, the ſame faculty by which we diſtinguiſh between truth and falſehood, enables us to diſtinguiſh between what is fit and unfit both in actions and affections: according to others this diſtinction is altogether the effect of immediate ſentiment and feeling, and ariſes from the ſatisfaction or diſguſt with which the view of certain actions or affections inſpires us. Self-love, reaſon, and ſentiment, therefore, are the three different ſources which have been aſſigned for the principle of approbation.

Before I proceed to give an account of thoſe different ſyſtems, I muſt obſerve, that the determination of this ſecond queſtion, though of the greateſt importance in ſpeculation, is of none in practice. The queſtion concerning the nature of virtue neceſſarily has ſome influence upon our notions of right and wrong in many particular caſes. That concerning the principle of approbation can poſſibly have no ſuch effect. To examine from what contrivance or mechaniſm within, thoſe different notions or ſentiments ariſe, is a mere matter of philoſophical curioſity.

CHAP. I.

Of those Systems which deduce the Principle of Approbation from Self-Love.

THOSE who account for the principle of approbation from self-love, do not all account for it in the same manner, and there is a good deal of confusion and inaccuracy in all their different systems. According to Mr. Hobbes, and many of his followers*, man is driven to take refuge in society, not by any natural love which he bears to his own kind, but because without the assistance of others he is incapable of subsisting with ease or safety. Society, upon this account, becomes necessary to him, and whatever tends to its support and welfare, he considers as having a remote tendency to his own interest; and, on the contrary, whatever is likely to disturb or destroy it, he regards as in some measure hurtful or pernicious to himself. Virtue is the great support and vice the great disturber of human society. The former, therefore, is agreeable and the latter offensive to every man; as from the one he foresees

* Puffendorff, Mandeville.

the proſperity, and from the other the ruin and diſorder of what is ſo neceſſary for the comfort and ſecurity of his exiſtence.

That the tendency of virtue to promote, and of vice to diſturb the order of ſociety, when we conſider it coolly and philoſophically, reflects a very great beauty upon the one, and a very great deformity upon the other, cannot, as I have obſerved upon a former occaſion, be called in queſtion. Human ſociety, when we contemplate it in a certain abſtract and philoſophical light, appears like a great, an immenſe machine, whoſe regular and harmonious movements produce a thouſand agreeable effects. As in any other beautiful and noble machine that was the production of human art, whatever tended to render its movements more ſmooth and eaſy, would derive a beauty from this effect, and, on the contrary, whatever tended to obſtruct them would diſpleaſe upon that account: ſo virtue, which is, as it were, the fine poliſh to the wheels of ſociety, neceſſarily pleaſes; while vice, like the vile ruſt, which makes them jar and grate upon one another, is as neceſſarily offenſive. This account, therefore, of the origin of approbation and diſapprobation, ſo far as it derives them from a regard to the order of ſociety, runs into that principle which

which gives beauty to utility, and which I have explained upon a former occasion; and it is from thence that this system derives all that appearance of probability which it possesses. When those authors describe the innumerable advantages of a cultivated and social, above a savage and solitary life; when they expatiate upon the necessity of virtue and good order for the maintenance of the one, and demonstrate how infallibly the prevalence of vice and disobedience to the laws tend to bring back the other, the reader is charmed with the novelty and grandeur of those views which they open to him: he sees plainly a new beauty in virtue, and a new deformity in vice, which he had never taken notice of before, and is commonly so delighted with the discovery, that he seldom takes time to reflect, that this political view having never occurred to him in his life before, cannot possibly be the ground of that approbation and disapprobation with which he has always been accustomed to consider those different qualities.

When those authors, on the other hand, deduce from self-love the interest which we take in the welfare of society, and the esteem which upon that account we bestow upon virtue, they do not mean, that when we in this

this age applaud the virtue of Cato, and deteſt the villany of Catiline, our ſentiments are influenced by the notion of any benefit we receive from the one, or of any detriment we ſuffer from the other. It was not becauſe the proſperity or ſubverſion of ſociety, in thoſe remote ages and nations, was apprehended to have any influence upon our happineſs or miſery in the preſent times; that according to theſe philoſophers, we eſteemed the virtuous, and blamed the diſorderly character. They never imagined that our ſentiments were influenced by any benefit or damage which we ſuppoſed actually to redound to us, from either; but by that which might have redounded to us, had we lived in thoſe diſtant ages and countries; or by that which might ſtill redound to us, if in our own times we ſhould meet with characters of the ſame kind. The idea, in ſhort, which thoſe authors were groping about, but which they were never able to unfold diſtinctly, was that indirect ſympathy which we feel with the gratitude or reſentment of thoſe who received the benefit or ſuffered the damage reſulting from ſuch oppoſite characters: and it was this which they were indiſtinctly pointing at, when they ſaid, that it was not the thought of what we had gained or ſuffered which prompted

prompted our applaufe or indignation, but the conception or imagination of what we might gain or fuffer if we were to act in fociety with fuch affociates.

Sympathy, however, cannot, in any fenfe, be regarded as a felfifh principle. When I fympathize with your forrow or your indignation, it may be pretended, indeed, that my emotion is founded in felf-love, becaufe it arifes from bringing your cafe home to myfelf, from putting myfelf in your fituation, and thence conceiving what I fhould feel in the like circumftances. But though fympathy is very properly faid to arife from an imaginary change of fituations with the perfon principally concerned, yet this imaginary change is not fuppofed to happen to me in my own perfon and character, but in that of the perfon with whom I fympathize. When I condole with you for the lofs of your only fon, in order to enter into your grief I do not confider what I, a perfon of fuch a character and profeffion, fhould fuffer, if I had a fon, and if that fon was unfortunately to die: but I confider what I fhould fuffer if I was really you, and I not only change circumftances with you, but I change perfons and characters. My grief, therefore, is entirely upon your account, and not in the leaft

upon

upon my own. It is not, therefore, in the leaft felfifh. How can that be regarded as a felfifh paffion, which does not arife even from the imagination of any thing that has befallen, or that relates to myfelf, in my own proper perfon and character, but which is entirely occupied about what relates to you? A man may fympathize with a woman in child-bed; though it is impoffible that he fhould conceive himfelf as fuffering her pains in his own proper perfon and character. That whole account of human nature, however, which deduces all fentiments and affections from felf-love, which has made fo much noife in the world, but which, fo far as I know, has never yet been fully and diftinctly explained, feems to me to have arifen from fome confufed mifapprehenfion of the fyftem of fympathy.

CHAP. II.

Of thofe Syftems which make Reafon the Principle of Approbation.

IT is well known to have been the doctrine of Mr. Hobbes, that a ftate of nature is a ftate of war; and that antecedent to the inftitution of civil government, there could be no fafe or peaceable fociety among men. To

To preserve society, therefore, according to him, was to support civil government, and to destroy civil government was the same thing as to put an end to society. But the existence of civil government depends upon the obedience that is paid to the supreme magistrate. The moment he loses his authority, all government is at an end. As self-preservation, therefore, teaches men to applaud whatever tends to promote the welfare of society, and to blame whatever is likely to hurt it; so the same principle, if they would think and speak consistently, ought to teach them to applaud upon all occasions obedience to the civil magistrate, and to blame all disobedience and rebellion. The very ideas of laudable and blameable, ought to be the same with those of obedience and disobedience. The laws of the civil magistrate, therefore, ought to be regarded as the sole ultimate standards of what was just and unjust, of what was right and wrong.

It was the avowed intention of Mr. Hobbes, by propagating these notions, to subject the consciences of men immediately to the civil, and not to the ecclesiastical powers, whose turbulence and ambition, he had been taught, by the example of his own times, to regard as the principal source of the disor-

ders of society. His doctrine, upon this account, was peculiarly offensive to theologians, who accordingly did not fail to vent their indignation against him with great asperity and bitterness. It was likewise offensive to all sound moralists, as it supposed that there was no natural distinction between right and wrong, that these were mutable and changeable, and depended upon the mere arbitrary will of the civil magistrate. This account of things, therefore, was attacked from all quarters and by all sorts of weapons, by sober reason as well as by furious declamation.

In order to confute so odious a doctrine, it was necessary to prove, that antecedent to all law or positive institution, the mind was naturally endowed with a faculty, by which it distinguished in certain actions and affections, the qualities of right, laudable, and virtuous, and in others those of wrong, blameable, and vicious.

Law, it was justly observed by Dr. Cudworth*, could not be the original source of those distinctions; since, upon the supposition of such a law, it must either be right to obey it, and wrong to disobey it, or indiffer-

* Immutable Morality, l. 1.

ent whether we obeyed it, or disobeyed it. That law which it was indifferent whether we obeyed or disobeyed, could not, it was evident, be the source of those distinctions; neither could that which it was right to obey and wrong to disobey, since even this still supposed the antecedent notions or ideas of right and wrong, and that obedience to the law was conformable to the idea of right, and disobedience to that of wrong.

Since the mind, therefore, had a notion of those distinctions, antecedent to all law, it seemed necessarily to follow, that it derived this notion from reason, which pointed out the difference between right and wrong, in the same manner in which it did that between truth and falsehood: and this conclusion, which, though true in some respects, is rather hasty in others, was more easily received at a time when the abstract science of human nature was but in its infancy, and before the distinct offices and powers of the different faculties of the human mind had been carefully examined and distinguished from one another. When this controversy with Mr. Hobbes was carried on with the greatest warmth and keenness, no other faculty had been thought of from which any such ideas could possibly be supposed to arise. It became

at

at this time, therefore, the popular doctrine, that the eſſence of virtue and vice did not conſiſt in the conformity or diſagreement of human actions with the law of a ſuperior, but in their conformity or diſagreement with reaſon, which was thus conſidered as the original ſource and principle of approbation and diſapprobation.

That virtue conſiſts in conformity to reaſon, is true in ſome reſpects, and this faculty may very juſtly be conſidered as, in ſome ſenſe, the ſource and principle of approbation and diſapprobation, and of all ſolid judgments concerning right and wrong. It is by reaſon that we diſcover thoſe general rules of juſtice by which we ought to regulate our actions: and it is by the ſame faculty that we form thoſe more vague and indeterminate ideas of what is prudent, of what is decent, of what is generous or noble, which we carry conſtantly about with us, and according to which we endeavour, as well as we can, to model the tenor of our conduct. The general maxims of morality are formed, like all other general maxims, from experience and induction. We obſerve in a great variety of particular caſes what pleaſes or diſpleaſes our moral faculties, what theſe approve or diſapprove of, and, by induction from

from this experience, we establish those general rules. But induction is always regarded as one of the operations of reason. From reason, therefore, we are very properly said to derive all those general maxims and ideas. It is by these, however, that we regulate the greater part of our moral judgments, which would be extremely uncertain and precarious if they depended altogether upon what is liable to so many variations as immediate sentiment and feeling, which the different states of health and humour are capable of altering so essentially. As our most solid judgments, therefore, with regard to right and wrong, are regulated by maxims and ideas derived from an induction of reason, virtue may very properly be said to consist in a conformity to reason, and so far this faculty may be considered as the source and principle of approbation and disapprobation.

But though reason is undoubtedly the source of the general rules of morality, and of all the moral judgments which we form by means of them; it is altogether absurd and unintelligible to suppose that the first perceptions of right and wrong can be derived from reason, even in those particular cases upon the experience of which the general rules are formed. These first perceptions, as well as

all other experiments upon which any general rules are founded, cannot be the object of reason but of immediate sense and feeling. It is by finding in a vast variety of instances that one tenor of conduct constantly pleases in a certain manner, and that another as constantly displeases the mind, that we form the general rules of morality. But reason cannot render any particular object either agreeable or disagreeable to the mind for its own sake. Reason may show that this object is the means of obtaining some other which is naturally either pleasing or displeasing, and in this manner may render it either agreeable or disagreeable for the sake of something else. But nothing can be agreeable or disagreeable for its own sake, which is not rendered such by immediate sense and feeling. If virtue, therefore, in every particular instance, necessarily pleases for its own sake, and if vice as certainly displeases the mind, it cannot be reason, but immediate sense and feeling, which, in this manner, reconciles us to the one, and alienates us from the other.

Pleasure and pain are the great objects of desire and aversion: but these are distinguished not by reason, but by immediate sense and feeling. If virtue, therefore, be desirable for its own sake, and if vice be, in the

the ſame manner, the object of averſion, it cannot be reaſon which originally diſtinguiſhes thoſe different qualities, but immediate ſenſe and feeling.

As reaſon, however, in a certain ſenſe, may juſtly be conſidered as the principle of approbation and diſapprobation, theſe ſentiments were, through inattention, long regarded as originally flowing from the operations of this faculty. Dr. Hutcheſon had the merit of being the firſt who diſtinguiſhed with any degree of preciſion in what reſpect all moral diſtinctions may be ſaid to ariſe from reaſon, and in what reſpect they are founded upon immediate ſenſe and feeling. In his illuſtrations upon the moral ſenſe he has explained this ſo fully, and, in my opinion, ſo unanſwerably, that, if any controverſy is ſtill kept up about this ſubject, I can impute it to nothing, but either to inattention to what that gentleman has written, or to a ſuperſtitious attachment to certain forms of expreſſion, a weakneſs not very uncommon among the learned, eſpecially in ſubjects ſo deeply intereſting as the preſent, in which a man of virtue is often loath to abandon, even the propriety of a ſingle phraſe which he has been accuſtomed to.

CHAP. III.

Of those Systems which make Sentiment the Principle of Approbation.

THOSE systems which make sentiment the principle of approbation may be divided into two different classes.

I. According to some, the principle of approbation is founded upon a sentiment of a peculiar nature, upon a particular power of perception exerted by the mind at the view of certain actions or affections; some of which affecting this faculty in an agreeable and others in a disagreeable manner, the former are stamped with the characters of right, laudable, and virtuous; the latter with those of wrong, blamable, and vicious. This sentiment being of a peculiar nature distinct from every other, and the effect of a particular power of perception, they give it a particular name, and call it a moral sense.

II. According to others, in order to account for the principle of approbation, there is no occasion for supposing any new power of perception which had never been heard of before:

before: Nature, they imagine, acts here, as in all other cases, with the strictest œconomy, and produces a multitude of effects from one and the same cause; and sympathy, a power which has always been taken notice of, and with which the mind is manifestly endowed, is, they think, sufficient to account for all the effects ascribed to this peculiar faculty.

I. Dr. Hutcheson had been at great pains to prove that the principle of approbation was not founded on self-love. He had demonstrated too that it could not arise from any operation of reason. Nothing remained, he thought, but to suppose it a faculty of a peculiar kind, with which Nature had endowed the human mind, in order to produce this one particular and important effect. When self-love and reason were both excluded, it did not occur to him that there was any other known faculty of the mind which could in any respect answer this purpose.

This new power of perception he called a moral sense*, and supposed it to be somewhat analogous to the external senses. As the bodies around us, by affecting these in a certain manner, appear to possess the different qualities of sound, taste, odour, colour; so the

* Inquiry concerning Virtue.

various affections of the human mind, by touching this particular faculty in a certain manner, appear to poſſeſs the different qualities of amiable and odious, of virtuous and vicious, of right and wrong.

The various ſenſes or powers of perception *, from which the human mind derives all its ſimple ideas, were, according to this ſyſtem, of two different kinds, of which the one were called the direct or antecedent, the other, the reflex or conſequent ſenſes. The direct ſenſes were thoſe faculties from which the mind derived the perception of ſuch ſpecies of things as did not preſuppoſe the antecedent perception of any other. Thus ſounds and colours were objects of the direct ſenſes. To hear a ſound or to ſee a colour does not preſuppoſe the antecedent perception of any other quality or object. The reflex or conſequent ſenſes on the other hand, were thoſe faculties from which the mind derived the perception of ſuch ſpecies of things as preſuppoſed the antecedent perception of ſome other. Thus harmony and beauty were objects of the reflex ſenſes. In order to perceive the harmony of a ſound, or the beauty of a colour, we muſt firſt perceive the ſound or the colour.

* Treatiſe of the Paſſions.

colour. The moral ſenſe was conſidered as a faculty of this kind. That faculty which Mr. Locke calls reflection, and from which he derived the ſimple ideas of the different paſſions and emotions of the human mind, was, according to Dr. Hutcheſon, a direct internal ſenſe. That faculty again by which we perceived the beauty or deformity, the virtue or vice of thoſe different paſſions or emotions, was a reflex, internal ſenſe.

Dr. Hutcheſon endeavoured ſtill farther to ſupport this doctrine, by ſhewing that it was agreeable to the analogy of nature, and that the mind was endowed with a variety of other reflex ſenſes exactly ſimilar to the moral ſenſe; ſuch as a ſenſe of beauty and deformity in external objects; a public ſenſe, by which we ſympathize with the happineſs or miſery of our fellow-creatures; a ſenſe of ſhame and honour, and a ſenſe of ridicule.

But notwithſtanding all the pains which this ingenious philoſopher has taken to prove that the principle of approbation is founded in a peculiar power of perception, ſomewhat analogous to the external ſenſes, there are ſome conſequences which he acknowledges to follow from this doctrine, that will, perhaps, be regarded by many as a ſufficient

confutation of it. The qualities, he allows*, which belong to the objects of any ſenſe, cannot, without the greateſt abſurdity, be aſcribed to the ſenſe itſelf. Who ever thought of calling the ſenſe of ſeeing black or white, the ſenſe of hearing loud or low, or the ſenſe of taſting ſweet or bitter? And, according to him, it is equally abſurd to call our moral faculties virtuous or vicious, morally good or evil. Theſe qualities belong to the objects of thoſe faculties, not to the faculties themſelves. If any man, therefore, was ſo abſurdly conſtituted as to approve of cruelty and injuſtice as the higheſt virtues, and to diſapprove of equity and humanity as the moſt pitiful vices, ſuch a conſtitution of mind might indeed be regarded as inconvenient both to the individual and to the ſociety, and likewiſe as ſtrange, ſurpriſing, and unnatural in itſelf; but it could not, without the greateſt abſurdity, be denominated vicious or morally evil.

Yet ſurely if we ſaw any man ſhouting with admiration and applauſe at a barbarous and unmerited execution, which ſome inſolent tyrant had ordered, we ſhould not think

* Illuſtrations upon the Moral Senſe, ſect. 1. p. 237, et ſeq. third edition.

we were guilty of any great absurdity in denominating this behaviour vicious and morally evil in the highest degree, though it expressed nothing but depraved moral faculties, or an absurd approbation of this horrid action, as of what was noble, magnanimous, and great. Our heart, I imagine, at the sight of such a spectator, would forget for a while its sympathy with the sufferer, and feel nothing but horror and detestation, at the thought of so execrable a wretch. We should abominate him even more than the tyrant who might be goaded on by the strong passions of jealousy, fear, and resentment, and upon that account be more excusable. But the sentiments of the spectator would appear altogether without cause or motive, and therefore most perfectly and completely detestable. There is no perversion of sentiment or affection which our heart would be more averse to enter into, or which it would reject with greater hatred and indignation than one of this kind; and so far from regarding such a constitution of mind as being merely something strange or inconvenient, and not in any respect vicious or morally evil, we should rather consider it as the very last and most dreadful stage of moral depravity.

Correct

Correct moral sentiments, on the contrary, naturally appear in some degree laudable and morally good. The man, whose censure and applause are upon all occasions suited with the greatest accuracy to the value or unworthiness of the object, seems to deserve a degree even of moral approbation. We admire the delicate precision of his moral sentiments: they lead our own judgments, and, upon account of their uncommon and surprising justness, they even excite our wonder and applause. We cannot indeed be always sure that the conduct of such a person would be in any respect correspondent to the precision and accuracy of his judgments concerning the conduct of others. Virtue requires habit and resolution of mind, as well as delicacy of sentiment; and unfortunately the former qualities are sometimes wanting, where the latter is in the greatest perfection. This disposition of mind, however, though it may sometimes be attended with imperfections, is incompatible with any thing that is grossly criminal, and is the happiest foundation upon which the superstructure of perfect virtue can be built. There are many men who mean very well, and seriously purpose to do what they think their duty, who notwithstanding are

disagree-

diſagreeable on account of the coarſeneſs of their moral ſentiments.

It may be ſaid, perhaps, that though the principle of approbation is not founded upon any power of perception that is in any reſpect analogous to the external ſenſes, it may ſtill be founded upon a peculiar ſentiment which anſwers this one particular purpoſe and no other. Approbation and diſapprobation, it may be pretended, are certain feelings or emotions which ariſe in the mind upon the view of different characters and actions; and as reſentment might be called a ſenſe of injuries, or gratitude a ſenſe of benefits, ſo theſe may very properly receive the name of a ſenſe of right and wrong, or of a moral ſenſe.

But this account of things, though it may not be liable to the ſame objections with the foregoing, is expoſed to others which are equally unanſwerable.

Firſt of all, whatever variations any particular emotion may undergo, it ſtill preſerves the general features which diſtinguiſh it to be an emotion of ſuch a kind, and theſe general features are always more ſtriking and remarkable than any variation which it may undergo in particular caſes. Thus anger is an emotion of a particular kind: and accordingly its general features are always more diſtinguiſh-

able than all the variations it undergoes in particular cases. Anger against a man is, no doubt, somewhat different from anger against a woman, and that again from anger against a child. In each of those three cases, the general passion of anger receives a different modification from the particular character of its object, as may easily be observed by the attentive. But still the general features of the passion predominate in all these cases. To distinguish these, requires no nice observation: a very delicate attention, on the contrary, is necessary to discover their variations: every body takes notice of the former; scarce any body observes the latter. If approbation and disapprobation, therefore, were, like gratitude and resentment, emotions of a particular kind, distinct from every other, we should expect that in all the variations which either of them might undergo, it would still retain the general features which mark it to be an emotion of such a particular kind, clear, plain, and easily distinguishable. But in fact it happens quite otherwise. If we attend to what we really feel when upon different occasions we either approve or disapprove, we shall find that our emotion in one case is often totally different from that in another, and that no common features can possibly be discovered

diſcovered between them. Thus the approbation with which we view a tender, delicate, and humane ſentiment, is quite different from that with which we are ſtruck by one that appears great, daring, and magnanimous. Our approbation of both may, upon different occaſions, be perfect and entire; but we are ſoftened by the one, and we are elevated by the other, and there is no ſort of reſemblance between the emotions which they excite in us. But, according to that ſyſtem which I have been endeavouring to eſtabliſh, this muſt neceſſarily be the caſe. As the emotions of the perſon whom we approve of, are, in thoſe two caſes, quite oppoſite to one another, and as our approbation ariſes from ſympathy with thoſe oppoſite emotions, what we feel upon the one occaſion, can have no ſort of reſemblance to what we feel upon the other. But this could not happen if approbation conſiſted in a peculiar emotion which had nothing in common with the ſentiments we approved of, but which aroſe at the view of thoſe ſentiments, like any other paſſion at the view of its proper object. The ſame thing holds true with regard to diſapprobation. Our horror for cruelty has no ſort of reſemblance to our contempt for mean-ſpiritedneſs. It is quite a different ſpecies of

diſcor

difcord which we feel at the view of thofe two different vices, between our own minds and thofe of the perfon whofe fentiments and behaviour we confider.

Secondly, I have already obferved, that not only the different paffions or affections of the human mind which are approved or difapproved of, appear morally good or evil, but that proper and improper approbation appear to our natural fentiments, to be ftamped with the fame characters. I would afk, therefore, how it is, that, according to this fyftem, we approve or difapprove of proper or improper approbation? To this queftion there is, I imagine, but one reafonable anfwer, which can poffibly be given. It muft be faid, that when the approbation with which our neighbour regards the conduct of a third perfon coincides with our own, we approve of his approbation, and confider it as, in fome meafure, morally good; and that on the contrary, when it does not coincide with our own fentiments, we difapprove of it, and confider it as, in fome meafure, morally evil. It muft be allowed, therefore, that, at leaft in this one cafe, the coincidence or oppofition of fentiments, between the obferver and the perfon obferved, conftitutes moral approbation or difapprobation. And if it does fo in this one cafe, I would

would ask, why not in every other? to what purpose imagine a new power of perception in order to account for those sentiments?

Against every account of the principle of approbation, which makes it depend upon a peculiar sentiment, distinct from every other, I would object; that it is strange that this sentiment, which Providence undoubtedly intended to be the governing principle of human nature, should hitherto have been so little taken notice of, as not to have got a name in any language. The word moral sense is of very late formation, and cannot yet be considered as making part of the English tongue. The word approbation has but within these few years been appropriated to denote peculiarly any thing of this kind. In propriety of language we approve of whatever is entirely to our satisfaction, of the form of a building, of the contrivance of a machine, of the flavour of a dish of meat. The word conscience does not immediately denote any moral faculty by which we approve or disapprove. Conscience supposes, indeed, the existence of some such faculty, and properly signifies our consciousness of having acted agreeably or contrary to its directions. When love, hatred, joy, sorrow gratitude, resentment, with so many other

passions

paſſions which are all ſuppoſed to be the ſubjects of this principle, have made themſelves conſiderable enough to get titles to know them by, is it not ſurpriſing that the ſovereign of them all ſhould hitherto have been ſo little heeded, that, a few philoſophers excepted, nobody has yet thought it worth while to beſtow a name upon it?

When we approve of any character or action, the ſentiments which we feel are, according to the foregoing ſyſtem, derived from four ſources, which are in ſome reſpects different from one another. Firſt, we ſympathize with the motives of the agent; ſecondly, we enter into the gratitude of thoſe who receive the benefit of his actions; thirdly, we obſerve that his conduct has been agreeable to the general rules by which thoſe two ſympathies generally act; and, laſt of all, when we conſider ſuch actions as making a part of a ſyſtem of behaviour which tends to promote the happineſs either of the individual or of the ſociety, they appear to derive a beauty from this utility, not unlike that which we aſcribe to any well-contrived machine. After deducting, in any one particular caſe, all that muſt be acknowledged to proceed from ſome one or other of theſe four principles, I ſhould be glad to know what remains, and

and I ſhall freely allow this overplus to be aſcribed to a moral ſenſe, or to any other peculiar faculty, provided any body will aſcertain preciſely what this overplus is. It might be expected, perhaps, that if there was any ſuch peculiar principle, ſuch as this moral ſenſe is ſuppoſed to be, we ſhould feel it, in ſome particular caſes, ſeparated and detached from every other, as we often feel joy, ſorrow, hope, and fear, pure and unmixed with any other emotion. This however, I imagine, cannot even be pretended. I have never heard any inſtance alleged in which this principle could be ſaid to exert itſelf alone and unmixed with ſympathy or antipathy, with gratitude or reſentment, with the perception of the agreement or diſagreement of any action to an eſtabliſhed rule, or laſt of all with that general taſte for beauty and order which is excited by inanimated as well as by animated objects.

II. There is another ſyſtem which attempts to account for the origin of our moral ſentiments from ſympathy, diſtinct from that which I have been endeavouring to eſtabliſh. It is that which places virtue in utility, and accounts for the pleaſure with which the ſpectator ſurveys the utility of any quality from ſympathy with the happineſs of thoſe who are

affected by it. This ſympathy is different both from that by which we enter into the motives of the agent, and from that by which we go along with the gratitude of the perſons who are benefited by his actions. It is the ſame principle with that by which we approve of a well-contrived machine. But no machine can be the object of either of thoſe two laſt-mentioned ſympathies. I have already, in the fourth part of this diſcourſe, given ſome account of this ſyſtem.

SECTION IV.

Of the Manner in which different Authors have treated of the practical Rules of Morality.

It was obſerved in the third part of this diſcourſe, that the rules of juſtice are the only rules of morality which are preciſe and accurate; that thoſe of all the other virtues are looſe, vague, and indeterminate; that the firſt may be compared to the rules of grammar; the others to thoſe which critics lay down for the attainment of what is ſublime and elegant in compoſition, and which preſent us rather with a general idea of the perfection we ought to aim at, than afford us any certain and infallible directions for acquiring it.

As the different rules of morality admit ſuch different degrees of accuracy, thoſe authors who have endeavoured to collect and digeſt them into ſyſtems have done it in two different manners; and one ſet has followed through the whole that looſe method to which they were naturally directed by the conſider-

ation of one species of virtues; while another has as universally endeavoured to introduce into their precepts that sort of accuracy of which only some of them are susceptible. The first have wrote like critics, the second like grammarians.

I. The first, among whom we may count all the ancient moralists, have contented themselves with describing in a general manner the different vices and virtues, and with pointing out the deformity and misery of the one disposition as well as the propriety and happiness of the other, but have not affected to lay down many precise rules that are to hold good unexceptionably in all particular cases. They have only endeavoured to ascertain, as far as language is capable of ascertaining, first, wherein consists the sentiment of the heart, upon which each particular virtue is founded, what sort of internal feeling or emotion it is which constitutes the essence of friendship, of humanity, of generosity, of justice, of magnanimity, and of all the other virtues, as well as of the vices which are opposed to them: and, secondly, what is the general way of acting, the ordinary tone and tenor of conduct to which each of those sentiments would direct us, or how it is that a friendly, a generous, a brave, a just, and a

humane

humane man, would, upon ordinary occaſions, chooſe to act.

To characterize the ſentiment of the heart, upon which each particular virtue is founded, though it requires both a delicate and an accurate pencil, is a taſk, however, which may be executed with ſome degree of exactneſs. It is impoſſible, indeed, to expreſs all the variations which each ſentiment either does or ought to undergo, according to every poſſible variation of circumſtances. They are endleſs, and language wants names to mark them by. The ſentiment of friendſhip, for example, which we feel for an old man is different from that which we feel for a young: that which we entertain for an auſtere man different from that which we feel for one of ſofter and gentler manners. and that again from what we feel for one of gay vivacity and ſpirit. The friendſhip which we conceive for a man is different from that with which a woman affects us, even where there is no mixture of any groſſer paſſion. What author could enumerate and aſcertain theſe and all the other infinite varieties which this ſentiment is capable of undergoing? But ſtill the general ſentiment of friendſhip and familiar attachment which is common to them all, may be aſcertained with a ſufficient degree of

accuracy. The picture which is drawn of it, though it will always be in many respects incomplete, may, however, have such a resemblance as to make us know the original when we meet with it, and even distinguish it from other sentiments to which it has a considerable resemblance, such as good-will, respect, esteem, admiration.

To describe, in a general manner, what is the ordinary way of acting to which each virtue would prompt us, is still more easy. It is, indeed, scarce possible to describe the the internal sentiment or emotion upon which it is founded, without doing something of this kind. It is impossible by language to express, if I may say so, the invisible features of all the different modifications of passion as they show themselves within. There is no other way of marking and distinguishing them from one another, but by describing the effects which they produce without, the alterations which they occasion in the countenance, in the air and external behaviour, the resolutions they suggest, the actions they prompt to. It is thus that Cicero, in the first book of his Offices, endeavours to direct us to the practice of the four cardinal virtues, and that Aristotle in the practical parts of his Ethics, points out to us the different habits by which he would have

us regulate our behaviour, ſuch as liberality, magnificence, magnanimity, and even jocularity and good-humour, qualities which that indulgent philoſopher has thought worthy of a place in the catalogue of the virtues, though the lightneſs of that approbation which we naturally beſtow upon them, ſhould not ſeem to entitle them to ſo venerable a name.

Such works preſent us with agreeable and lively pictures of manners. By the vivacity of their deſcriptions they inflame our natural love of virtue, and increaſe our abhorrence of vice: by the juſtneſs as well as delicacy of their obſervations they may often help both to correct and to aſcertain our natural ſentiments with regard to the propriety of conduct, and ſuggeſting many nice and delicate attentions, form us to a more exact juſtneſs of behaviour, than what, without ſuch inſtruction, we ſhould have been apt to think of. In treating of the rules of morality, in this manner, conſiſts the ſcience which is properly called Ethics, a ſcience which, though like criticiſm it does not admit of the moſt accurate preciſion, is, however, both highly uſeful and agreeable. It is of all others the moſt ſuſceptible of the embelliſhments of eloquence, and by means of them of beſtowing, if that

be possible, a new importance upon the smallest rules of duty. Its precepts, when thus dressed and adorned, are capable of producing upon the flexibility of youth, the noblest and most lasting impressions, and as they fall in with the natural magnanimity of that generous age, they are able to inspire, for a time at least, the most heroic resolutions, and thus tend both to establish and confirm the best and most useful habits of which the mind of man is susceptible. Whatever precept and exhortation can do to animate us to the practice of virtue, is done by this science delivered in this manner.

II. The second set of moralists, among whom we may count all the casuists of the middle and latter ages of the christian church, as well as all those who in this and in the preceding century have treated of what is called natural jurisprudence, do not content themselves with characterizing in this general manner that tenor of conduct which they would recommend to us, but endeavour to lay down exact and precise rules for the direction of every circumstance of our behaviour. As justice is the only virtue with regard to which such exact rules can properly be given, it is this virtue that has chiefly fallen

fallen under the conſideration of thoſe two different ſets of writers. They treat of it, however, in a very different manner.

Thoſe who write upon the principles of juriſprudence, conſider only what the perſon to whom the obligation is due, ought to think himſelf entitled to exact by force; what every impartial ſpectator would approve of him for exacting, or what a judge or arbiter, to whom he had ſubmitted his caſe, and who had undertaken to do him juſtice, ought to oblige the other perſon to ſuffer or to perform. The caſuiſts, on the other hand, do not ſo much examine what it is, that might properly be exacted by force, as what it is, that the perſon who owes the obligation ought to think himſelf bound to perform from the moſt ſacred and ſcrupulous regard to the general rules of juſtice, and from the moſt conſcientious dread, either of wronging his neighbour, or of violating the integrity of his own character. It is the end of juriſprudence to preſcribe rules for the deciſions of judges and arbiters. It is the end of caſuiſtry to preſcribe rules for the conduct of a good man. By obſerving all the rules of juriſprudence, ſuppoſing them ever ſo perfect, we ſhould deſerve nothing but to be free from external puniſhment. By obſerving thoſe of caſuiſtry,

ſuppoſing

ſuppoſing them ſuch as they ought to be, we ſhould be entitled to conſiderable praiſe by the exact and ſcrupulous delicacy of our behaviour.

It may frequently happen that a good man ought to think himſelf bound, from a ſacred and conſcientious regard to the general rules of juſtice, to perform many things which it would be the higheſt injuſtice to extort from him, or for any judge or arbiter to impoſe upon him by force. To give a trite example; a highwayman, by the fear of death, obliges a traveller to promiſe him a certain ſum of money. Whether ſuch a promiſe, extorted in this manner by unjuſt force, ought to be regarded as obligatory, is a queſtion that has been very much debated.

If we conſider it merely as a queſtion of juriſprudence, the deciſion can admit of no doubt. It would be abſurd to ſuppoſe that the highwayman can be entitled to uſe force to conſtrain the other to perform. To extort the promiſe was a crime which deſerved the higheſt puniſhment, and to extort the performance would only be adding a new crime to the former. He can complain of no injury who has been only deceived by the perſon by whom he might juſtly have been killed. To ſuppoſe that a judge ought to enforce the obligation

obligation of ſuch promiſes, or that the magiſtrate ought to allow them to ſuſtain action at law, would be the moſt ridiculous of all abſurdities. If we conſider this queſtion, therefore, as a queſtion of juriſprudence, we can be at no loſs about the deciſion.

But if we conſider it as a queſtion of caſuiſtry, it will not be ſo eaſily determined. Whether a good man, from a conſcientious regard to that moſt ſacred rule of juſtice, which commands the obſervance of all ſerious promiſes, would not think himſelf bound to perform, is at leaſt much more doubtful. That no regard is due to the diſappointment of the wretch who brings him into this ſituation, that no injury is done to the robber, and conſequently that nothing can be extorted by force, will admit of no ſort of diſpute. But whether ſome regard is not, in this caſe, due to his own dignity and honour, to the inviolable ſacredneſs of that part of his character which makes him reverence the law of truth and abhor every thing that approaches to treachery and falſehood, may, perhaps, more reaſonably be made a queſtion. The caſuiſts accordingly are greatly divided about it. One party, with whom we may count Cicero among the ancients, among the moderns, Puffendorf, Barbeyrac his commentator, and

above

above all the late Dr. Hutcheſon, one who in moſt caſes was by no means a looſe caſuiſt, determine, without any heſitation, that no ſort of regard is due to any ſuch promiſe, and that to think otherwiſe is mere weakneſs and ſuperſtition. Another party, among whom we may reckon* ſome of the ancient fathers of the church, as well as ſome very eminent modern caſuiſts, have been of another opinion, and have judged all ſuch promiſes obligatory.

If we conſider the matter according to the common ſentiments of mankind, we ſhall find that ſome regard would be thought due even to a promiſe of this kind; but that it is impoſſible to determine how much, by any general rule, that will apply to all caſes without exception. The man who was quite frank and eaſy in making promiſes of this kind, and who violated them with as little ceremony, we ſhould not chooſe for our friend and companion. A gentleman who ſhould promiſe a highwayman five pounds and not perform, would incur ſome blame. If the ſum promiſed, however, was very great, it might be more doubtful what was proper to be done. If it was ſuch, for exam-

* St. Auguſtine, La Placette.

ple,

ple, that the payment of it would entirely ruin the family of the promiser, if it was so great as to be sufficient for promoting the most useful purposes, it would appear in some measure criminal, at least extremely improper to throw it, for the sake of a punctilio, into such worthless hands. The man who should beggar himself, or who should throw away an hundred thousand pounds, though he could afford that vast sum, for the sake of observing such a parole with a thief, would appear to the common sense of mankind, absurd and extravagant in the highest degree. Such profusion would seem inconsistent with his duty, with what he owed both to himself and others, and what, therefore, regard to a promise extorted in this manner, could by no means authorise. To fix, however, by any precise rule, what degree of regard ought to be paid to it, or what might be the greatest sum which could be due from it, is evidently impossible. This would vary according to the characters of the persons, according to their circumstances, according to the solemnity of the promise, and even according to the incidents of the rencounter: and if the promiser had been treated with a great deal of that sort of gallantry, which is sometimes to be met with in persons of the most abandoned character,

characters, more would seem due than upon other occasions. It may be said in general, that exact propriety requires the observance of all such promises, wherever it is not inconsistent with some other duties that are more sacred; such as regard to the public interest, to those whom gratitude, whom natural affection, or whom the laws of proper beneficence should prompt us to provide for. But, as was formerly taken notice of, we have no precise rules to determine what external actions are due from a regard to such motives, nor, consequently, when it is that those virtues are inconsistent with the observance of such promises.

It is to be observed, however, that whenever such promises are violated, though for the most necessary reasons, it is always with some degree of dishonour to the person who made them. After they are made, we may be convinced of the impropriety of observing them. But still there is some fault in having made them. It is at least a departure from the highest and noblest maxims of magnanimity and honour. A brave man ought to die, rather than make a promise which he can neither keep without folly, nor violate without ignominy. For some degree of ignominy always attends a situation of this kind. Treachery and falsehood are vices so dangerous,

ſo dreadful, and, at the ſame time, ſuch as may ſo eaſily, and, upon many occaſions, ſo ſafely be indulged, that we are more jealous of them than of almoſt any other. Our imagination therefore attaches the idea of ſhame to all violations of faith, in every circumſtance and in every ſituation. They reſemble, in this reſpect, the violations of chaſtity in the fair ſex, a virtue of which, for the like reaſons, we are exceſſively jealous; and our ſentiments are not more delicate with regard to the one, than with regard to the other. Breach of chaſtity diſhonours irretrievably. No circumſtances, no ſolicitation can excuſe it; no ſorrow, no repentance, atone for it. We are ſo nice in this reſpect that even a rape diſhonours, and the innocence of the mind cannot, in our imagination, waſh out the pollution of the body. It is the ſame caſe with the violation of faith when it has been ſolemnly pledged, even to the moſt worthleſs of mankind. Fidelity is ſo neceſſary a virtue, that we apprehend it in general to be due even to thoſe to whom nothing elſe is due, and whom we think it lawful to kill and deſtroy. It is to no purpoſe that the perſon who has been guilty of the breach of it, urges that he promiſed in order to ſave his life, and that he broke his promiſe becauſe it was inconſiſtent

consistent with some other respectable duty to keep it. These circumstances may alleviate, but cannot entirely wipe out his dishonour. He appears to have been guilty of an action with which, in the imaginations of men, some degree of shame is inseparably connected. He has broke a promise which he had solemnly averred he would maintain; and his character if not irretrievably stained and polluted, has at least a ridicule affixed to it, which it will be very difficult entirely to efface; and no man, I imagine, who had gone through an adventure of this kind would be fond of telling the story.

This instance may serve to show wherein consists the difference between casuistry and jurisprudence, even when both of them consider the obligations of the general rules of justice.

But though this difference be real and essential, though those two sciences propose quite different ends, the sameness of the subject has made such a similarity between them, that the greater part of authors whose professed design was to treat of jurisprudence, have determined the different questions they exa[illegible], sometimes according to the principles of that [illegible], and sometimes according to [illegible], without distinguishing, and, perhaps,

perhaps, without being themselves aware when they did the one, and when the other.

The doctrine of the casuists, however, is by no means confined to the consideration of what a conscientious regard to the general rules of justice would demand of us. It embraces many other parts of Christian and moral duty. What seems principally to have given occasion to the cultivation of this species of science was the custom of auricular confession, introduced by the Roman Catholic superstition, in times of barbarism and ignorance. By that institution, the most secret actions, and even the thoughts of every person, which could be suspected of receding in the smallest degree from the rules of Christian purity, were to be revealed to the confessor. The confessor informed his penitents whether, and in what respect, they had violated their duty, and what penance it behoved them to undergo, before he could absolve them in the name of the offended Deity.

The consciousness, or even the suspicion of having done wrong, is a load upon every mind, and is accompanied with anxiety and terror in all those who are not hardened by long habits of iniquity. Men, in this, as in all other distresses, are naturally eager to disburthen themselves of the oppression which

they feel upon their thoughts, by unboſoming the agony of their mind to ſome perſon whoſe ſecrecy and diſcretion they can confide in. The ſhame which they ſuffer from this acknowledgment, is fully compenſated by that alleviaton of their uneaſineſs which the ſympathy of their confident ſeldom fails to occaſion. It relieves them to find that they are not altogether unworthy of regard, and that however their paſt conduct may be cenſured, their preſent diſpoſition is at leaſt approved of, and is perhaps ſufficient to compenſate the other, at leaſt to maintain them in ſome degree of eſteem with their friend. A numerous and artful clergy had, in thoſe times of ſuperſtition, inſinuated themſelves into the confidence of almoſt every private family. They poſſeſſed all the little learning which the times could afford, and their manners, though in many reſpects rude and diſorderly, were poliſhed and regular compared with thoſe of the age they lived in. They were regarded, therefore, not only as the great directors of all religious, but of all moral duties. Their familiarity gave reputation to whoever was ſo happy as to poſſeſs it, and every mark of their diſapprobation ſtamped the deepeſt ignominy upon all who had the miſfortune to fall under it. Being conſidered as the great judges

judges of right and wrong, they were naturally consulted about all scruples that occurred, and it was reputable for any person to have it known that he made those holy men the confidents of all such secrets, and took no important or delicate step in his conduct without their advice and approbation. It was not difficult for the clergy, therefore, to get it established as a general rule, that they should be entrusted with what it had already become fashionable to entrust them, and with what they generally would have been entrusted, though no such rule had been established. To qualify themselves for confessors became thus a necessary part of the study of churchmen and divines, and they were thence led to collect what are called cases of conscience, nice and delicate situations in which it is hard to determine whereabouts the propriety of conduct may lie. Such works, they imagined, might be of use both to the directors of consciences and to those who were to be directed; and hence the origin of books of casuistry.

The moral duties which fell under the consideration of the casuists were chiefly those which can, in some measure at least, be circumscribed within general rules, and of which the violation is naturally attended with some degree of remorse and some dread of suffering

puniſhment. The deſign of that inſtitution which gave occaſion to their works, was to appeaſe thoſe terrors of conſcience which attend upon the infringement of ſuch duties. But it is not every virtue of which the defect is accompanied with any very ſevere compunctions of this kind, and no man applies to his confeſſor for abſolution, becauſe he did not perform the moſt generous, the moſt friendly, or the moſt magnanimous action which, in his circumſtances, it was poſſible to perform. In failures of this kind, the rule that is violated is commonly not very determinate, and is generally of ſuch a nature too, that though the obſervance of it might entitle to honour and reward, the violation ſeems to expoſe to no poſitive blame, cenſure, or puniſhment. The exerciſe of ſuch virtues the caſuiſts ſeem to have regarded as a ſort of works of ſupererogation, which could not be very ſtrictly exacted, and which it was therefore unneceſſary for them to treat of.

The breaches of moral duty, therefore, which came before the tribunal of the confeſſor, and upon that account fell under the cognizance of the caſuiſts, were chiefly of three different kinds.

Firſt and principally, breaches of the rules of juſtice. The rules here are all expreſs and poſitive,

positive, and the violation of them is naturally attended with the consciousness of deserving, and the dread of suffering punishment both from God and man.

Secondly, breaches of the rules of chastity. These in all grosser instances are real breaches of the rules of justice, and no person can be guilty of them without doing the most unpardonable injury to some other. In smaller instances, when they amount only to a violation of those exact decorums which ought to be observed in the conversation of the two sexes, they cannot indeed justly be considered as violations of the rules of justice. They are generally, however, violations of a pretty plain rule, and, at least in one of the sexes, tend to bring ignominy upon the person who has been guilty of them, and consequently to be attended in the scrupulous with some degree of shame and contrition of mind.

Thirdly, breaches of the rules of veracity. The violation of truth, it is to be observed, is not always a breach of justice, though it is so upon many occasions, and consequently cannot always expose to any external punishment. The vice of common lying, though a most miserable meanness, may frequently do hurt to nobody, and in this case no claim of vengeance or satisfaction can be due either to the

perſons impoſed upon, or to others. But though the violation of truth is not always a breach of juſtice, it is always a breach of a very plain rule, and what naturally tends to cover with ſhame the perſon who has been guilty of it.

There ſeems to be in young children an inſtinctive diſpoſition to believe whatever they are told. Nature ſeems to have judged it neceſſary for their preſervation that they ſhould, for ſome time at leaſt, put implicit confidence in thoſe to whom the care of their childhood, and of the earlieſt and moſt neceſſary parts of their education, is intruſted. Their credulity, accordingly, is exceſſive, and it requires long and much experience of the falſehood of mankind to reduce them to a reaſonable degree of diffidence and diſtruſt. In grown-up people the degrees of credulity are, no doubt, very different. The wiſeſt and moſt experienced are generally the leaſt credulous. But the man ſcarce lives who is not more credulous than he ought to be, and who does not, upon many occaſions, give credit to tales, which not only turn out to be perfectly falſe, but which a very moderate degree of reflection and attention might have taught him could not well be true. The natural diſpoſition is always to believe. It is acquired wiſdom and experience

experience only that teach incredulity, and they very seldom teach it enough. The wisest and most cautious of us all frequently gives credit to stories which he himself is afterwards both ashamed and astonished that he could possibly think of believing.

The man whom we believe is necessarily, in the things concerning which we believe him, our leader and director, and we look up to him with a certain degree of esteem and respect. But as from admiring other people we come to wish to be admired ourselves; so from being led and directed by other people we learn to wish to become ourselves leaders and directors. And as we cannot always be satisfied merely with being admired, unless we can at the same time persuade ourselves that we are in some degree really worthy of admiration; so we cannot always be satisfied merely with being believed, unless we are at the same time conscious that we are really worthy of belief. As the desire of praise, and that of praise-worthiness, though very much a-kin, are yet distinct and separate desires; so the desire of being believed and that of being worthy of belief, though very much a-kin too, are equally distinct and separate desires.

The desire of being believed, the desire of persuading, of leading and directing other

people, ſeems to be one of the ſtrongeſt of all our natural deſires. It is, perhaps, the inſtinct upon which is founded the faculty of ſpeech, the characteriſtical faculty of human nature. No other animal poſſeſſes this faculty, and we cannot diſcover in any other animal any deſire to lead and direct the judgment and conduct of its fellows. Great ambition, the deſire of real ſuperiority, of leading and directing, ſeems to be altogether peculiar to man, and ſpeech is the great inſtrument of ambition, of real ſuperiority, of leading and directing the judgments and conduct of other people.

It is always mortifying not to be believed, and it is doubly ſo when we ſuſpect that it is becauſe we are ſuppoſed to be unworthy of belief and capable of ſeriouſly and wilfully deceiving. To tell a man that he lies, is of all affronts the moſt mortal. But whoever ſeriouſly and wilfully deceives, is neceſſarily conſcious to himſelf that he merits this affront, that he does not deſerve to be believed, and that he forfeits all title to that ſort of credit from which alone he can derive any ſort of eaſe, comfort, or ſatisfaction in the ſociety of his equals. The man who had the misfortune to imagine that nobody believed a ſingle word he ſaid, would feel himſelf the outcaſt

of

of human society, would dread the very thought of going into it, or of presenting himself before it, and could scarce fail, I think, to die of despair. It is probable, however, that no man ever had just reason to entertain this humiliating opinion of himself. The most notorious liar, I am disposed to believe, tells the fair truth at least twenty times for once that he seriously and deliberately lies; and, as in the most cautious, the disposition to believe is apt to prevail over that to doubt and distrust; so in those who are the most regardless of truth, the natural disposition to tell it prevails upon most occasions over that to deceive, or in any respect to alter or disguise it.

We are mortified when we happen to deceive other people, though unintentionally, and from having been ourselves deceived. Though this involuntary falsehood may frequently be no mark of any want of veracity, of any want of the most perfect love of truth, it is always in some degree a mark of want of judgment, of want of memory, of improper credulity, of some degree of precipitancy and rashness. It always diminishes our authority to persuade, and always brings some degree of suspicion upon our fitness to lead and direct. The man who sometimes misleads from

mistake,

miſtake, however, is widely different from him who is capable of wilfully deceiving. The former may ſafely be truſted upon many occaſions; the latter very ſeldom upon any.

Frankneſs and openneſs conciliate confidence. We truſt the man who ſeems willing to truſt us. We ſee clearly, we think, the road by which he means to conduct us, and we abandon ourſelves with pleaſure to his guidance and direction. Reſerve and concealment, on the contrary, call forth diffidence. We are afraid to follow the man who is going we do not know where. The great pleaſure of converſation and ſociety, beſides, ariſes from a certain correſpondence of ſentiments and opinions, from a certain harmony of minds, which like ſo many muſical inſtruments coincide and keep time with one another. But this moſt delightful harmony cannot be obtained unleſs there is a free communication of ſentiments and opinions. We all deſire, upon this account, to feel how each other is affected, to penetrate into each other's boſoms, and to obſerve the ſentiments and affections which really ſubſiſt there. The man who indulges us in this natural paſſion, who invites us into his heart, who, as it were, ſets open the gates of his breaſt to us, ſeems to exerciſe a ſpecies of hoſpitality more delightful

delightful than any other. No man, who is in ordinary good temper, can fail of pleaſing, if he has the courage to utter his real ſentiments as he feels them, and becauſe he feels them. It is this unreſerved ſincerity which renders even the prattle of a child agreeable. How weak and imperfect ſoever the views of the open-hearted, we take pleaſure to enter into them, and endeavour, as much as we can, to bring down our own underſtanding to the level of their capacities, and to regard every ſubject in the particular light in which they appear to have conſidered it. This paſſion to diſcover the real ſentiments of others is naturally ſo ſtrong, that it often degenerates into a troubleſome and impertinent curioſity to pry into thoſe ſecrets of our neighbours which they have very juſtifiable reaſons for concealing; and, upon many occaſions, it requires prudence and a ſtrong ſenſe of propriety to govern this, as well as all the other paſſions of human nature, and to reduce it to that pitch which any impartial ſpectator can approve of. To diſappoint this curioſity, however, when it is kept within proper bounds, and aims at nothing which there can be any juſt reaſon for concealing, is equally diſagreeable in its turn. The man who eludes our moſt innocent queſtions, who gives no ſatiſ-

ſatisfaction to our moſt inoffenſive inquiries, who plainly wraps himſelf up in impenetrable obſcurity, ſeems, as it were, to build a wall about his breaſt. We run forward to get within it, with all the eagerneſs of harmleſs curioſity; and feel ourſelves all at once puſhed back with the rudeſt and moſt offenſive violence.

The man of reſerve and concealment, though ſeldom a very amiable character, is not diſreſpected or deſpiſed. He ſeems to feel coldly towards us, and we feel as coldly towards him. He is not much praiſed or beloved, but he is as little hated or blamed. He very ſeldom, however, has occaſion to repent of his caution, and is generally diſpoſed rather to value himſelf upon the prudence of his reſerve. Though his conduct, therefore, may have been very faulty, and ſometimes even hurtful, he can very ſeldom be diſpoſed to lay his caſe before the caſuiſts, or to fancy that he has any occaſion for their acquittal or approbation.

It is not always ſo with the man, who, from falſe information, from inadvertency, from precipitancy and raſhneſs, has involuntarily deceived. Though it ſhould be in a matter of little conſequence, in telling a piece of common news, for example, if he is a real lover

lover of truth, he is ashamed of his own carelessness, and never fails to embrace the first opportunity of making the fullest acknowledgments. If it is in a matter of some consequence, his contrition is still greater; and if any unlucky or fatal consequence has followed from his misinformation, he can scarce ever forgive himself. Though not guilty, he feels himself to be in the highest degree what the ancients called, piacular, and is anxious and eager to make every sort of atonement in his power. Such a person might frequently be disposed to lay his case before the casuists, who have in general been very favourable to him, and though they have sometimes justly condemned him for rashness, they have universally acquitted him of the ignominy of falsehood.

But the man who had the most frequent occasion to consult them, was the man of equivocation and mental reservation, the man who seriously and deliberately meant to deceive, but who, at the same time wished to flatter himself that he had really told the truth. With him they have dealt variously. When they approved very much of the motives of his deceit, they have sometimes acquitted him, though, to do them justice, they have in general and much more frequently condemned him.

The chief ſubjects of the works of the caſuiſts, therefore, were the conſcientious regard that is due to the rules of juſtice; how far we ought to reſpect the life and property of our neighbour; the duty of reſtitution; the laws of chaſtity and modeſty, and wherein conſiſted what, in their language, are called the ſins of concupiſcence; the rules of veracity, and the obligation of oaths, promiſes, and contracts of all kinds.

It may be ſaid in general of the works of the caſuiſts, that they attempted, to no purpoſe, to direct by preciſe rules what it belongs to feeling and ſentiment only to judge of. How is it poſſible to aſcertain by rules the exact point at which, in every caſe, a delicate ſenſe of juſtice begins to run into a frivolous and weak ſcrupuloſity of conſcience? When it is that ſecrecy and reſerve begin to grow into diſſimulation? How far an agreeable irony may be carried, and at what preciſe point it begins to degenerate into a deteſtable lie? What is the higheſt pitch of freedom and eaſe of behaviour which can be regarded as graceful and becoming, and when it is that it firſt begins to run into a negligent and thoughtleſs licentiouſneſs? With regard to all ſuch matters, what would hold good in any one caſe would ſcarce do ſo exactly in any other,

and what conſtitutes the propriety and happineſs of behaviour varies in every caſe with the ſmalleſt variety of ſituation. Books of caſuiſtry, therefore, are generally as uſeleſs as they are commonly tireſome. They could be of little uſe to one who ſhould conſult them upon occaſion, even ſuppoſing their deciſions to be juſt; becauſe, notwithſtanding the multitude of caſes collected in them, yet upon account of the ſtill greater variety of poſſible circumſtances, it is a chance, if among all thoſe caſes there be found one exactly parallel to that under conſideration. One who is really anxious to do his duty, muſt be very weak, if he can imagine that he has much occaſion for them; and with regard to one who is negligent of it, the ſtyle of thoſe writings is not ſuch as is likely to awaken him to more attention. None of them tend to animate us to what is generous and noble. None of them tend to ſoften us to what is gentle and humane. Many of them, on the contrary, tend rather to teach us to chicane with our own conſciences, and by their vain ſubtilties ſerve to authoriſe innumerable evaſive refinements with regard to the moſt eſſential articles of our duty. That frivolous accuracy which they attempted to introduce into ſubjects which do not admit of it, almoſt ne-

ceſſarily

cessarily betrayed them into those dangerous errors, and at the same time rendered their works dry and disagreeable, abounding in abstruse and metaphysical distinctions, but incapable of exciting in the heart any of those emotions which it is the principal use of books of morality to excite.

The two useful parts of moral philosophy, therefore, are Ethics and Jurisprudence: casuistry ought to be rejected altogether; and the ancient moralists appear to have judged much better, who in treating of the same subjects, did not affect any such nice exactness, but contented themselves with describing, in a general manner, what is the sentiment upon which justice, modesty, and veracity are founded, and what is the ordinary way of acting to which those virtues would commonly prompt us.

Something, indeed, not unlike the doctrine of the casuists, seems to have been attempted by several philosophers. There is something of this kind in the third book of Cicero's Offices, where he endeavours like a casuist to give rules for our conduct in many nice cases, in which it is difficult to determine whereabouts the point of propriety may lie. It appears too, from many passages in the same book, that several other philosophers had

had attempted something of the same kind before him. Neither he nor they, however, appear to have aimed at giving a complete system of this sort, but only meant to show how situations may occur, in which it is doubtful, whether the highest propriety of conduct consists in observing or in receding from what, in ordinary cases, are the rules of duty.

Every system of positive law may be regarded as a more or less imperfect attempt towards a system of natural jurisprudence, or towards an enumeration of the particular rules of justice. As the violation of justice is what men will never submit to from one another, the public magistrate is under a necessity of employing the power of the commonwealth to enforce the practice of this virtue. Without this precaution, civil society would become a scene of bloodshed and disorder, every man revenging himself at his own hand, whenever he fancied he was injured. To prevent the confusion which would attend upon every man's doing justice to himself, the magistrate, in all governments that have acquired any considerable authority, undertakes to do justice to all, and promises to hear and to redress every complaint of injury. In all well-governed states too, not only judges are appointed for determining the

controverſies of individuals, but rules are preſcribed for regulating the deciſions of thoſe judges; and theſe rules are, in general, intended to coincide with thoſe of natural juſtice. It does not, indeed, always happen that they do ſo in every inſtance. Sometimes what is called the conſtitution of the ſtate, that is, the intereſt of the government; ſometimes the intereſt of particular orders of men who tyrannize the government, warp the poſitive laws of the country from what natural juſtice would preſcribe. In ſome countries, the rudeneſs and barbariſm of the people hinder the natural ſentiments of juſtice from arriving at that accuracy and preciſion which, in more civilized nations, they naturally attain to. Their laws are, like their manners, groſs and rude and undiſtinguiſhing. In other countries the unfortunate conſtitution of their courts of judicature hinders any regular ſyſtem of juriſprudence from ever eſtabliſhing itſelf among them, though the improved manners of the people may be ſuch as would admit of the moſt accurate. In no country do the deciſions of poſitive law coincide exactly, in every caſe, with the rules which the natural ſenſe of juſtice would dictate. Syſtems of poſitive law, therefore, though they deſerve the greateſt authority, as the records of the ſentiments of mankind in

in different ages and nations, yet can never be regarded as accurate ſyſtems of the rules of natural juſtice.

It might have been expected that the reaſonings of lawyers, upon the different imperfections and improvements of the laws of different countries, ſhould have given occaſion to an inquiry into what were the natural rules of juſtice independent of all poſitive inſtitution. It might have been expected that theſe reaſonings ſhould have led them to aim at eſtabliſhing a ſyſtem of what might properly be called natural juriſprudence, or a theory of the general principles which ought to run through and be the foundation of the laws of all nations. But though the reaſonings of lawyers did produce ſomething of this kind, and though no man has treated ſyſtematically of the laws of any particular country, without intermixing in his work many obſervations of this ſort; it was very late in the world before any ſuch general ſyſtem was thought of, or before the philoſophy of law was treated of by itſelf, and without regard to the particular inſtitutions of any one nation. In none of the ancient moraliſts, do we find any attempt towards a particular enumeration of the rules of juſtice. Cicero in his Offices, and Ariſtotle in his Ethics, treat of juſtice in the

the ſame general manner in which they treat of all the other virtues. In the laws of Cicero and Plato, where we might naturally have expected ſome attempts towards an enumeration of thoſe rules of natural equity, which ought to be enforced by the poſitive laws of every country, there is, however, nothing of this kind. Their laws are laws of police, not of juſtice. Grotius ſeems to have been the firſt who attempted to give the world any thing like a ſyſtem of thoſe principles which ought to run through, and be the foundation of the laws of all nations; and his treatiſe of the laws of war and peace, with all its imperfections, is perhaps at this day the moſt complete work that has yet been given upon the ſubject. I ſhall in another diſcourſe endeavour to give an account of the general principles of law and government, and of the different revolutions they have undergone in the different ages and periods of ſociety, not only in what concerns juſtice, but in what concerns police, revenue, and arms, and whatever elſe is the object of law. I ſhall not, therefore, at preſent enter into any further detail concerning the hiſtory of juriſprudence.

THE END.

CONSIDERATIONS

CONCERNING THE FIRST

FORMATION OF LANGUAGES,

AND THE

Different Genius of original and compounded

LANGUAGES.

CONSIDERATIONS

CONCERNING THE FIRST

FORMATION OF LANGUAGES,

&c. &c. &c.

THE aſſignation of particular names, to denote particular objects, that is, the inſtitution of nouns ſubſtantive, would probably be one of the firſt ſteps towards the formation of language. Two ſavages, who had never been taught to ſpeak, but had been bred up remote from the ſocieties of men, would naturally begin to form that language by which they would endeavour to make their mutual wants intelligible to each other, by uttering certain ſounds, whenever they meant to denote certain objects. Thoſe objects only which were moſt familiar to them, and which

they had moſt frequent occaſion to mention, would have particular names aſſigned to them. The particular cave whoſe covering ſheltered them from the weather, the particular tree whoſe fruit relieved their hunger, the particular fountain whoſe water allayed their thirſt, would firſt be denominated by the words *cave*, *tree*, *fountain*, or by whatever other appellations they might think proper, in that primitive jargon, to mark them. Afterwards, when the more enlarged experience of theſe ſavages had led them to obſerve, and their neceſſary occaſions obliged them to make mention of other caves, and other trees, and other fountains, they would naturally beſtow, upon each of thoſe new objects, the ſame name, by which they had been accuſtomed to expreſs the ſimilar object they were firſt acquainted with. The new objects had none of them any name of its own, but each of them exactly reſembled another object, which had ſuch an appellation. It was impoſſible that thoſe ſavages could behold the new objects, without recollecting the old ones; and the name of the old ones, to which the new bore ſo cloſe a reſemblance. When they had occaſion, therefore, to mention, or to point out to each other, any of the new objects, they would naturally utter the name of the correſ-

2 pondent

ſpondent old one, of which the idea could not fail, at that inſtant, to preſent itſelf to their memory in the ſtrongeſt and livelieſt manner. And thus, thoſe words, which were originally the proper names of individuals, would each of them inſenſibly become the common name of a multitude. A child that is juſt learning to ſpeak, calls every perſon who comes to the houſe its papa, or its mama; and thus beſtows upon the whole ſpecies thoſe names which it had been taught to apply to two individuals. I have known a clown, who did not know the proper name of the river which ran by his own door. It was *the river*, he ſaid, and he never heard any other name for it. His experience, it ſeems, had not led him to obſerve any other river. The general word *river*, therefore, was, it is evident, in his acceptance of it, a proper name ſignifying an individual object. If this perſon had been carried to another river, would he not readily have called it a river? Could we ſuppoſe any perſon living on the banks of the Thames ſo ignorant, as not to know the general word *river*, but to be acquainted only with the particular word *Thames*, if he was brought to any other river, would he not readily call it a *Thames?* This, in reality, is no more than what they, who are well acquainted with the general word,

word, are very apt to do. An Englishman, describing any great river which he may have seen in some foreign country, naturally says, that it is another Thames. The Spaniards, when they first arrived upon the coast of Mexico, and observed the wealth, populousness, and habitations, of that fine country, so much superior to the savage nations which they had been visiting for some time before, cried out that it was another Spain. Hence it was called New Spain; and this name has stuck to that unfortunate country ever since. We say, in the same manner, of a hero, that he is an Alexander; of an orator, that he is a Cicero; of a philosopher, that he is a Newton. This way of speaking, which the grammarians call an Antonomasia, and which is still extremely common, though now not at all necessary, demonstrates how much mankind are naturally disposed to give to one object the name of any other, which nearly resembles it, and thus to denominate a multitude, by what originally was intended to express an individual.

It is this application of the name of an individual to a great multitude of objects, whose resemblance naturally recalls the idea of that individual, and of the name which expresses it, that seems originally to have given occasion

to

to the formation of thoſe claſſes and aſſortments, which, in the ſchools, are called genera and ſpecies, and of which the ingenious and eloquent M. Rouſſeau of Geneva * finds himſelf ſo much at a loſs to account for the origin. What conſtitutes a ſpecies is merely a number of objects, bearing a certain degree of reſemblance to one another, and on that account denominated by a ſingle appellation, which may be applied to expreſs any one of them.

When the greater part of objects had thus been arranged under their proper claſſes and aſſortments, diſtinguiſhed by ſuch general names, it was impoſſible that the greater part of that almoſt infinite number of individuals, comprehended under each particular aſſortment or ſpecies, could have any peculiar or proper names of their own, diſtinct from the general name of the ſpecies. When there was occaſion, therefore, to mention any particular object, it often became neceſſary to diſtinguiſh it from the other objects comprehended under the ſame general name, either, firſt, by its peculiar qualities; or, ſecondly, by the peculiar relation which it ſtood in to ſome other things. Hence the neceſſary origin of two

* Origine de l'Inegalité. Partie Premiere, p. 376, 377. Edition d'Amſterdam des Oeuvres diverſes de J. J. Rouſſeau.

other

other ſets of words, of which the one ſhould expreſs quality; the other, relation.

Nouns adjective are the words which expreſs quality conſidered as qualifying, or, as the ſchoolmen ſay, in concrete with, ſome particular ſubject. Thus the word *green* expreſſes a certain quality conſidered as qualifying, or as in concrete with, the particular ſubject to which it may be applied. Words of this kind, it is evident, may ſerve to diſtinguiſh particular objects from others comprehended under the ſame general appellation. The words *green tree*, for example, might ſerve to diſtinguiſh a particular tree from others that were withered or blaſted.

Prepoſitions are the words which expreſs relation conſidered, in the ſame manner, in concrete with the co-relative object. Thus the prepoſitions *of*, *to*, *for*, *with*, *by*, *above*, *below*, &c. denote ſome relation ſubſiſting between the objects expreſſed by the words between which the prepoſitions are placed; and they denote that this relation is conſidered in concrete with the co-relative object. Words of this kind ſerve to diſtinguiſh particular objects from others of the ſame ſpecies, when thoſe particular objects cannot be ſo properly marked out by any peculiar qualities of their own. When we ſay *the green tree of the meadow*,

meadow, for example, we diſtinguiſh a particular tree, not only by the quality which belongs to it but by the relation which it ſtands in to another object.

As neither quality nor relation can exiſt in abſtract, it is natural to ſuppoſe that the words which denote them conſidered in concrete, the way in which we always ſee them ſubſiſt, would be of much earlier invention than thoſe which expreſs them conſidered in abſtract, the way in which we never ſee them ſubſiſt. The words *green* and *blue* would, in all probability, be ſooner invented than the words *greenneſs* and *blueneſs*; the words *above* and *below*, than the words *ſuperiority* and *inferiority*. To invent words of the latter kind requires a much greater effort of abſtraction than to invent thoſe of the former. It is probable, therefore, that ſuch abſtract terms would be of much later inſtitution. Accordingly, their etymologies generally ſhew that they are ſo, they being generally derived from others that are concrete.

But though the invention of nouns adjective be much more natural than that of the abſtract nouns ſubſtantive derived from them, it would ſtill, however, require a conſiderable degree of abſtraction and generalization. Thoſe, for example, who firſt invented the words

words *green*, *blue*, *red*, and the other names of colours, muſt have obſerved and compared together a great number of objects, muſt have remarked their reſemblances and diſſimilitudes in reſpect of the quality of colour, and muſt have arranged them, in their own minds, into different claſſes and aſſortments, according to thoſe reſemblances and diſſimilitudes. An adjective is by nature a general, and in ſome meaſure an abſtract word, and neceſſarily preſuppoſes the idea of a certain ſpecies or aſſortment of things, to all of wich it is equally applicable. The word *green* could not, as we were ſuppoſing might be the caſe of the word *cave*, have been originally the name of an individual, and afterwards have become, by what grammarians call an Antonomaſia, the name of a ſpecies. The word *green* denoting, not the name of a ſubſtance, but the peculiar quality of a ſubſtance, muſt from the very firſt have been a general word, and conſidered as equally applicable to any other ſubſtance poſſeſſed of the ſame quality. The man who firſt diſtinguiſhed a particular object by the epithet of *green*, muſt have obſerved other objects that were not *green* from which he meant to ſeparate it by this appellation. The inſtitution of this name, therefore, ſuppoſes compariſon. It likewiſe ſuppoſes ſome degree

degree of abſtraction. The perſon who firſt invented this appellation muſt have diſtinguiſhed the quality from the object to which it belonged, and muſt have conceived the object as capable of ſubſiſting without the quality. The invention, therefore, even of the ſimpleſt nouns adjective, muſt have required more metaphyſics than we are apt to be aware of. The different mental operations, of arrangement or claſſing, of compariſon, and of abſtraction, muſt all have been employed, before even the names of the different colours, the leaſt metaphyſical of all nouns adjective, could be inſtituted. From all which I infer, that when languages were beginning to be formed, nouns adjective would by no means be the words of the earlieſt invention.

There is another expedient for denoting the different qualities of different ſubſtances, which as it requires no abſtraction, nor any conceived ſeparation of the quality from the ſubject, ſeems more natural than the invention of nouns adjective, and which, upon this account, could hardly fail, in the firſt formation of language, to be thought of before them. This expedient is to make ſome variation upon the noun ſubſtantive itſelf, according to the different qualities which it is endowed with. Thus, in many languages, the qualities both

both of ſex and of the want of ſex, are expreſſed by different terminations in the nouns ſubſtantive, which denote objects ſo qualified. In Latin, for example, *lupus*, *lupa*; *equus*, *equa*; *juvencus*, *juvenca*; *Julius*, *Julia*; *Lucretius*, *Lucretia*, &c. denote the qualities of male and female in the animals and perſons to whom ſuch appellations belong, without needing the addition of any adjective for this purpoſe. On the other hand, the words *forum*, *pratum*, *plauſtrum*, denote by their peculiar termination the total abſence of ſex in the different ſubſtances which they ſtand for. Both ſex, and the want of all ſex, being naturally conſidered as qualities modifying and inſeparable from the particular ſubſtances to which they belong, it was natural to expreſs them rather by a modification in the noun ſubſtantive, than by any general and abſtract word expreſſive of this particular ſpecies of quality. The expreſſion bears, it is evident, in this way, a much more exact analogy to the idea or object which it denotes, than in the other. The quality appears, in nature, as a modification of the ſubſtance, and as it is thus expreſſed, in language, by a modification of the noun ſubſtantive, which denotes that ſubſtance, the quality and the ſubject are, in this caſe, blended together, if I may ſay ſo, in

in the expreſſion, in the ſame manner as they appear to be in the object and in the idea. Hence the origin of the maſculine, feminine, and neutral genders, in all the ancient languages. By means of theſe the moſt important of all diſtinctions, that of ſubſtances into animated and inanimated, and that of animals into male and female, ſeem to have been ſufficiently marked without the aſſiſtance of adjectives, or of any general names denoting this moſt extenſive ſpecies of qualifications.

There are no more than theſe three genders in any of the languages with which I am acquainted; that is to ſay, the formation of nouns ſubſtantive can, by itſelf, and without the accompaniment of adjectives, expreſs no other qualities but thoſe three above mentioned, the qualities of male, of female, of neither male nor female. I ſhould not, however, be ſurpriſed, if, in other languages with which I am unacquainted, the different formations of nouns ſubſtantive ſhould be capable of expreſſing many other different qualities. The different diminutives of the Italian, and of ſome other languages, do, in reality, ſometimes, expreſs a great variety of different modifications in the ſubſtances denoted by thoſe nouns which undergo ſuch variations.

It was impoſſible, however, that nouns ſubſtantive could, without loſing altogether their original form, undergo ſo great a number of variations, as would be ſufficient to expreſs that almoſt infinite variety of qualities, by which it might, upon different occaſions, be neceſſary to ſpecify and diſtinguiſh them. Though the different formation of nouns ſubſtantive, therefore, might, for ſome time, foreſtall the neceſſity of inventing nouns adjective, it was impoſſible that this neceſſity could be foreſtalled altogether. When nouns adjective came to be invented, it was natural that they ſhould be formed with ſome ſimilarity to the ſubſtantives to which they were to ſerve as epithets or qualifications. Men would naturally give them the ſame terminations with the ſubſtantives to which they were firſt applied, and from that love of ſimilarity of ſound, from that delight in the returns of the ſame ſyllables, which is the foundation of analogy in all languages, they would be apt to vary the termination of the ſame adjective, according as they had occaſion to apply it to a maſculine, to a feminine, or to a neutral ſubſtantive. They would ſay, *magnus lupus*, *magna lupa*, *magnum pratum*, when they meant to expreſs a great *he wolf*, a great *ſhe wolf*, a great *meadow*.

This

This variation, in the termination of the noun adjective, according to the gender of the ſubſtantive, which takes place in all the ancient languages, ſeems to have been introduced chiefly for the ſake of a certain ſimilarity of ſound, of a certain ſpecies of rhyme, which is naturally ſo very agreeable to the human ear. Gender, it is to be obſerved, cannot properly belong to a noun adjective, the ſignification of which is always preciſely the ſame, to whatever ſpecies of ſubſtantives it is applied. When we ſay, *a great man*, *a great woman*, the word *great* has preciſely the ſame meaning in both caſes, and the difference of the ſex in the ſubjects to which it may be applied, makes no ſort of difference in its ſignification. *Magnus*, *magna*, *magnum*, in the ſame manner, are words which expreſs preciſely the ſame quality, and the change of the termination is accompanied with no ſort of variation in the meaning. Sex and gender are qualities which belong to ſubſtances, but cannot belong to the qualities of ſubſtances. In general, no quality, when conſidered in concrete, or as qualifying ſome particular ſubject, can itſelf be conceived as the ſubject of any other quality, though when conſidered in abſtract it may. No adjective therefore can qualify any other adjective. A *great good man*,

means a man who is both *great* and *good*. Both the adjectives qualify the ſubſtantive; they do not qualify one another. On the other hand, when we ſay, the *great goodneſs* of the man, the word *goodneſs* denoting a quality conſidered in abſtract, which may itſelf be the ſubject of other qualities, is upon that account capable of being qualified by the word *great*.

If the original invention of nouns adjective would be attended with ſo much difficulty, that of prepoſitions would be accompanied with yet more. Every prepoſition, as I have already obſerved, denotes ſome relation conſidered in concrete with the co-relative object. The prepoſition *above*, for example, denotes the relation of ſuperiority, not in abſtract, as it is expreſſed by the word *ſuperiority*, but in concrete with ſome co-relative object. In this phraſe, for example, *the tree above the cave*, the word *above* expreſſes a certain relation between the *tree* and the *cave*, and it expreſſes this relation in concrete with the co-relative object, *the cave*. A prepoſition always requires, in order to complete the ſenſe, ſome other word to come after it; as may be obſerved in this particular inſtance. Now, I ſay, the original invention of ſuch words would require a yet greater effort of abſtraction and general-

generalization, than that of nouns adjective. First of all, a relation is, in itself, a more metaphysical object than a quality. Nobody can be at a loss to explain what is meant by a quality; but few people will find themselves able to express, very distinctly, what is understood by a relation. Qualities are almost always the objects of our external senses; relations never are. No wonder, therefore, that the one set of objects should be so much more comprehensible than the other. Secondly, though prepositions always express the relation which they stand for, in concrete with the co-relative object, they could not have originally been formed without a considerable effort of abstraction. A preposition denotes a relation and nothing but a relation. But before men could institute a word, which signified a relation, and nothing but a relation, they must have been able, in some measure, to consider this relation abstractedly from the related objects; since the idea of those objects does not, in any respect, enter into the signification of the preposition. The invention of such a word, therefore, must have required a considerable degree of abstraction. Thirdly, a preposition is from its nature a general word, which, from its very first institution, must have been considered as equally applicable

to denote any other similar relation. The man who first invented the word *above*, must not only have distinguished, in some measure, the relation of *superiority* from the objects which were so related, but he must have also distinguished this relation from other relations, such as, from the relation of *inferiority* denoted by the word *below*, from the relation of *juxtaposition*, expressed by the word *beside*, and the like. He must have conceived this word, therefore, as expressive of a particular sort or species of relation distinct from every other, which could not be done without a considerable effort of comparison and generalization.

Whatever were the difficulties, therefore, which embarrassed the first invention of nouns adjective, the same, and many more, must have embarrassed that of prepositions. If mankind, therefore, in the first formation of languages, seem to have, for some time, evaded the necessity of nouns adjective, by varying the termination of the names of substances, according as these varied in some of their most important qualities, they would much more find themselves under the necessity of evading, by some similar contrivance, the yet more difficult invention of prepositions. The different cases in the ancient lan-

guages is a contrivance of precisely the same kind. The genitive and dative cases, in Greek and Latin, evidently supply the place of the prepositions; and by a variation in the noun substantive, which stands for the co-relative term, express the relation which subsists between what is denoted by that noun substantive, and what is expressed by some other word in the sentence. In these expressions, for example, *fructus arboris, the fruit of the tree; sacer Herculi, sacred to Hercules*, the variations made in the co-relative words, *arbor* and *Hercules*, express the same relations which are expressed in English by the prepositions *of* and *to*.

To express a relation in this manner, did not require any effort of abstraction. It was not here expressed by a peculiar word denoting relation and nothing but relation, but by a variation upon the co-relative term. It was expressed here, as it appears in nature, not as something separated and detached, but as thoroughly mixed and blended with the co-relative object.

To express relation in this manner, did not require any effort of generalization. The words *arboris* and *Herculi*, while they involve in their signification the same relation expressed by the English prepositions *of* and *to*,

are not like those prepositions, general words, which can be applied to express the same relation between whatever other objects it might be observed to subsist.

To express relation in this manner did not require any effort of comparison. The words *arboris* and *Herculis* are not general words intended to denote a particular species of relation which the inventors of those expressions meant, in consequence of some sort of comparison, to separate and distinguish from every other sort of relation. The example, indeed, of this contrivance would soon probably be followed, and whoever had occasion to express a similar relation between any other objects would be very apt to do it by making a similar variation on the name of the co-relative object. This, I say, would probably, or rather certainly happen; but it would happen without any intention or foresight in those who first set the example, and who never meant to establish any general rule. The general rule would establish itself insensibly, and by slow degrees, in consequence of that love of analogy and similarity of sound, which is the foundation of by far the greater part of the rules of grammar.

To express relation, therefore, by a variation in the name of the co-relative object, requiring

requiring neither abſtraction, nor generalization, nor compariſon of any kind, would, at firſt, be much more natural and eaſy, than to expreſs it by thoſe general words called prepoſitions, of which the firſt invention muſt have demanded ſome degree of all thoſe operations.

The number of caſes is different in different languages. There are five in the Greek, ſix in the Latin, and there are ſaid to be ten in the Armenian language. It muſt have naturally happened that there ſhould be a greater or a ſmaller number of caſes, according as in the terminations of nouns ſubſtantive the firſt formers of any language happened to have eſtabliſhed a greater or a ſmaller number of variations, in order to expreſs the different relations they had occaſion to take notice of, before the invention of thoſe more general and abſtract prepoſitions which could ſupply their place.

It is, perhaps, worth while to obſerve that thoſe prepoſitions, which in modern languages hold the place of the ancient caſes, are of all others, the moſt general, and abſtract, and metaphyſical; and of conſequence would probably be the laſt invented. Aſk any man of common acuteneſs, What relation is expreſſed by the prepoſition *above*? He will readily

readily answer, that of *superiority*. By the preposition *below*? He will as quickly reply, that of *inferiority*. But ask him, What relation is expressed by the preposition *of*? and, if he has not beforehand employed his thoughts a good deal upon these subjects, you may safely allow him a week to consider of his answer. The prepositions *above* and *below* do not denote any of the relations expressed by the cases in the ancient languages. But the preposition *of*, denotes the same relation, which is in them expressed by the genitive case; and which it is easy to observe, is of a very metaphysical nature. The preposition *of*, denotes relation in general, considered in concrete with the co-relative object. It marks that the noun substantive which goes before it, is somehow or other related to that which comes after it, but without in any respect ascertaining, as is done by the preposition *above*, what is the peculiar nature of that relation. We often apply it, therefore, to express the most opposite relations; because, the most opposite relations agree so far that each of them comprehends in it the general idea or nature of a relation. We say, *the father of the son*, and *the son of the father*; *the fir-trees of the forest*, and the *forest of the fir-trees*. The relation in which the father stands to the

son

ſon is, it is evident, a quite oppoſite relation to that in which the ſon ſtands to the father; that in which the parts ſtand to the whole, is quite oppoſite to that in which the whole ſtands to the parts. The word *of*, however, ſerves very well to denote all thoſe relations, becauſe in itſelf it denotes no particular relation, but only relation in general; and ſo far as any particular relation is collected from ſuch expreſſions, it is inferred by the mind, not from the prepoſition itſelf, but from the nature and arrangement of the ſubſtantives, between which the prepoſition is placed.

What I have ſaid concerning the prepoſition *of*, may in ſome meaſure be applied to the prepoſitions *to*, *for*, *with*, *by*, and to whatever other prepoſitions are made uſe of in modern languages, to ſupply the place of the ancient caſes. They all of them expreſs very abſtract and metaphyſical relations, which any man who takes the trouble to try it, will find it extremely difficult to expreſs by nouns ſubſtantive, in the ſame manner as we may expreſs the relation denoted by the prepoſition *above*, by the noun ſubſtantive *ſuperiority*. They all of them, however, expreſs ſome ſpecific relation, and are, conſequently, none of them ſo abſtract as the prepoſition *of*, which may be regarded as by far the moſt metaphy-

metaphyſical of all prepoſitions. The prepoſitions, therefore, which are capable of ſupplying the place of the ancient caſes, being more abſtract than the other prepoſitions, would naturally be of more difficult invention. The relations at the ſame time, which thoſe prepoſitions expreſs, are, of all others, thoſe which we have moſt frequent occaſion to mention. The prepoſitions *above*, *below*, *near*, *within*, *without*, *againſt*, &c. are much more rarely made uſe of, in modern languages, than the prepoſitions *of*, *to*, *for*, *with*, *from*, *by*. A prepoſition of the former kind will not occur twice in a page; we can ſcarce compoſe a ſingle ſentence without the aſſiſtance of one or two of the latter. If theſe latter prepoſitions, therefore, which ſupply the place of the caſes, would be of ſuch difficult invention on account of their abſtractedneſs, ſome expedient, to ſupply their place, muſt have been of indiſpenſable neceſſity, on account of the frequent occaſion which men have to take notice of the relations which they denote. But there is no expedient ſo obvious, as that of varying the termination of one of the principal words.

It is, perhaps, unneceſſary to obſerve, that there are ſome of the caſes in the ancient languages, which, for particular reaſons, cannot

be

be reprefented by any prepofitions. Thefe are the nominative, accufative, and vocative cafes. In thofe modern languages which do not admit of any fuch variety in the terminations of their nouns fubftantive, the correfpondent relations are expreffed by the place of the words, and by the order and conftruction of the fentence.

As men have frequently occafion to make mention of multitudes as well as of fingle objects, it became neceffary that they fhould have fome method of expreffing number. Number may be expreffed either by a particular word, expreffing number in general, fuch as the words *many*, *more*, &c. or by fome variation upon the words which exprefs the things numbered. It is this laft expedient which mankind would probably have recourfe to, in the infancy of language. Number, confidered in general, without relation to any particular fet of objects numbered, is one of the moft abftract and metaphyfical ideas, which the mind of man is capable of forming; and, confequently, is not an idea which would readily occur to rude mortals, who were juft beginning to form a language. They would naturally, therefore, diftinguifh when they talked of a fingle, and when they talked of a multitude of objects, not by any

metaphyſical adjectives, ſuch as the Engliſh *a*, *an*, *many*, but by a variation, upon the termination of the word which ſignified the objects numbered. Hence the origin of the ſingular and plural numbers in all the ancient languages; and the ſame diſtinction has likewiſe been retained in all the modern languages, at leaſt, in the greater part of words.

All primitive and uncompounded languages ſeem to have a dual as well as a plural, number. This is the caſe of the Greek, and I am told of the Hebrew, of the Gothic, and of many other languages. In the rude beginnings of ſociety, *one*, *two*, and *more*, might poſſibly be all the numeral diſtinctions which mankind would have any occaſion to take notice of. Theſe they would find it more natural to expreſs, by a variation upon every particular noun ſubſtantive, than by ſuch general and abſtract words as *one*, *two*, *three*, *four*, &c. Theſe words, though cuſtom has rendered them familiar to us, expreſs, perhaps, the moſt ſubtile and refined abſtractions, which the mind of man is capable of forming. Let any one conſider within himſelf, for example, what he means by the word *three*, which ſignifies neither three ſhillings, nor three pence, nor three perſons, nor three horſes, but three in general; and he will eaſily ſatisfy himſelf that a word,

a word, which denotes ſo very metaphyſical an abſtraction, could not be either a very obvious or a very early invention. I have read of ſome ſavage nations, whoſe language was capable of expreſſing no more than the three firſt numeral diſtinctions. But whether it expreſſed thoſe diſtinctions by three general words, or by variations upon the nouns ſubſtantive, denoting the things numbered, I do not remember to have met with any thing which could determine.

As all the ſame relations which ſubſiſt between ſingle may likewiſe ſubſiſt between numerous objects, it is evident there would be occaſion for the ſame number of caſes, in the dual and in the plural, as in the ſingular number. Hence the intricacy and complexneſs of the declenſions in all the ancient languages. In the Greek there are five caſes in each of the three numbers, conſequently fifteen in all.

As nouns adjective, in the ancient languages, varied their terminations according to the gender of the ſubſtantive to which they were applied, ſo did they likewiſe, according to the caſe and the number. Every noun adjective in the Greek language, therefore, having three genders, and three numbers, and five caſes in each number, may be conſidered

as having five and forty different variations. The firſt formers of language ſeem to have varied the termination of the adjective, according to the caſe and the number of the ſubſtantive, for the ſame reaſon which made them vary it according to the gender; the love of analogy, and of a certain regularity of ſound. In the ſignification of adjectives there is neither caſe nor number, and the meaning of ſuch words is always preciſely the ſame, notwithſtanding all the variety of termination under which they appear. *Magnus vir*, *magni viri*, *magnorum virorum*, *a great man*, *of a great man*, *of great men*; in all theſe expreſſions the words *magnus*, *magni*, *magnorum*, as well as the word *great*, have preciſely one and the ſame ſignification, though the ſubſtantives to which they are applied have not. The difference of termination in the noun adjective is accompanied with no ſort of difference in the meaning. An adjective denotes the qualification of a noun ſubſtantive. But the different relations in which that noun ſubſtantive may occaſionally ſtand, can make no ſort of difference upon its qualification.

If the declenſions of the ancient languages are ſo very complex, their conjugations are infinitely more ſo. And the complexneſs of the one is founded upon the ſame principle with

with that of the other, the difficulty of forming, in the beginnings of language, abstract and general terms.

Verbs must necessarily have been coëval with the very first attempts towards the formation of language. No affirmation can be expressed without the assistance of some verb. We never speak but in order to express our opinion that something either is or is not. But the word denoting this event, or this matter of fact, which is the subject of our affirmation, must always be a verb.

Impersonal verbs, which express in one word a complete event, which preserve in the expression that perfect simplicity and unity, which there always is in the object and in the idea, and which suppose no abstraction, or metaphysical division of the event into its several constituent members of subject and attribute, would, in all probability, be the species of verbs first invented. The verbs *pluit*, *it rains*, *ningit*, *it snows*, *tonat*, *it thunders*, *lucet*, *it is day*, *turbatur*, *there is a confusion*, &c. each of them express a complete affirmation, the whole of an event, with that perfect simplicity and unity with which the mind conceives it in nature. On the contrary, the phrases, *Alexander ambulat*, *Alexander walks*, *Petrus sedet*, *Peter sits*, divide the event, as it

were, into two parts, the perſon or ſubject, and the attribute, or matter of fact, affirmed of that ſubject. But in nature, the idea or conception of Alexander walking, is as perfectly and completely one ſimple conception, as that of Alexander not walking. The diviſion of this event, therefore, into two parts, is altogether artificial, and is the effect of the imperfection of language, which, upon this, as upon many other occaſions, ſupplies, by a number of words, the want of one, which could expreſs at once the whole matter of fact that was meant to be affirmed. Every body muſt obſerve how much more ſimplicity there is in the natural expreſſion, *pluit*, than in the more artificial expreſſions, *imber decidit*, *the rain falls*; or *tempeſtas eſt pluvia*, *the weather is rainy*. In theſe two laſt expreſſions, the ſimple event, or matter of fact, is artificially ſplit and divided in the one, into two; in the other into three parts. In each of them it is expreſſed by a ſort of grammatical circumlocution, of which the ſignificancy is founded upon a certain metaphyſical analyſis of the component parts of the idea expreſſed by the word *pluit*. The firſt verbs, therefore, perhaps even the firſt words, made uſe of in the beginnings of language, would in all probability be ſuch impersonal verbs. It is obſerved

ferved accordingly, I am told by the Hebrew grammarians, that the radical words of their language, from which all the others are derived, are all of them verbs and imperfonal verbs.

It is eafy to conceive how, in the progrefs of language, thofe imperfonal verbs fhould become perfonal. Let us fuppofe, for example, that the word *venit*, *it comes*, was originally an imperfonal verb, and that it denoted, not the coming of fomething in general, as at prefent, but the coming of a particular object, fuch as *the Lion*. The firft favage inventors of language, we fhall fuppofe, when they obferved the approach of this terrible animal, were accuftomed to cry out to one another, *venit*, that is, *the lion comes*, and that this word thus expreffed a complete event, without the affiftance of any other. Afterwards, when, on the further progrefs of language, they had begun to give names to particular fubftances, whenever they obferved the approach of any other terrible object, they would naturally join the name of that object, to the word *venit*, and cry out, *venit urfus*, *venit lupus*. By degrees the word *venit* would thus come to fignify the coming of any terrible object, and not merely the coming of the lion. It would now, therefore, exprefs, not

 the

the coming of a particular object, but the coming of an object of a particular kind. Having become more general in its ſignification, it could no longer repreſent any particular diſtinct event by itſelf, and without the aſſiſtance of a noun ſubſtantive, which might ſerve to aſcertain and determine its ſignification. It would now, therefore, have become a perſonal inſtead of an imperſonal verb. We may eaſily conceive how, in the further progreſs of ſociety, it might ſtill grow more general in its ſignification, and come to ſignify, as at preſent, the approach of any thing whatever, whether good, bad, or indifferent.

It is probably in ſome ſuch manner as this, that almoſt all verbs have become perſonal, and that mankind have learned by degrees to ſplit and divide almoſt every event into a great number of metaphyſical parts, expreſſed by the different parts of ſpeech, variouſly combined in the different members of every phraſe and ſentence.* The ſame ſort of progreſs

* As the far greater part of verbs expreſs, at preſent, not an event, but the attribute of an event, and, conſequently, require a ſubject, or nominative caſe, to complete their ſignification, ſome grammarians, not having attended to this progreſs of nature, and being deſirous to make their common rules quite univerſal, and without any exception, have inſiſted that

gress seems to have been made in the art of speaking as in the art of writing. When mankind first began to attempt to express their ideas by writing, every character represented a whole word. But the number of words being almost infinite, the memory found itself quite loaded and oppressed by the multitude of characters which it was obliged to retain. Necessity taught them, therefore, to divide words into their elements, and to invent characters which should represent, not the words themselves, but the elements of which they were composed. In consequence of this invention, every particular word came to be represented, not by one character, but by a multitude of characters; and the expression of it in writing became much more intricate and complex than before. But though particular words were thus represented by a greater number of characters, the whole language was expressed by a much smaller, and about four and twenty letters were found capable of supplying the place of that immense

[illegible]

multitude of characters, which were requisite before. In the same manner, in the beginnings of language, men seem to have attempted to express every particular event, which they had occasion to take notice of, by a particular word, which expressed at once the whole of that event. But as the number of words must, in this case, have become really infinite, in consequence of the really infinite variety of events, men found themselves partly compelled by necessity, and partly conducted by nature, to divide every event into what may be called its metaphysical elements, and to institute words, which should denote not so much the events, as the elements of which they were composed. The expression of every particular event, became in this manner more intricate and complex, but the whole system of the language became more coherent, more connected, more easily retained and comprehended.

When verbs, from being originally impersonal, had thus, by the division of the event into its metaphysical elements, become personal, it is natural to suppose that they would first be made use of in the third person singular. No verb is ever used impersonally in our language, nor, so far as I know, in any other modern tongue. But in the ancient languages,

guages, whenever any verb is used impersonally, it is always in the third person singular. The termination of those verbs, which are still always impersonal, is constantly the same with that of the third person singular of personal verbs. The consideration of these circumstances, joined to the naturalness of the thing itself, may serve to convince us that verbs first became personal in what is now called the third person singular.

But as the event, or matter of fact, which is expressed by a verb, may be affirmed either of the person who speaks, or of the person who is spoken to, as well as of some third person or object, it became necessary to fall upon some method of expressing these two peculiar relations of the event. In the English language this is commonly done, by prefixing, what are called the personal pronouns, to the general word which expresses the event affirmed. *I came, you came, he or it came*; in these phrases the event of having come is, in the first, affirmed of the speaker; in the second, of the person spoken to; in the third, of some other person or object. The first formers of language, it may be imagined, might have done the same thing, and prefixing in the same manner the two first personal pronouns, to the same termination of the verb,

 which

which expressed the third person singular, might have said *ego venit*, *tu venit*, as well as *ille* or *illud venit*. And I make no doubt but they would have done so, if at the time when they had first occasion to express these relations of the verb, there had been any such words as either *ego* or *tu* in their language. But in this early period of the language which we are now endeavouring to describe, it is extremely improbable that any such words would be known. Though custom has now rendered them familiar to us, they, both of them, express ideas extremely metaphysical and abstract. The word *I*, for example, is a word of a very particular species. Whatever speaks may denote itself by this personal pronoun. The word *I*, therefore, is a general word, capable of being predicated, as the logicians say, of an infinite variety of objects. It differs, however, from all other general words in this respect; that the objects of which it may be predicated, do not form any particular species of objects distinguished from all others. The word *I*, does not, like the word *man*, denote a particular class of objects, separated from all others by peculiar qualities of their own. It is far from being the name of a species, but, on the contrary, whenever it is made use of, it always denote a precise individual,

dividual, the particular perſon who then ſpeaks. It may be ſaid to be, at once, both what the logicians call, a ſingular, and what they call, a common term; and to join in its ſignification the ſeemingly oppoſite qualities of the moſt preciſe individuality, and the moſt extenſive generalization. This word, therefore, expreſſing ſo very abſtract and metaphyſical an idea, would not eaſily or readily occur to the firſt formers of language. What are called the perſonal pronouns, it may be obſerved, are among the laſt words of which children learn to make uſe. A child, ſpeaking of itſelf, ſays, *Billy walks*, *Billy ſits*, inſtead of *I walk*, *I ſit*. As in the beginnings of language, therefore, mankind ſeem to have evaded the invention of at leaſt the more abſtract prepoſitions, and to have expreſſed the ſame relations which theſe now ſtand for, by varying the termination of the co-relative term, ſo they likewiſe would naturally attempt to evade the neceſſity of inventing thoſe more abſtract pronouns by varying the termination of the verb, according as the event which it expreſſed was intended to be affirmed of the firſt, ſecond, or third perſon. This ſeems, accordingly, to be the univerſal practice of all the ancient languages. In Latin, *veni*, *veniſti*, *venit*, ſufficiently denote, without any other addition,

addition, the different events expreſſed by the Engliſh phraſes, *I came*, *you came*, *he or it came*. The verb would, for the ſame reaſon, vary its termination, according as the event was intended to be affirmed of the firſt, ſecond, or third perſons plural; and what is expreſſed by the Engliſh phraſes, *we came*, *ye came*, *they came*, would be denoted by the Latin words, *venimus*, *veniſtis*, *venerunt*. Thoſe primitive languages too, which, upon account of the difficulty of inventing numeral names, had introduced a dual, as well as a plural number, into the declenſion of their nouns ſubſtantive, would probably, from analogy, do the ſame thing in the conjugations of their verbs. And thus in all thoſe original languages, we might expect to find, at leaſt ſix, if not eight or nine variations, in the termination of every verb, according as the event which it denoted was meant to be affirmed of the firſt, ſecond, or third perſons ſingular, dual, or plural. Theſe variations again being repeated, along with others, through all its different tenſes, through all its different modes, and through all its different voices, muſt neceſſarily have rendered their conjugations ſtill more intricate and complex than their declenſions.

Language would probably have continued upon this footing in all countries, nor would ever

ever have grown more ſimple in its declenſions and conjugations, had it not become more complex in its compoſition, in conſequence of the mixture of ſeveral languages with one another, occaſioned by the mixture of different nations. As long as any language was ſpoke by thoſe only who learned it in their infancy, the intricacy of its declenſions and conjugations could occaſion no great embarraſſment. The far greater part of thoſe who had occaſion to ſpeak it, had acquired it at ſo very early a period of their lives, ſo inſenſibly and by ſuch ſlow degrees, that they were ſcarce ever ſenſible of the difficulty. But when two nations came to be mixed with one another, either by conqueſt or migration, the caſe would be very different. Each nation, in order to make itſelf intelligible to thoſe with whom it was under the neceſſity of converſing, would be obliged to learn the language of the other. The greater part of individuals too, learning the new language, not by art, or by remounting to its rudiments and firſt principles, but by rote, and by what they commonly heard in converſation, would be extremely perplexed by the intricacy of its declenſions and conjugations. They would endeavour, therefore, to ſupply their ignorance of theſe by whatever ſhift the language could

could afford them. Their ignorance of the declenſions they would naturally ſupply by the uſe of prepoſitions; and a Lombard, who was attempting to ſpeak Latin, and wanted to expreſs that ſuch a perſon was a citizen of Rome, or a benefactor to Rome, if he happened not to be acquainted with the genitive and dative caſes of the word *Roma*, would naturally expreſs himſelf by prefixing the prepoſitions *ad* and *de* to the nominative; and, inſtead of *Romæ*, would ſay, *ad Roma* and *de Roma*. *Al Roma* and *di Roma*, accordingly, is the manner in which the preſent Italians, the deſcendants of the ancient Lombards and Romans, expreſs this and all other ſimilar relations. And in this manner prepoſitions ſeem to have been introduced, in the room of the ancient declenſions. The ſame alteration has, I am informed, been produced, upon the Greek language, ſince the taking of Conſtantinople by the Turks. The words are, in a great meaſure, the ſame as before; but the grammar is entirely loſt, prepoſitions having come in the place of the old declenſions. This change is undoubtedly a ſimplification of the language, in point of rudiments and principle. It introduces, inſtead of a great variety of declenſions, one univerſal declenſion, which is the ſame in every

every word, of whatever gender, number, or termination.

A similar expedient enables men, in the situation above mentioned, to get rid of almost the whole intricacy of their conjugations. There is in every language a verb, known by the name of the substantive verb; in Latin, *sum*, in English, *I am*. This verb denotes not the existence of any particular event, but existence in general. It is, upon this account, the most abstract and metaphysical of all verbs; and consequently, could by no means be a word of early invention. When it came to be invented, however, as it had all the tenses and modes of any other verb, by being joined with the passive participle, it was capable of supplying the place of the whole passive voice, and of rendering this part of their conjugations as simple and uniform as the use of prepositions had rendered their declensions. A Lombard, who wanted to say, *I am loved*, but could not recollect the word *amor*, naturally endeavoured to supply his ignorance, by saying, *Ego sum amatus*. *Io sono amato*, is at this day the Italian expression, which corresponds to the English phrase above mentioned.

There is another verb, which, in the same manner, runs through all languages, and

which is distinguished by the name of the possessive verb; in Latin, *habeo*; in English, *I have*. This verb, likewise, denotes an event of an extremely abstract and metaphysical nature, and, consequently, cannot be supposed to have been a word of the earliest invention. When it came to be invented, however, by being applied to the passive participle, it was capable of supplying a great part of the active voice, as the substantive verb had supplied the whole of the passive. A Lombard, who wanted to say, *I had loved*, but could not recollect the word *amaveram*, would endeavour to supply the place of it, by saying either *ego habebam amatum*, or *ego habui amatum*. *Io aveva amato*, or *Io ebbi amato*, are the correspondent Italian expressions at this day. And thus upon the intermixture of different nations with one another, the conjugations, by means of different auxiliary verbs, were made to approach towards the simplicity and uniformity of the declensions.

In general it may be laid down for a maxim, that the more simple any language is in its composition, the more complex it must be in its declensions and conjugations; and on the contrary, the more simple it is in its declensions and conjugations, the more complex it must be in its composition.

The

The Greek ſeems to be, in a great meaſure, a ſimple, uncompounded language, formed from the primitive jargon of thoſe wandering ſavages, the ancient Hellenians and Pelaſgians, from whom the Greek nation is ſaid to have been deſcended. All the words in the Greek language are derived from about three hundred primitives, a plain evidence that the Greeks formed their language almoſt entirely among themſelves, and that when they had occaſion for a new word, they were not accuſtomed, as we are, to borrow it from ſome foreign language, but to form it, either by compoſition, or derivation from ſome other word or words, in their own. The declenſions and conjugations, therefore, of the Greek are much more complex than thoſe of any other European language with which I am acquainted.

The Latin is a compoſition of the Greek and of the ancient Tuſcan languages. Its declenſions and conjugations accordingly are much leſs complex than thoſe of the Greek; it has dropt the dual number in both. Its verbs have no optative mood diſtinguiſhed by any peculiar termination. They have but one future. They have no aoriſt diſtinct from the preterit-perfect; they have no middle voice; and even many of their tenſes in

in the paſſive voice are eked out, in the ſame manner as in the modern languages, by the help of the ſubſtantive verb joined to the paſſive participle. In both the voices, the number of infinitives and participles is much ſmaller in the Latin than in the Greek.

The French and Italian languages are each of them compounded, the one of the Latin, and the language of the ancient Franks, the other of the ſame Latin, and the language of the ancient Lombards. As they are both of them, therefore, more complex in their compoſition than the Latin, ſo are they likewiſe more ſimple in their declenſions and conjugations. With regard to their declenſions, they they have both of them loſt their caſes altogether; and with regard to their conjugations, they have both of them loſt the whole of the paſſive, and ſome part of the active voices, of their verbs. The want of the paſſive voice they ſupply entirely by the ſubſtantive verb joined to the paſſive participle; and they make out part of the active, in the ſame manner, by the help of the poſſeſſive verb and the ſame paſſive participle.

The Engliſh is compounded of the French and the ancient Saxon languages. The French was introduced into Britain by the Norman conqueſt, and continued, till the time

time of Edward III. to be the ſole language of the law as well as the principal language of the court. The Engliſh, which came to be ſpoken afterwards, and which continues to be ſpoken now, is a mixture of the ancient Saxon and this Norman French. As the Engliſh language, therefore, is more complex in its compoſition than either the French or the Italian, ſo is it likewiſe more ſimple in its declenſions and conjugations. Thoſe two languages retain, at leaſt, a part of the diſtinction of genders, and their adjectives vary their termination according as they are applied to a maſculine or to a feminine ſubſtantive. But there is no ſuch diſtinction in the Engliſh language, whoſe adjectives admit of no variety of termination. The French and Italian languages have, both of them, the remains of a conjugation; and all thoſe tenſes of the active voice which cannot be expreſſed by the poſſeſſive verb joined to the paſſive participle, as well as many of thoſe which can, are, in thoſe languages, marked by varying the termination of the principal verb. But almoſt all thoſe other tenſes are in the Engliſh eked out by other auxiliary verbs, ſo that there is in this language ſcarce even the remains of a conjugation. *I love*, *I loved*, *loving*, are all the varieties of termination which the greater part

 of

of Engliſh verbs admit of. All the different modifications of meaning, which cannot be expreſſed by any of thoſe three terminations, muſt be made out by different auxiliary verbs joined to ſome one or other of them. Two auxiliary verbs ſupply all the deficiencies of the French and Italian conjugations; it requires more than half a dozen to ſupply thoſe of the Engliſh, which, beſides the ſubſtantive and poſſeſſive verbs, makes uſe of *do, did, will, would, ſhall, ſhould, can, could, may, might.*

It is in this manner that language becomes more ſimple in its rudiments and principles, juſt in proportion as it grows more complex in its compoſition, and the ſame thing has happened in it, which commonly happens with regard to mechanical engines. All machines are generally, when firſt invented, extremely complex in their principles, and there is often a particular principle of motion for every particular movement which it is intended they ſhould perform. Succeeding improvers obſerve, that one principle may be ſo applied as to produce ſeveral of thoſe movements; and thus the machine becomes gradually more and more ſimple, and produces its effects with fewer wheels, and fewer principles of motion. In language, in the ſame manner, every caſe of every noun,

noun, and every tenſe of every verb, was originally expreſſed by a particular diſtinct word, which ſerved for this purpoſe and for no other. But ſucceeding obſervation diſcovered, that one ſet of words was capable of ſupplying the place of all that infinite number, and that four or five prepoſitions, and half a dozen auxiliary verbs, were capable of anſwering the end of all the declenſions and of all the conjugations in the ancient languages.

But this ſimplification of languages, though it ariſes, perhaps, from ſimilar cauſes, has by no means ſimilar effects with the correſpondent ſimplification of machines. The ſimplification of machines renders them more and more perfect, but this ſimplification of the rudiments of languages renders them more and more imperfect, and leſs proper for many of the purpoſes of language: and this for the following reaſons.

Firſt of all, languages are by this ſimplification rendered more prolix, ſeveral words having become neceſſary to expreſs what could have been expreſſed by a ſingle word before. Thus the words, *Dei* and *Deo*, in the Latin, ſufficiently ſhew, without any addition, what relation the object ſignified is underſtood to ſtand in to the objects expreſſed by the other words in the ſentence. But to expreſs the

ſame relation in Engliſh, and in all other modern languages, we muſt make uſe of, at leaſt, two words, and ſay, *of God, to God.* So far as the declenſions are concerned, therefore, the modern languages are much more prolix than the ancient. The difference is ſtill greater with regard to the conjugations. What a Roman expreſſed by the ſingle word, *amaviſſem*, an Engliſhman is obliged to expreſs by four different words, *I ſhould have loved.* It is unneceſſary to take any pains to ſhow how much this prolixneſs muſt enervate the eloquence of all modern languages. How much the beauty of any expreſſion depends upon its conciſeneſs, is well known to thoſe who have any experience in compoſition.

Secondly, this ſimplification of the principles of languages renders them leſs agreeable to the ear. The variety of termination in the Greek and Latin, occaſioned by their declenſions and conjugations, gives a ſweetneſs to their language altogether unknown to ours, and a variety unknown to any other modern language. In point of ſweetneſs, the Italian, perhaps, may ſurpaſs the Latin, and almoſt equal the Greek; but in point of variety, it is greatly inferior to both.

Thirdly, this ſimplification, not only renders the ſounds of our language leſs agreeable

to

to the ear, but it alſo reſtrains us from diſpoſing ſuch ſounds as we have, in the manner that might be moſt agreeable. It ties down many words to a particular ſituation, though they might often be placed in another with much more beauty. In the Greek and Latin, though the adjective and ſubſtantive were ſeparated from one another, the correſpondence of their terminations ſtill ſhowed their mutual reference, and the ſeparation did not neceſſarily occaſion any ſort of confuſion. Thus in the firſt line of Virgil,

> Tityre tu patulæ recubans ſub tegmine fagi;

we eaſily ſee that *tu* refers to *recubans*, and *patulæ* to *fagi*; though the related words are ſeparated from one another by the intervention of ſeveral others; becauſe the terminations, ſhowing the correſpondence of their caſes, determine their mutual reference. But if we were to tranſlate this line literally into Engliſh, and ſay, *Tityrus, thou of ſpreading reclining under the ſhade beech*, Œdipus himſelf could not make ſenſe of it; becauſe there is here no difference of termination, to determine which ſubſtantive each adjective belongs to. It is the ſame caſe with regard to verbs. In Latin

the verb may be often placed, without any inconveniency or ambiguity, in any part of the ſentence. But in Engliſh its place is almoſt always preciſely determined. It muſt follow the ſubjective and precede the objective member of the phraſe in almoſt all caſes. Thus in Latin whether you ſay, *Joannem verberavit Robertus*, or *Robertus verberavit Joannem*, the meaning is preciſely the ſame, and the termination fixes John to be the ſufferer in both caſes. But in Engliſh *John beat Robert*, and *Robert beat John*, have by no means the ſame ſignification. The place therefore of the three principal members of the phraſe is in the Engliſh, and for the ſame reaſon in the French and Italian languages, almoſt always preciſely determined; whereas in the ancient languages a greater latitude is allowed, and the place of theſe members is often, in a great meaſure, indifferent. We muſt have recourſe to Horace, in order to interpret ſome parts of Milton's literal tranſlation;

> Who now enjoys thee credulous all gold,
> Who always vacant, always amiable
> Hopes thee, of flattering gales
> Unmindful —

are

the verses which it is impossible to interpret by any rules of our language. There are no rules in our language, by which any man could discover, that, in the first line, *credulous* referred to *who*, and not to *thee*; or that *all gold* referred to any thing; or that in the fourth line, *unmindful* referred to *who* in the second, and not to *thee* in the third; or on the contrary, that, in the second line, *always vacant, always amiable*, referred to *thee* in the third, and not to *who* in the same line with it. In the Latin, indeed, all this is perfectly plain.

> Qui nunc te fruitur credulus aurea,
> Qui semper vacuam, semper amabilem
> Sperat, nescius auræ fallacis.

Because the terminations in the Latin determine the reference of each adjective to its proper substantive, which it is impossible for any thing in the English to do. How much this power of transposing the order of their words must have facilitated the composition of the ancients, both in verse and prose, can hardly be imagined. That it must greatly have facilitated their versification it is needless to observe; and in prose, whatever beauty depends

depends upon the arrangement and construction of the several members of the period, must to them have been acquirable with much more ease, to much greater perfection, than it can be to those whose expression is constantly confined by the prolixness, constraint, and monotony of modern languages.

FINIS.

Printed by A. Strahan, Printers-Street, London.

Ingram Content Group UK Ltd.
Milton Keynes UK
UKHW020118200523
422059UK00005B/106